# Transitional Justice and the Kurdish Conflict

Centralising the experience of victims-survivors and other grassroots actors, this book examines how transitional justice can be used in transforming the Kurdish conflict in Turkey.

Despite 40 years of armed conflict, its violent effects on Kurdish people and the wider society, and strong demands for justice, there is little work on transitional justice in the context of the Kurdish conflict. In response, this book explores the limits and potentials of transitional justice in Turkey's ongoing conflict by focusing on the perspectives of victims-survivors and grassroots justice activists. Such perspectives have received little attention in the transitional justice literature, even as it has exhibited an increasing interest in contexts where no formal transition has taken place. But, as this book demonstrates, the Kurdish conflict reveals the importance, not only of documenting these perspectives, but in seeing how those most affected by conflict are able to transform their experience into political action. Drawing on Kurdish victim-survivors' own understandings of their experiences and activists' perceptions of the potential of transitional justice, the book thereby addresses, and advocates, the transformative potential of bottom-up, grassroots-level efforts to deliver transitional justice goals.

This book will appeal to transitional justice scholars and practitioners, those with interests in the role of social movements, as well as others with interests in the Kurdish conflict or in Middle Eastern politics more generally.

**Nisan Alıcı** is Lecturer at the Centre for Applied Social Sciences, Policy, Practice and Research (CASSPPR), University of Derby, UK.

Part of the Transitional Justice Series
Series editor Kieran McEvoy
*Queen's University Belfast, UK*

A GlassHouse book

For information about the series and details of previous and forthcoming titles, see https://www.routledge.com/Transitional-Justice/book-series/TRANJ

# Transitional Justice and the Kurdish Conflict

## A Grassroots Approach

Nisan Alıcı

Routledge
Taylor & Francis Group
a GlassHouse Book

First published 2026
by Routledge
4 Park Square, Milton Park, Abingdon, Oxon OX14 4RN

and by Routledge
605 Third Avenue, New York, NY 10158

*Routledge is an imprint of the Taylor & Francis Group, an informa business*

*A GlassHouse book*



*British Library Cataloguing-in-Publication Data*
A catalogue record for this book is available from the British Library

*Library of Congress Cataloging-in-Publication Data*
Names: Alıcı, Nisan, 1989– author.
Title: Transitional justice and the Kurdish conflict : a grassroots approach / Nisan Alıcı
Description: Abingdon, Oxon [UK] ; New York, NY : Routledge, 2026. | Series: Transitional justice | Includes bibliographical references and index.
Identifiers: LCCN 2025012193 (print) | LCCN 2025012194 (ebook)
Subjects: LCSH: Transitional justice—Turkey. | Political crimes and offenses—Turkey. | Victims of political violence—Legal status, laws, etc.—Turkey. | Turkey—History—Turkish-Kurdish Conflict, 1978– | Kurds—Legal status, laws, etc.—Turkey. | Kurds—Turkey—History—Autonomy and independence movements. | Partiya Karkerel,n Kurdistanel,—History. | Human rights—Turkey.
Classification: LCC KKX4415 .A94 2026 (print) | LCC KKX4415 (ebook) | DDC 956.103—dc23/eng/20250320
LC record available at https://lccn.loc.gov/2025012193
LC ebook record available at https://lccn.loc.gov/2025012194

ISBN: 978-1-032-55851-6 (hbk)
ISBN: 978-1-032-55852-3 (pbk)
ISBN: 978-1-003-43257-9 (ebk)

DOI: 10.4324/9781003432579

Typeset in Sabon
by Apex CoVantage, LLC

# Contents

# Acknowledgement

This book is the culmination of years of research, reflection, and collaboration. It began as a PhD project at Ulster University's Transitional Justice Institute and has since evolved through the support and insights of many individuals and institutions. I am deeply grateful to everyone who contributed to this journey, whether through academic guidance, intellectual exchanges, or personal encouragement.

I owe special thanks to my interlocutors, who generously shared their time and perspectives, enriching this work with their lived experiences.

Institutionally, this book's journey began at Ulster University and continued through Nottingham Trent University (NTU), Cambridge University, Trinity College Dublin (TCD), and Queen's University Belfast (QUB) before being completed at the University of Derby. I am deeply grateful to colleagues and mentors at these institutions for providing me the space to engage meaningfully with this research. In particular, I owe much to my PhD supervisors at Ulster University, Professor Siobhan Wills and Professor Brandon Hamber, whose invaluable guidance and support shaped this work in countless ways. I am also grateful to Professor Rory O'Connell, whose encouragement as a research director fostered a collaborative and supportive research environment, as well as for his continued mentorship throughout my academic growth.

The guidance and encouragement of mentors, including Professor Jonathan Doak at NTU, Dr. Lauren Dempster at QUB, and Professor Alessio D'Angelo at University of Derby, have been incredibly helpful in navigating research challenges.

My fellow post-doctoral researchers at the QUB, Dr. Erika Jimenez and Dr. Chulani Kodikara, were a highlight of my time at QUB—our writing sessions provided both motivation and structure. My students at various institutions have also been a source of inspiration throughout this journey, whose enthusiasm for learning reinforced the significance of academic work. Thought-provoking discussions in the Transitional Justice module at TCD Belfast and the Peace and Conflict module at QUB further expanded the intellectual scope of this research.

I am fortunate to have a long list of friends to thank. My time at Ulster University gifted me some of my closest friends, whose love and care made Belfast feel like home. My heartfelt gratitude goes to Dr. Cira Pallí-Asperó, Cristal Palacios Yumar, Dr. Laura Sirabella, Mariana Espinós-Blasco., Nevena Klobucar, Nicole Marinaro, Dr. Priyam Yarnell, Dr. Selbi Durdiyeva, and Professor Bill Rolston. Their companionship through shared meals, deep conversations, and endless laughter has been a source of immense joy. Special thanks to Dr. Cecilia Gialdini, Dr. Nada Ahmed, and Dr. Marc Olivier-Loiseau for sharing the challenges and joys of completing a PhD and simply navigating life. I am so lucky to feel their constant love and support.

The intellectual and personal support of colleagues at DEMOS Research Collective has played a fundamental role in shaping this academic journey. My experience with DEMOS has been foundational to my identity as a researcher, and I remain proud of the work we have accomplished there. Special thanks to Dr. Güneş Daslı, Güley Bor, and Mertcan Doğan for their intellectual companionship and unwavering friendship. Their brilliance and kindness continue to inspire me.

Unwavering support across time and distance came from my friends from back home, many of whom now live abroad. The daily messages of Asiye Duman and Uğur Çalışkan have brightened many gloomy days. The intellectual and personal influence of Işıl Su Erdoğan over more than two decades has been profound. From teenage discussions to the life paths she has chosen, her perspectives have shaped my emotional and academic growth in countless ways.

I owe a deep depth of gratitude to my psychotherapist Arzu Uyar, whose support made my journey—not just as an academic, but as a person—immeasurably easier. The therapeutic space she held for me over the years and across countries has helped me become a stronger, more independent, and ultimately happier migrant academic. I will always appreciate the avenues opened through this work.

I am immensely grateful to my mother, Ülkü Akgün Alıcı, and my father, Hasan Alıcı, for nurturing my political curiosity and supporting my intellectual pursuits. I am keenly aware of the privilege of having parents who actively encouraged me to pursue a career aligned with my values. My sister, Asya Alıcı, is one of my greatest sources of joy. Her unconditional love, warmth, and unwavering support are a constant reminder of how lucky I am to have her in my life. I also want to thank my cat, Meredith, who joined me just after I signed the book contract. Her companionship brought comfort and joy during long nights of writing.

Finally, the deepest gratitude goes to my partner, Abdullah Zeytun. His love and support have been invaluable throughout this process, from deep conversations that sharpened my arguments to his unwavering commitment to justice, human rights, and the Kurdish struggle. It is the dedication and resilience of countless individuals like him that inspired me to write this book. I have done my best to honour their efforts. My sincere hope is that this book contributes to their struggle and serves as a step toward a peaceful and just society in Turkey.

Chapter 1

# Introduction

## Situating Turkey within the Field of Transitional Justice

### 1.1 Introduction

This book is one of the first to provide a rigourous and detailed analysis of the Kurdish conflict through the lens of transitional justice, drawing on an empirical study grounded in grassroots approaches. The seeds of the book were sown in the aftermath of Turkey's failed 2013–2015 peace process—a moment of lost opportunity that reshaped the country's political trajectory. Over the past decade, Turkey has moved further away from any prospects of peace, replaced by deepening authoritarianism and escalating state violence. Yet, just as I was finalising this book, a new phase of negotiations surfaced. On 27 February 2025, imprisoned PKK (*Partiya Karkerên Kurdistan*, Kurdistan Workers' Party) leader Abdullah Öcalan issued a historic call for the PKK to lay down arms. This announcement was met with hope, excitement, and caution by the Kurdish population and those advocating for a political resolution to the conflict. Whether this call will lead to concrete political developments remains uncertain. What is clear, however, is that even in the absence of a formal peace process, justice-seeking efforts have persisted.

This book analyses these grassroots, community-driven efforts in transitional justice, challenging the notion that such processes are confined to post-conflict periods. Instead, it argues that transitional justice can emerge in fragmented, grassroots-led forms even amid ongoing violence. Drawing on extensive empirical research, this book disrupts dominant narratives on transitional justice and conflict transformation, offering novel theoretical and practical insights into the applicability and implications of transitional justice mechanisms during an ongoing conflict.

Addressing two critical gaps in the field, the book first examines how transitional justice can be applied in ongoing conflicts and authoritarian regimes, with a particular focus on Turkey's Kurdish conflict—an often-overlooked case with significant regional and international implications. It provides valuable lessons for the field, especially in contexts where neither a formal peace process nor a political transition has taken place. Second, it highlights the crucial role of grassroots actors and organised victims in advancing transitional

DOI: 10.4324/9781003432579-1

justice, even in highly repressive political environments. Through in-depth analyses of the Saturday Mothers movement and the unofficial Truth and Justice Commission for Diyarbakır Prison, the book illustrates how community level activism continues to drive demands for justice despite state-imposed constraints. In doing so, it speaks directly to contemporary global conflicts and the rise of authoritarian regimes, where human rights violations persist, yet grassroots movements remain vital forces in the pursuit of justice. The Turkish-Kurdish case is perfectly suited to build a differentiated approach for transitional justice to respond to the grassroots movements' needs and demands to be better equipped in such challenging contexts.

## 1.2 The Central Argument

This book argues that transitional justice is not solely confined to post-conflict settings; rather, it is a contested process shaped through fragmented, grassroots-led initiatives in protracted violence and authoritarian contexts. In such cases where there is no official transitional justice agenda, civil society actors hold a solid potential to stimulate transformation and implement transitional justice mechanisms, at least in incremental steps. However, as I demonstrate in this book, authoritarian regimes present additional limitations to transitional justice imaginaries, as human rights violations and criminalisation of peace efforts creates a narrow civic space. In Turkey, despite a wealth of experience and widespread grassroots efforts in the absence of an official transitional justice agenda, there has been a decline in interest in transitional justice, leading to a limited and inert transitional justice civic space. Strengthening the connections between civil society actors in Turkey and international transitional justice scholarship and practice can provide civil society activists with innovative tools and strategies to overcome existing challenges and increasing their effectiveness in achieving their goals. The transitional justice scholarship, in return, should dedicate more attention to ongoing conflict cases, such as Turkey, where the social and political landscape is shaped by an authoritarian regime. As authoritarian regimes proliferate around the world, there is a growing need for transitional justice literature to address the complexities faced by civil society actors in pursuing transitional justice in non-transitions (Chapter 3), namely under authoritarian regimes where state violence and human rights violations continue.

Traditionally, transitional justice has been implemented in the aftermath of conflict, often as an integral part of peace agreements—such as in Colombia—where comprehensive mechanisms like truth commissions, reparations, and institutional reforms are introduced to facilitate reconciliation and prevent future violence. Turkey, however, does not fit this conventional model. The country has neither undergone a formal peace process nor experienced a clear political transition. As this book demonstrates, transitional justice is increasingly applied in contexts of protracted conflict and repression, where grassroots movements and limited state initiatives seek justice despite ongoing violence. The Turkish case offers valuable insights into both the potential and constraints of implementing justice mechanisms under an authoritarian regime and an unresolved armed conflict. It exemplifies a case of fragmented transitional justice, where a myriad of grassroots-initiated justice efforts and some limited state-led attempts have emerged despite the absence of a formal transition. Therefore, the Turkish-Kurdish case offers valuable lessons for transitional justice theory and practice, particularly in understanding both the possibilities and constraints of implementing justice mechanisms while an ongoing conflict and authoritarian regime continues.

This book makes three key interventions in transitional justice scholarship. First, it challenges the assumption that transitional justice is only possible after conflict ends by showing how justice-seeking efforts persist even in non-transition and repressive contexts. By providing a close examination of a case that has not been on the radar of transitional justice scholarship, it opens new avenues for learning. Second, it foregrounds the voices and agency of grassroots actors and organised victims as central forces in shaping justice initiatives. Their persistence in the absence of formal mechanisms exemplifies the transformative potential of bottom-up justice initiatives, offering critical insights into how victims' agency can shape transitional justice goals. Third, it advances the research agenda by advocating for a more nuanced transitional justice understanding of how ongoing conflict and authoritarianism shape and constrain community-driven approaches. This much-needed expansion of transitional justice scholarship is grounded in an in-depth examination of past initiatives, current grassroots mobilisation, complexities of victimhood, and civil society's evolving justice demands. By offering a rigorous analysis of the Kurdish experience of conflict, justice, and accountability, this book makes a significant contribution to both transitional justice scholarship and Kurdish Studies.

## 1.3 Why Address the Kurdish Conflict through a Transitional Justice Lens?

Since the founding of the Republic in 1923, Turkey's political trajectory has been shaped by recurrent cycles of state violence, repression, and impunity. The early years of the Republic saw efforts to forge a unitary national identity centred on Turkishness and Sunni Islam, leading to the marginalisation and persecution of ethnic and religious minorities. From the 1915 Armenian Genocide to the forced displacement and massacres of Kurds, Alevis, Greeks, and Assyrians, successive governments have employed violence as a means of consolidating state power and silencing opposition. These patterns of repression deepened as military coups and authoritarian governance further criminalised political dissent, curtailed civil liberties, and entrenched a culture of impunity.

A defining feature of this context is the decades-long armed conflict between the Turkish state and the PKK, which erupted in 1984. The conflict has caused immense loss of life and mass displacement, leaving a profound and lasting impact on Turkey and the wider region. The state's response to the conflict has been marked by enforced disappearances, village burnings, forced displacement, torture, and arbitrary imprisonment, with denial and impunity characterising the official stance on these abuses (Yıldız and Baert, 2021). Yet, despite this long history of violence and repression, Turkey has never undertaken a comprehensive transitional justice process to confront past atrocities or provide redress for victims. Instead, denial, impunity, and the suppression of truth-seeking initiatives have allowed cycles of repression to persist, shaping both the present and future of the country's political landscape.

Given this historical trajectory, the question of how societies confront past and ongoing violence becomes particularly pressing. In many post-authoritarian and post-conflict settings, transitional justice mechanisms—such as truth commissions, criminal accountability measures, reparations, and institutional reforms—have played a crucial role in addressing historical injustices. However, in Turkey, where neither a formal political transition nor a negotiated peace process has taken place, transitional justice has remained largely absent from state policy.

Yet, despite this absence, grassroots justice actors, victim-survivor movements, and human rights advocates have mobilised to seek truth, accountability, and recognition, often employing the language and strategies of transitional justice. These bottom-up initiatives challenge dominant assumptions in transitional justice scholarship, particularly the idea that justice mechanisms can only emerge after conflict ends. By examining Turkey's Kurdish conflict through a transitional justice lens, this book highlights how justice-seeking efforts persist even amid state repression and ongoing violence—offering critical insights for both the field of transitional justice and global justice movements more broadly.

In the absence of an official framework for truth, justice, and accountability, civil society actors began to mobilise more actively around transitional justice goals in the early 2000s, using the language of 'dealing with the past' to address these critical issues. This mobilisation reached its peak during the 2013–2015 peace process, which raised hopes for formally confronting Turkey's violent past through established mechanisms. However, following the collapse of the peace process and the rise of authoritarianism post-2015, efforts toward transitional justice were increasingly marginalised and ultimately faded from the public agenda.

Transitional justice emerged as a distinct field in the late 1980s and early 1990s, primarily in response to the challenges human rights activists faced during transitions from authoritarian regimes to more democratic ones in countries such as Argentina and Chile (Arthur, 2009). The term transitional justice was coined to describe a new form of human rights activity addressing the political dilemmas activists encountered in these transitional contexts.

Scholars, activists, lawyers, policymakers, and civil society representatives came together in conferences to explore avenues for achieving justice for victims and facilitating the transition in question. These conferences, firstly held in the aftermath of authoritarian regime collapses in South America and then to discuss similar issues for post-Apartheid South Africa, set out the newly emerging field's conceptual framework (Arthur, 2009).

Initially, transitional justice literature focused on addressing past injustices and violence by examining mechanisms such as truth, justice, and accountability employed by successor regimes to confront abuses. Over time, the field expanded to reflect the complexities of political transitions, incorporating a diversity of approaches, instruments, and agents (Aboueldahab, 2024; Lawther and Moffett, 2017; Quinn, 2017). Criminal prosecutions, truth telling, reparations, institutional reform, and memorialisation became widely recognised as key components of transitional justice (de Greiff, 2012). Today, international organisations and policymakers acknowledge transitional justice as a critical tool for peacebuilding and enabling transitions from conflict to non-violence (Lawther and Moffett, 2017; Nagy, 2008).

Although transitional justice has traditionally been used in post-conflict settings, scholars and practitioners have started to investigate the implications of using transitional justice during an ongoing conflict and its potential to facilitate conflict transformation Engstrom, 2013; Hansen, 2011; Sarkin, 2016; Van Nievelt, 2016). Implementing transitional justice mechanisms amid ongoing violence requires a strong commitment and involvement of grassroots such as the victims of the conflict, local communities, human rights advocates, and civil and political organisations (Sarkin, 2016). These groups play a vital role where official peace process and state mechanisms are absent, often advancing justice initiatives through bottom-up mobilisation. This book highlights the complexities of victimhood in such settings, exploring how organised victims and grassroots actors conceptualise their experiences and mobilise for justice.

Transitional justice emerged as an international field shaped by comparative practices, continuously evolving through empirical case studies (Arthur, 2009). This book contributes to this knowledge base by examining the underexplored Kurdish conflict—a highly topical and significant case study. The absence of a formal conflict resolution and an official transitional justice process in Turkey has led to the Kurdish case being largely overlooked in transitional justice scholarship. Civil society-led initiatives, which are vital in the absence of state-led mechanisms, have received limited academic attention, both nationally and internationally.

For example, despite a growing scholarly interest in unofficial truth commissions,[1] especially in contexts where formal commissions are politi-

1 Greensboro Truth Commission is one of the most widely studied unofficial, community-led truth commissions. For some of the recent works, see for example Nicole Fox and

cally infeasible (Bickford, 2007), the civil society-led Truth and Justice Commission for Diyarbakır Prison has not gained sufficient traction within transitional justice literature (Alici, 2024). The Truth and Justice Commission for the Diyarbakır Prison is one of the most remarkable transitional justice initiatives in Turkey as its actors mobilised around the transitional justice discourse and contributed to recognition and accountability in the absence of an overarching transitional justice framework. This neglect of cases such as Turkey in the transitional justice literature is striking given that such initiatives demonstrate the ability of grassroots actors to pursue transitional justice objectives without a formal, state-backed framework. The lack of focus on transitional justice in non-paradigmatic settings—where political transition is absent—reflects a persistent gap in the field, which this book directly addresses (Hansen, 2011).

The Kurdish conflict holds profound national, regional, and international dimensions that impact millions of lives. Rooted in colonial histories and unresolved violence, the conflict manifests through systemic state repression, displacement, and ongoing struggles for justice. At the time of writing, Turkey's involvement in northern Syria, aiming to dismantle the democratic gains of the Kurdish movement in the Autonomous Administration of North and East Syria (AANES), further underscores the transnational nature of the conflict. Additionally, the Kurdish diaspora, as the world's largest stateless population and one of Europe's most politically active migrant groups, amplifies the relevance of this case for global justice debates (Baser, 2011).

Although this book focuses on northern Kurdistan (*Bakur* in Kurdish) within Turkey's borders, its findings resonate beyond national boundaries, addressing cross-border dimensions of the Kurdish issue in Turkey, Syria, Iraq, and Iran. Transitional justice scholarship has only recently begun exploring *"aparadigmatic cases"* in the Middle East, yet the Kurdish conflict remains insufficiently studied as a stand-alone case.[2]

## 1.4 Key Contributions

This book fills a critical gap by offering a rigourous, empirically grounded analysis of the Kurdish conflict through a transitional justice lens. By

David Cunningham, "Transitional Justice in Public and Private: Truth Commission Narratives in Greensboro," *The International Journal of Transitional Justice* (2022).

2 See for example: Aboueldahab, N., 2023. Transitional Justice as Repression and Resistance: Practices in the Arab World. *Journal of International Criminal Justice*, 21, 701–717. https://doi.org/10.1093/jicj/mqac027;

Herremans, B., Destrooper, T., 2023. Moving Beyond Formal Truth Practices and Forensic Truth in the Syrian Conflict: How Informal Truth Practices Contribute to Thicker Understandings of Truth. Social & Legal Studies 32, 519–539. https://doi.org/10.1177/09646639221134965; Salehi, M., 2022. Transitional justice in process: Plans and politics in Tunisia. Manchester University Press.

examining the role of civil society initiatives, grassroots mobilisation, and the construction and complexities of victimhood, it demonstrates how justice initiatives can persist in the absence of political transition. In doing so, this book not only sheds light on the Kurdish experience but also lays a foundation for future studies to build on—particularly those exploring the regional and global implications of this ongoing conflict. This book's unique contributions lie in three interlinked areas:

### *Situating the Kurdish Conflict within Transitional Justice Literature*

Despite four decades of conflict and its devastating impacts, transitional justice scholarship has largely overlooked the Kurdish conflict. While several studies have addressed related themes, such as conflict transformation, peace processes, and reconciliation (Arslan, 2019; Başer and Çelik, 2014; Baser and Ozerdem, 2019; Celik, 2010; Günes, 2013; Yegen, 2016), these analyses do not have a transitional justice lens. Transitional justice-specific analyses, where they exist, tend to focus on institutional mechanisms, dealing with the past, and memory politics (Bakiner, 2013; Budak, 2015; Jongerden, 2016; Kaya, 2015; Mihr, 2017; Uçarlar, 2015). However, there is little focus on grassroots mobilisation or bottom-up justice initiatives in the context of non-transition, and the ongoing conflict, along with the perceptions of affected communities and grassroots actors regarding transitional justice, remains largely unexamined. This book addresses these gaps by offering a comprehensive analysis of transitional justice in the context of the Kurdish conflict, examining how grassroots actors and civil society initiatives respond to systemic injustices in the absence of formal transitional justice mechanisms. By situating these efforts within the broader framework of "transitional justice in deeply conflicted societies" (Hansen, 2011), this book demonstrates the potential of bottom-up justice practices to challenge state denial and impunity, even in non-transition contexts. In doing so, this study offers a fresh perspective on transitional justice in Turkey, foregrounding the agency of victims and grassroots actors while expanding the theoretical and empirical scope of transitional justice literature to include protracted conflicts like the Kurdish case.

### *Expanding Transitional Justice to Non-Transitions and Ongoing Conflicts*

This book advances the understanding of transitional justice by critically engaging with its application in non-transition contexts—settings where political change is limited, conflicts persist, or democratic backsliding occurs (Aboueldahab, 2018; Destrooper et al., 2023; Engstrom, 2013; Quinn, 2014). Recent scholarship has begun to explore the innovative ways grassroots actors pursue justice when formal mechanisms are inaccessible (Herremans and Bellintani, 2023). However, transitional justice literature does not yet fully capture cases marked by varying levels of fragmented transitions and ongoing abuses (Hansen, 2014). By situating the Kurdish conflict within these emerging debates, this book demonstrates how transitional justice mechanisms—typically associated with post-conflict settings—can be adapted and implemented through grassroots initiatives during an ongoing conflict. It reveals how victims and survivors, civil society actors, and local communities creatively navigate the constraints imposed by repressive regimes to pursue justice and accountability.

This contribution pushes transitional justice scholarship beyond its normative boundaries, offering a nuanced understanding of how justice initiatives can function in "deeply conflicted societies" (Hansen, 2011, p. 23) where state denial and impunity are entrenched. By expanding the theoretical and practical scope of transitional justice to include protracted conflicts like the Kurdish case, this study challenges the field to rethink its assumptions and provides a fresh perspective on the adaptability of transitional justice mechanisms to ongoing violence and political stagnation.

### *Highlighting the Role of Grassroots Movements: The Saturday Mothers*

This book uniquely analyses the Saturday Mothers' long-standing mobilisation as a key grassroots movement through a transitional justice framework. Since 1995, the Saturday Mothers—relatives of those forcibly disappeared during the 1980s and 1990s and activists—have held sit-ins in Istanbul's Galatasaray Square to demand truth, justice, and accountability. Despite ongoing arrests and police violence, their persistence highlights the resilience of organised victims in confronting state denial and impunity. By situating the Saturday Mothers within transitional justice, this book demonstrates how organised victims' agency drives demands for truth-telling, accountability, and memorialisation in the absence of formal mechanisms. Their activism challenges systemic silencing, creates alternative spaces for memory, and raises public awareness of Turkey's legacy of enforced disappearances. This analysis underscores the transformative role of organised victim groups in advancing transitional justice goals, particularly in non-transition contexts. It reframes those most affected by conflict-related human rights violations as key agents of justice, offering a powerful example of how grassroots mobilisation can challenge impunity and foster truth-seeking and social transformation in the face of systemic denial.

## 1.5 Reflections on Methodologies and Ethics

My background—a Turkish mother, Kurdish father, professional and activist engagement with the Kurdish political movement, and a member of the

DEMOS Research Association[3]—shaped the research process at every stage. As a researcher with Turkish-Kurdish heritage, I have occupied a dual position as both an insider and outsider to the research context.

My multiple identities meant different things to different participants in this research, thus creating both advantages and disadvantages (Mwambari, 2019). I remained reflexive of this, which influenced how participants perceived me and shaped the flow of our interactions. These dynamics often reflected broader socio-political hierarchies, including those tied to ethnicity, professional roles, and lived experiences of the conflict. For instance, my Kurdish heritage and professional background granted me familiarity and access, yet my lack of personal victimisation or fluency in Kurdish positioned me as an outsider in certain contexts. Similarly, power dynamics fluctuated during interviews, with participants sometimes deferring to me as an academic authority, while in other cases, their deeper local expertise or lived experience placed them in a position of greater influence over the direction of the conversation.

This study adopted a qualitative research approach, conducting a two-phase fieldwork that included in-depth and semi-structured interviews with the aim of "learning about people in depth and on their own terms, and in the context of their situations" (Schutt, 2019, p. 391). This approach allowed a context-sensitive and nuanced analysis, centring the perspectives of those most affected: victims, activists, and practitioners. Understanding how individuals make sense of themselves, their place in the world, and their interactions requires engaging with their perspectives directly (Jongerden, 2016). This approach necessitates a researcher's deep, internal comprehension of the subject, developed through an extended dialogue with those whose narratives shape the research. By adopting qualitative methods, I sought to uncover how relatives of the disappeared and advocates for peace and justice conceptualise their experiences and the surrounding socio-political context.

Data collection involved two phases of fieldwork that allowed for an iterative process of data collection and analysis. In the first phase, conducted in 2019, I carried out 13 semi-structured, in-depth expert interviews with lawyers, human rights advocates, and researchers. Ten of them were conducted in-person in Istanbul, while two of them were on Skype due to the interlocutors' location of residency. These participants were selected for their expertise in working with victims of conflict-related human rights violations, such as forced disappearances, gender-based violence, and memory initiatives. The expertise, or the special knowledge that my interlocutors[4] had, was gained

3 DEMOS Research Association was founded in Ankara in 2015 to foreground a collective approach to knowledge production. Ever since its founding, it has conducted research within the broad purview of peace studies and examined examples from Turkey and abroad, adopting a gender perspective while doing so. https://en.demos.org.tr/

4 Krystalli (2019) argues that the word interlocutor refers to a dialogic relationship, because interlocution is a conversation, and it leads to theoretical insights. Following her, I also refer to those whom I interviewed as interlocutors.

"through their activity—and not necessarily through their training—because they have privileged access to information" (Meuser and Nagel, 2009, p. 24).

The second phase of the fieldwork took place during the Covid pandemic in 2020. Due to safety concerns and travel restrictions, the fieldwork moved online. It involved interviews with activist leaders,[5] journalists, lawyers, and practitioners in this phase. It included seven additional expert interviews and four interviews with relatives of the disappeared, who are part of an active struggle for truth and justice. Among my 24 interlocutors are participants in the Saturday sit-ins in Istanbul or Kurdish cities, including human rights defenders, relatives of the disappeared, and lawyers providing legal support to families in their fight for justice. In these interviews I explored how the movement's justice demands were articulated, sustained, and linked to transitional justice goals.

I chose participants based on their leadership roles, experience in human rights advocacy, and ability to provide insights into the evolution and broader significance of the movement. The sampling strategy ensured diversity among participants, incorporating perspectives from lawyers, practitioners, and activist leaders. At the end of the book, I provide a list of these interviews. To uphold anonymity, I identify participants by their organisation rather than by their specific roles. When additional context is necessary, I include only non-identifying details that help situate a quotation without risking exposure of the speaker's identity.

Given the politically sensitive nature of the research, I conducted data analysis with a strong awareness of the socio-political context shaping participants' narratives. I triangulated the interview data with secondary sources, such as reports, archival materials, and existing literature, to ensure a rigourous and comprehensive interpretation. This process helped contextualise participants' accounts, particularly regarding the authoritarian regime and its impact on civil society's demands for justice.

Prior to beginning fieldwork, ethical approval was obtained from my institution. Ethical considerations were central to this research, given its focus on a sensitive political topic. Such conditions posed significant challenges concerning the safety, confidentiality, and well-being of participants. Many of my interlocutors were already at risk prior to this study—several had been arrested or prosecuted for their human rights work, and three were incarcerated during the period of my research. These arrests reflected the broader risks they faced due to their activism. Recognising these vulnerabilities, I took every possible measure to prevent placing participants at additional risk. Safeguarding their confidentiality and preserving their anonymity were

5 Activist leaders are those who have been part of the Saturday Mothers movement, but not necessarily with a victimisation experience themselves.

therefore of paramount importance. The research adhered to standard ethical principles, including do-no-harm, informed consent, and confidentiality.

Informed consent was obtained from all participants to ensure they fully understood the study's purpose, procedures, and risks. Each participant received an information sheet and consent form, with time to consider their involvement. The interviews were automatically labelled as confidential and anonymous. Participants' names and identifying information were omitted, and all data was anonymised.

When interviewing conflict-affected participants, it is possible that recalling stressful events may evoke emotional distress. Even without being asked directly about their experiences of victimisation, which was the case in this research, individuals might choose to share painful stories (Moss et al., 2019). To help ensure participants were prepared for this possibility, I selected interlocutors who had previously provided interviews to researchers and media outlets, and, in some cases, who had taken on 'activist leader' roles. Their experience in communicating frequently with the media and discussing sensitive subjects helped them navigate challenging emotional terrain.

Additionally, I took deliberate steps to safeguard participants. I underwent specialised training on trauma-informed interviewing and working with vulnerable individuals, and I consulted experts during the first phase of fieldwork. These measures deepened my understanding of ethical considerations and equipped me with knowledge of available support mechanisms, ensuring that participants would have appropriate avenues for assistance should they need it following our interviews.

## 1.6 Structure of the Book

Chapter 2, 'The Kurdish Conflict, Transitional Justice and Victimhood in Turkey', provides essential background on the Kurdish conflict to contextualise grassroots actors' motivations and demands. It examines the root causes of the conflict, which shape and construct notions of victimhood, and outlines Turkey's current socio-political context. It highlights the intersection of an authoritarian regime and ongoing conflict, where peace and transitional justice efforts are increasingly criminalised, silenced, and rendered invisible. Understanding this context offers insights into how civic space is constrained and how these dynamics influence the prospects for implementing transitional justice in non-transition settings. This chapter also explores specific practices of state violence targeting the dead and rituals surrounding death. It identifies a continuum between the enforced disappearances and extrajudicial killings of the 1990s and recent actions that humiliate and desecrate Kurdish bodies, depriving families of the ability to perform cultural and religious rituals. Such practices create profound uncertainty, preventing families from fulfilling their duties toward the dead, which are central to the grieving process. The Saturday Mothers' movement emerged from this 'space of in-betweenness'—the absence of bodies or gravestones to mourn—highlighting how unresolved disappearances and disrupted mourning rituals prolong grief and amplify the families' struggles for justice and closure.

Chapter 3, 'Victimhood and Transitional Justice in Ongoing Conflicts', critically situates the book within existing transitional justice scholarship, particularly elaborating the victim-centred, agency-oriented, and context-specific approaches. Drawing on literature that highlights the significance of victims and survivors' active participation in shaping transitional justice processes (Lundy and McGovern, 2008; Mendez, 2016; Robins, 2011), the chapter interrogates the shortcomings of top-down, prescriptive frameworks (Gready and Robins, 2014; Sharp, 2013) and advocates for a model rooted in victims' agency. It addresses the contested nature of victimhood in conflict and post-conflict settings, emphasising the power dynamics involved in defining who qualifies as a victim and the political stakes of inclusion and exclusion. The chapter concludes by exploring the expanding scope of transitional justice scholarship to include ongoing conflicts, highlighting its relevance to the Kurdish case.

Chapter 4, 'Understanding the Saturday Mothers Movement', examines the emergence, evolution, and expansion of the Saturday Mothers/People as a grassroots justice movement and analyses the key tools and strategies they have employed. Persistently mobilising to demand truth, justice, and accountability since 1995, the Saturday Mothers have become the longest-lasting and most systematically organised social movement in Turkey. The chapter provides an in-depth analysis of the journey that the movement has established itself as a powerful political actor, including the role of mothers, its deliberate political independence, and the unique format of the Saturday gatherings. It situates the movement as a significant example of sustained grassroots agency advancing transitional justice goals outside a formal political transition.

Chapter 5, 'The Construction and Complexities of Victimhood in the Kurdish Conflict', investigates the multi-layered and complex nature of victimhood in the Kurdish conflict. It explores the divergent meanings and connotations of the term 'victim', unpacking how conflict-affected individuals navigate their experiences of victimisation while asserting themselves as political agents. By analysing the intersecting dimensions of gender and ethnicity the chapter highlights the complexities of victim identity. The chapter critiques binary understandings of victimhood and offers a more nuanced approach.

From this foundation, Chapter 6, 'Saturday Mothers' Contributions to the Pillars of Transitional Justice', connects the Saturday Mothers' grassroots mobilisation to the core pillars of transitional justice: truth, justice, guarantees of non-recurrence, and memorialisation. It demonstrates how organised victim movements can meaningfully advance transitional justice objectives, even in the absence of formal mechanisms or a political transition. By analysing the Saturday Mothers' persistent efforts, the chapter underscores their role in truth-seeking, advocating for accountability, creating spaces of memory, and challenging impunity—contributing to both the local struggle for justice and broader transitional justice scholarship.

Chapter 7, 'Fragmented Transitions: Civil Society, State Responses, and Transitional Justice in Turkey's Kurdish Conflict', maps significant transitional justice initiatives in Turkey, focusing on two key developments from the late 2000s and early 2010s: the unofficial, civil society-led Truth and Justice Commission for Diyarbakır Prison (2007) and the prime minister's apology for the Dersim Massacre (2011). These transitional justice instances help us understand the potential and limitations of implementing transitional justice measures without an overarching agenda. The chapter highlights how grassroots pressure and political acknowledgement have, at times, enabled partial transitional justice goals, even without an overarching framework. By analysing these examples, it demonstrates how truth-telling, accountability, and memorialisation can emerge through both bottom-up and top-down efforts in ongoing conflict settings.

Building on these analyses, Chapter 8, 'Transitional Justice Imaginaries in Turkey', explores civil society actors' current perceptions and conceptualisations of transitional justice within Turkey's authoritarian and conflicted context. Grassroots organisations, victim and survivor groups, lawyers, and activists recognise the continued importance and relevance of transitional justice even within the constraints of an ongoing conflict and authoritarian regime. Drawing on the perceptions of those actively involved in past and present justice efforts, the chapter examines their visions, challenges, and aspirations for transitional justice. It identifies opportunities for grassroots actors to reimagine justice while grappling with the limitations posed by ongoing violence and political repression.

Finally, Chapter 9 presents the book's key findings and offers a forward-looking analytical assessment. It responds directly to the overarching research questions, outlining the reasons why transformative justice is the future direction that transitional justice should take in Turkey. It emphasises the potential for a victim-centred, context-specific, and transformative approach to transitional justice to address justice demands in Turkey's Kurdish conflict. It concludes by outlining future research directions and offering recommendations for rethinking transitional justice in similar contexts.

## Reference List

Aboueldahab, N., 2018. *Writing Atrocities: Syrian Civil Society and Transitional Justice*. Doha, Qatar: Brookings Doha Center. Available at: https://www.brookings.edu/wp-content/uploads/2018/04/transitional-justice-english_web.pdf

Aboueldahab, N., 2024. Breaking the echo chambers of transitional justice and TWAIL: An intellectual and policy exchange. *International Journal of Transitional Justice*, ijae036. https://doi.org/10.1093/ijtj/ijae036

Alici, N., 2024. Learning from civil society actors in turkey: Using transitional justice in an ongoing conflict. *International Journal of Transitional Justice*, ijae015. https://doi.org/10.1093/ijtj/ijae015

Arslan, S., 2019. Transborder ethnic kin and the dynamics of peace processes: Insights from the Kurdish conflict transborder ethnic kin and the dynamics of peace processes: Insights from the Kurdish conflict. *Civil Wars*, 00, pp. 1–24. https://doi.org/10.1080/13698249.2019.1667721

Arthur, P., 2009. How "Transitions" reshaped human rights: A conceptual history of transitional justice. *Human Rights Quarterly*, 31(2), pp. 321–367.

Bakiner, O., 2013. Is Turkey coming to terms with its past? Politics of memory and majoritarian conservatism. *Nationalities Papers*, 41, pp. 691–708. https://doi.org/10.1080/00905992.2013.770732

Baser, B., 2011. Kurdish diaspora political activism in Europe with a particular focus on Great Britain. In *Diaspora Dialogues for Development and Peace Project*. Berlin: Berghof Peace Support/Luzern: Centre for Just Peace and Democracy. Available at: https://d1wqtxts1xzle7.cloudfront.net/30850887/SL_Diaspora_Papers_Baser-libre.pdf.

Baser, B. and Ozerdem, A., 2019. Conflict transformation and asymmetric conflicts: A critique of the failed Turkish-Kurdish peace process. *Terrorism and Political Violence*, 00, pp. 1–22. https://doi.org/10.1080/09546553.2019.1657844

Başer, Z. and Çelik, A.B., 2014. Imagining peace in a conflict environment: Kurdish youths' framing of the Kurdish issue in Turkey. *Patterns Prejudice*, 48, pp. 265–285. https://doi.org/10.1080/0031322X.2014.925197

Bickford, L., 2007. Unofficial truth projects. *Human Rights Quarterly*, 29, pp. 994–1035. https://doi.org/10.1353/hrq.2007.0036

Budak, Y., 2015. Dealing with the past: Transitional justice, ongoing conflict and the Kurdish issue in Turkey. *International Journal of Transitional Justice*, pp. 219–238. https://doi.org/10.1093/ijtj/ijv002

Celik, A.B., 2010. Turkey: Kurdish question and the coercive state. *Civil Society and Peacebuilding: A Critical Assessment*, pp. 153–179.

de Greiff, P., 2012. Theorizing transitional justice. In Melissa S. Williams (Ed.), Transitional Justice: NOMOS LI. New York, NY, online edn: NYU Press Scholarship Online. https://doi.org/10.18574/nyu/9780814794661.003.0002

DEMOS Research Association, 2024. *Geçiş Dönemi Adaleti Atölyeleri/Seminerleri*. Available at: https://demos.org.tr/projeler/gecis-donemi-adaleti-atolyeleri-seminerleri/ (Accessed: 19 December 2024).

Destrooper, T., Engbo Gissel, L. and Bree Carlson, K. (Eds.), 2023. *Transitional Justice in Aparadigmatic Contexts: Accountability, Recognition, and Disruption*. Routledge.

Engstrom, P., 2013. Transitional justice and ongoing conflict. In C.L. Sriram, J. Garcia-Godos, J. Herman and O. Martin-Ortega (Eds.), *Transitional Justice and Peacebuilding on the Ground: Victims and Ex-Combatants*. New York: Routledge, pp. 41–61.

Gready, P. and Robin, S., 2014. From transitional to transformative justice: A new Agenda for practice. *International Journal of Transitional Justice*. https://doi.org/10.1093/ijtj/iju013

Güneş, C., 2014. Political reconciliation in Turkey: Challenges and prospects. In C. Günes and W. Zeydanlıoğlu (Eds.), *The Kurdish Question in Turkey: New Perspectives on Violence, Representation, and Reconciliation*. London: Routledge, 258–281.

Hansen, T.O., 2011. Transitional justice: Toward a differentiated theory. *Oregon Review of International Law*, 13, pp. 1–46. https://doi.org/10.2307/840816

Hansen, T.O., 2014. The vertical and horizontal expansion of transitional justice: Explanations and implications for a contested field. In S. Buckley-Zistel, T.K. Beck, C. Braun, and F. Mieth (Eds.), *Transitional Justice Theories*. Oxon: Routledge, pp. 105–124.

Herremans, B. and Bellintani, V., 2023. Overcoming the justice impasse in Syria. In E. Tine Destrooper, L. Engbo Gissel, and K. Bree Carlson (Eds.), *Transitional Justice in Aparadigmatic Contexts: Accountability, Recognition, and Disruption*, 1st ed. Routledge, pp. 1–16.

Jongerden, J., 2016. Making sense: Research as active engagement. *Kurdish Studies*, 4, pp. 94–104. https://doi.org/10.33182/ks.v4i1.408

Kaya, D.G., 2015. Coming to terms with the past: Rewriting history through a therapeutic public discourse in turkey. *International Journal of Middle East Studies*, 47, pp. 681–700. https://doi.org/10.1017/S0020743815000938

Krystalli, R.C., 2019. *"We Are Not Good Victims": Hierarchies of Suffering and the Politics of Victimhood in Colombia*. Doctoral dissertation. The Fletcher School of Law and Diplomacy.

Lawther, C. and Moffett, L., 2017. Introduction. In C. Lawther, L. Moffett, and D. Jacobs (Eds.), *Research Handbook on Transitional Justice*. Cheltenham: Edward Elgar Publishing, 2017, pp. 1–17.

Lundy, P. and McGovern, M., 2008. Whose justice? rethinking transitional justice from the bottom up. *Journal of Law and Society*. https://doi.org/10.1111/j.1467-6478.2008.00438.x

Mendez, J.E., 2016. Victims as protagonists in transitional justice. *International Journal of Transitional Justice*, 10, pp. 1–5.

Meuser, M. and Nagel, U., 2009. The expert interview and changes in knowledge production. In A. Bogner, B. Littig, and W. Menz (Eds.), *Interviewing Experts*. London: Palgrave Macmillan, pp. 17–42.

Mihr, A., 2017. Regime consolidation through transitional justice in Europe: The cases of Germany, Spain and Turkey. *International Journal of Transitional Justice*. https://doi.org/10.1093/ijtj/ijx003

Moss, S.M., Uluğ, Ö.M. and Acar, Y.G., 2019. Doing research in conflict contexts: Practical and ethical challenges for researchers when conducting fieldwork. *Peace and Conflict: Journal of Peace Psychology*, 25, pp. 86–99. https://doi.org/10.1037/pac0000334

Mwambari, D., 2019. Local positionality in the production of knowledge in Northern Uganda. *International Journal of Qualitative Methods*, 18. https://doi.org/10.1177/1609406919864845

Nagy, R., 2008. Transitional justice as global project: Critical reflections. *Third World Quarterly*, 29(2), pp. 275–289.

Queen's University Belfast, 2024. *The Role of Organised Victims in Transitional Justice in Turkey: A Project Overview*. Available at: https://pure.qub.ac.uk/en/activities/the-role-of-organised-victims-in-transitional-justice-in-turkey-a (Accessed: 19 December 2024).

Quinn, J.R., 2014. Whiter the transition of transitional justice. *Interdisciplinary Journal of Human Rights Law*, 8(1), pp. 63–79.

Quinn, J.R., 2017. The development of transitional justice. In C. Lawther, L. Moffett, and D. Jacobs (Eds.), *Research Handbook on Transitional Justice*. Cheltenham: Edward Elgar Publishing, pp. 11–33.

Robins, S., 2011. Towards victim-centred transitional justice: Understanding the needs of families of the disappeared in postconflict Nepal. *International Journal of Transitional Justice*, 5, pp. 75–98. https://doi.org/10.1093/ijtj/ijq027

Sarkin, J., 2016. Refocusing transitional justice to focus not only on the past, but also to concentrate on ongoing conflicts and enduring human rights crises. *Journal of International Humanitarian Legal Studies*, 7(2), pp. 294–329.

Schutt, R.K., 2019. *Investigating the Social World: The Process and Practice of Research*. 9th ed. Los Angeles, CA: SAGE.

Sharp, D.N., 2013. Beyond the post-conflict checklist: Linking peacebuilding and transitional justice through the lens of critique. *Chicago Journal of International Law*, 14, p. 165.

Uçarlar, N., 2015. *Nothing in Its Right Place. Demands of Justice and Coming to Terms with the Past in the Post-Conflict Period*. DİSA Publications.

Van Nievelt, M.A., 2016. Transitional justice in ongoing conflict: Colombia's integrative approach to peace and justice. *Cornell International Affairs Review*, 11(2), pp. 1–20.

Yegen, M., 2016. Armed struggle to peace negotiations: Independent Kurdistan to democratic autonomy, or the PKK in context. *Middle East Critique*, 6149, pp. 1–19. https://doi.org/10.1080/19436149.2016.1218162

Yıldız, Y.Y. and Baert, P., 2021. Confessions without guilt: Public confessions of state violence in Turkey. *Theory and Society*, 50, pp. 125–149. https://doi.org/10.1007/s11186-020-09398-x

Chapter 2

# The Kurdish Conflict, Transitional Justice, and Victimhood in Turkey

## 2.1 Introduction

The early years of the Republic saw efforts to consolidate a homogenised national identity based on Turkishness and Sunni Islam, which resulted in systematic violence against ethnic and religious minorities. The Armenian Genocide (1915–1923), which predated the Republic's establishment, was followed by state-led atrocities against other communities, including the mass expulsions of Greeks, the massacres of Assyrians, and the Dersim Massacre of 1937–38, in which thousands of Kurds and Alevis were killed or forcibly displaced. These violent episodes set a precedent for the suppression of political and ethnic dissent in Turkey's modern history.

Throughout the 20th century, military coups and authoritarian governance reinforced this legacy. Political dissidents—particularly leftists, Kurds, Alevis, and those advocating for greater democratic freedoms—were systematically targeted through imprisonment, torture, and forced exile. The military coups of 1960, 1971, 1980, and 1997 played a central role in shaping Turkey's political landscape, with each intervention consolidating the state's repressive apparatus and curbing opposition movements. The 1980 coup, in particular, was marked by widespread torture, extrajudicial killings, and the mass incarceration of political activists, leaving a lasting impact on civil and political rights in the country.

This chapter provides the contextual background to the book by situating the organised victims of the Kurdish conflict in the wider conflict dynamics and current political context. To enable an understanding of the social and political dynamics of the Kurdish issue, I begin by drawing a detailed picture of the emergence, development, and the root causes of the armed conflict. The first section also sheds light on the recent developments regarding the Kurdish issue including the failed peace attempts in the last two decades. In the following section, I identify the critical turning points that led to the current political context, which is characterised by ongoing conflict and authoritarianism. Understanding how the intersection of authoritarian rule and the ongoing conflict shrinks the civic space is key to my analysis of

DOI: 10.4324/9781003432579-2

the grassroots actors' understandings and imaginaries of transitional justice as they are very much shaped by the political dynamics of the last couple of years (see Chapter 8). Following this chronological overview of the political developments, I move on to a detailed picture of necropolitics, which has heavily dominated the Kurdish political and social space. The Kurdish resistance including the organised victim movements emerged as part of this space. In Chapter 4 and Chapter 6, I analyse the Saturday Mothers movement and their contributions to pillars of transitional justice. Since Saturday Mothers was mobilised to demand truth and justice for enforced disappearances, I give a detailed account of these and their impact on the families in Section 2.4. In relation to this, Section 2.5 situates the Saturday Mothers movement within the broader scope of the organised victim groups who have challenged the state's politics of death. Finally, in Section 2.6, I provide an overview of the transitional justice-related efforts made by the state and the grassroots actors. This section sets the scene for the detailed analysis of Turkey's transitional justice trajectories analysed in Chapter 8.

## 2.2 Background to the Kurdish Conflict

### *Kurds in the Early Republic Era*

The total number of Kurds is estimated to be between 30 and 40 million in total, constituting the fourth-largest ethnic group in the Middle East. Most live in the area that has been historically named Kurdistan, which extends through south-eastern Turkey, western Iran, northern Iraq, and portions of northern Syria (Jongerden and Hamdi Akkaya, 2015). Between 15 and 20 million Kurds live in Turkey, constituting 20–25% of the total population. Following the collapse of the Ottoman Empire at the end of World War I, the 1920 Treaty of Sèvres and the 1923 Treaty of Lausanne redrew the map of the Middle East. The newly created borders established the new modern states of Turkey, Iraq, and Syria and left Kurds divided across four countries.

The Kurdish conflict has been one of the longest-lasting armed conflicts in the Middle East. It is rooted in the history of the Turkish Republic, which was founded in 1923, although the armed conflict started in 1984 when the PKK launched its first major attack against the Turkish military forces. The modern Turkey was founded as a nation-state based on the ambition to create a homogenous Turkish nation (Jongerden, 2017). The state's efforts to promote nationalism and turn the multi-ethnic and multireligious republic into a homogeneous nation created a particular cultural identity with which the citizens should comply. Ethno-religious diversity that was inherited from the Ottoman Empire was now considered an obstacle to stability and progress (Zeydanlıoğlu, 2008). Islam was no longer the social glue for the new Republic, which made the religious commonalities between Turks and Kurds irrelevant to the new context, while rendering ethno-linguistic differences more visible. To consolidate the power of the newly founded modern Turkey, this understanding required the Turkification of all peoples living within the borders of the country.

The state labelled ethno-religious minorities as others, saw them as potential threats to the established order, and implemented restrictions to their political rights (Kaya and Whiting, 2019). Alongside non-Muslims, Alevis, and Armenians, Kurds were among those minorities and were the largest group of non-Turkish people with a distinct culture and language (Zeydanlıoğlu, 2008). Hence, the state had the need to undertake a deliberate campaign to eradicate the distinctive Kurdish identity, with the objective of assimilating the Kurdish population into the Turkish identity through a variety of coercive measures. This forced assimilation, structural efforts to abolish Kurds' cultural identity, is explained at length in the next section.

### *Racism and Assimilationist Policies towards Kurds*

The state's policies towards Kurds are not limited to assimilation but also include denial and annihilation, implementing diverse strategies from a broad repertoire. Even though assimilation policies dominate, they give rise to various forms of racism (Göral and Benlisoy, 2024; Yarkın, 2022).

Identity has been at the centre of the Kurdish conflict. Shortly after the proclaiming of the Turkish Republic in 1923, the Turkish state adopted a dual discourse concerning its Kurdish population. On the one hand, it denied the very existence of the Kurds and identified them as a feudal and oppressive ethno-class on the other (Yeğen, 1999). The official state discourse framed the Turkish ethnicity as the founder of all Anatolian civilisations and situated the Kurdish people within the Turkish nation (Zeydanlıoğlu, 2008). According to this official narrative, Kurds had forgotten that they were Turks, and they were speaking some form of Persian (Beşikçi, 1990).

As will be explored in the next chapters, denial "as a macro-level political strategy" has remained as a state policy to date (Avci, 2019). For decades, successive Turkish governments refused to recognise its Kurdish population as a distinct people and denied them the linguistic, ethnic, cultural, religious, economic, and political rights (Bozarslan, 2008). It was hoped that the systematic assimilation policies toward the Kurdish identity would ensure the loyalty of the Kurdish citizens to the nation-state (Zeydanlıoğlu, 2008). On the contrary, preserving the identity became one of the central pillars of the Kurdish resistance (Yeğen, 1996). Those policies ultimately paved the way for the emergence of the Kurdish political movement, which grew to challenge denial and assimilation (Gunes, 2013).

The denial of the Kurdish identity for assimilationist purposes was materialised through the oppression on the Kurdish language, notably a policy of linguicide (Amir Hassanpour et al., 2012), the destruction of historical-cultural, social, and political accumulation of the Kurds, and restrictive and punitive policies on the production and consumption of cultural products of music and literature (Üstündağ, 2019; Coşkun et al., 2013). One example of linguicide was the ban on the usage of the words "Kurds", "Kurdistan", and "Kurdish". Zeydanlığlu (2008, p. 7) explains how the Kurdish culture and identity were denied at the initial stages of the new republic:

> The Kurdish language, traditional dress, folklore and any expression of Kurdish culture were banned and reconstructed as "Turkish". All references to a territory called "Kurdistan", which had been widely acknowledged during the Ottoman era, were removed from maps and official documents, and Turkish names gradually replaced the names of Kurdish towns and villages. Most rural Kurds only became aware of the new Turkish names of their villages through contact with the Turkish gendarmerie.

To date, there are significant political barriers preventing Kurdish speakers from transmitting their language to the next generations (Zeydanlioğlu, 2012). Although the government made some minor changes in this regard, these changes remained instrumentalised and calculated moves to respond to internal and external pressures before elections, without addressing the structural issues or root causes (Derince, 2013).

The roots of the armed conflict, characterised by some as an identity-driven conflict, thus stems from the state's lack of willingness to recognise the Kurdish identity (Mohammed and Romano, 2023). My interviewees' responses reflect the impact of the state's attitude towards Kurdish identity, especially assimilationist strategies, on the Kurdish issue. For example, an interlocutor stated that the conflict is essentially a matter of identity and status: "The issue is about Kurds not finding a place in the share of hegemony. It is a problem of fundamental human rights and freedoms . . . It [the state's oppression] is considered as the erasure of an identity" (Interview no:14, 2020). The next section elaborates on how assimilation as a root cause of the conflict has led a decades-long armed conflict to emerge in the 1980s.

## *The Emergence and Development of the Armed Conflict from the 1960s to 1990s*

The armed conflict is the manifestation of the "systematic denial and degradation of Kurds" (Jongerden, 2017, p. 3). Military coups in 1960, 1971, and 1980 augmented the assimilationist and repressive policies against Kurds. In addition to political repression, forced Turkification policies denied Kurds naming their children with Kurdish names. They included the opening of boarding schools in the Kurdish region where Kurdish children would more easily assimilated because they were separated from their families (Beşikçi, 1990; Zeydanlıoğlu, 2008). In the 1970s and 1980s, the national liberation discourse within the Kurdish political movement gained power and identified the Kurds as a colonised people and Kurdistan as an interstate and international colony which led to the idea that to achieve national unification, a revolutionary movement was required under the leadership of the Kurdish working class (Gunes, 2013).

The 1980 military coup was not only formative in a growing support for the Kurdish political movement, but it has also targeted left-wing organisations, trade unionists, politicians, university professors, teachers, journalists and lawyers, causing a long-term human and social cost (Zürcher, 2017). At the end of the first year following the coup, 122,600 individuals had been arrested (Zürcher, 2017). Torture was widespread during the detainees' interrogation and the following imprisonment, which was criticised by international human rights organisations at the time. Through the coup, the systemic assimilative and repressive state practices against Kurds also increased massively, which portrayed the Kurdish region as a specific threat to the national unity of the country (McDowall, 2007).

Following the 1989 coup, a heavy military presence was placed in the Kurdish region with the task of administering a major Turkification plan, including the arrest of 81,000 Kurds (McDowall, 2007). Military prisons became places where systematic torture was used against Kurds.[1] In 1982, the military junta authored a new constitution which included the articles that codified the assimilation. For example, Article 28/2 prohibited the use of "any language prohibited by law" in publications and broadcasts, and Article 42/9 banned the teaching of any other language than Turkish "as a native language to the citizens of Turkey" Constitution of Turkey, 1982). In effect, these articles, among others, targeted specifically the Kurdish language and constitutionalised the ban of it. The 1982 constitution was also problematic in terms of how it defined citizenship. Article 66 stated that "everyone bound to the Turkish state through the bond of citizenship is a Turk". This article has attracted a lot of criticism for defining citizenship based on the ethnic Turkish identity and discriminating against citizens of other ethnic origins.[2]

Yavuz (2001, p. 12) notes that "the 1980 coup and its oppressiveness helped to create a siege mentality among Kurds, compelling them to think that their future was constrained and contained by the Turkish state". A Human Rights Watch report published in July 1990 with the title "Destroying Ethnic

1 See Chapter 7 for a civil society-led transitional justice effort to deal with the legacy of the Diyarbakir Military Prison, the most notorious military prison of the post-1980 military coup period.

2 The Constitutional Reconciliation Commission was established in the parliament in 2011 to work on a new constitution. During that period, the Kurdish political movement and left-wing civil society organisations advocated for replacing the ethnicity-based citizenship with constitutional citizenship, which would mean that citizenship would be independent from race, ethnicity, gender or religion (Barkey and Kadıoğlu, 2011). The Commission was dissolved in 2013 without reaching any conclusion.

Identity: The Kurds of Turkey" reveals this mentality and addresses Kurdish community's outrage about the ongoing denial of their ethnic identity: "Kurds told us again and again that they want to be able to speak Kurdish officially, to read Kurdish books, to sing Kurdish songs, to dance Kurdish dances, to celebrate Kurdish holidays, and to give their children Kurdish names" (Human Rights Watch, 1990, p. 2).

The growing frustration with the oppressive policies coincided with the expansion in the Kurdish political scene. During the 1950s and 1960s, "individuals from all social groups of the Kurdish people" (Yeğen, 2016, p. 368) were involved in Kurdish resistance in urban areas, especially in major Kurdish and Turkish cities. Starting from the 1960s onwards, the profile of Kurds involved in the resistance began shifting towards Kurdish students and educated professionals who used a leftist and secular terminology. They saw the Kurdish issue as "a question of colonialism and championed a solution to it through a hybrid program in which the notions of national liberation and class emancipation were intertwined" (Yeğen, 2016, p. 369).

Among the Kurdish resistance groups who emerged at that period to challenge the political and cultural oppression, the PKK stood out by attracting a mass support, mobilisation, and activism during the 1980s and 1990s (Gunes, 2013; Yeğen, 2016). The PKK's formation started between the 1971 and 1980 military coups, but it was formally established in 1978 under Abdullah Öcalan's leadership. Since the PKK emerged from Turkey's revolutionary left tradition, there were both Kurds and Turks among the founding members (Jongerden and Hamdi Akkaya, 2015). They expressed their key objectives as "the right to self-determination, understood at the time as the establishment of an independent and united Kurdistan, and a socialist transformation of society" (Jongerden and Akkaya, 2015, p. 4). By the early 1990s, the PKK had reached to ten thousand guerrilla fighters who secured territorial dominance across wide rural areas in south-eastern Turkey Jongerden and Akkaya, 2015).

Within the context of the armed conflict, the armed forces and state-led paramilitaries employed indiscriminate violence towards civilians in the Kurdish-populated regions which were under the state of emergency between 1987 and 2002. According to the Human Rights Investigation Commission of the Grand National Assembly of Turkey (*Türkiye Büyük Millet Meclisi*), 35,567 people died due to the armed conflict between 1984 and 2013, 7,918 of whom were public servants, and the rest were Kurdish civilians and guerrilla fighters (Türkiye Büyük Millet Meclisi, 2013). In collaboration with paramilitary and extremist groups and intelligence organs, Special Forces (*Özel Timler*) murdered thousands of Kurdish intellectuals, human rights activists, and politicians while terrorising the population at large (McDowall, 2007). Similar to the resettlement programmes of the early decades of the republic, the 1990s saw mass-scale village evacuations where Kurdish peasants were exposed to "degrading behaviour, arbitrary arrest, violence, torture, extra-judicial killings, sexual violence or threats of violence and the wanton destruction (or plunder) of moveable property, livestock and food stocks" (McDowall, 2007, p. 440). What set the 1990s apart from the other decades of the armed conflict was the extreme violence targeted against civilians, turning the 1990s into the most violently turbulent decade in the century-long history of conflict in northern Kurdistan (Işık, 2020).

The PKK's activities have not remained limited to the military area. The PKK "has proven itself capable of simultaneous engagement in armed struggle and popular political mobilization, including by taking part in elections and controlling local governments" (Jongerden and Hamdi Akkaya, 2015, p. 5). As of the 1990s, the PKK has transformed into a transnational social and political movement Gunes, 2013). Its political and military actions led many Kurds to mobilise. Alongside the armed campaign by the PKK, many Kurds resisted political violence through peaceful means such as mass rallies, school boycotts, and shutdowns of shops (Çelik, 2014; Gunes, 2013). Therefore, the 1990s were not only the peak of state violence against Kurds but were also central to the political mobilisation and empowerment of the Kurdish people.

The rapid mobilisation and empowerment were also reflected in the fact that Kurdish political parties started to gain widespread support in Turkey in the 1990s. In the same period, the PKK mobilised the Kurdish diaspora in Europe and formed a large network of cultural centres and community organisations (Gunes, 2013). The Kurdish diaspora started to organise campaigns in Europe to expose state violence. In cooperation with their foreign colleagues, Kurdish lawyers filed lawsuits before the European Court of Human Rights (ECtHR), which became an essential tool for holding the Turkish state accountable in the eyes of a wider audience (Uçarlar, 2015). Kurdish lawyers used the ECtHR as a tool for legal mobilisation and social transformation (Kurban, 2020).

The end of the 1990s was marked by two critical developments for the Kurdish issue and Turkish politics. The PKK leader Abdullah Öcalan was captured in Kenya and brought back to Turkey, which sparked worldwide protests among Kurds and their allies. Following Öcalan's capture, the PKK announced a unilateral ceasefire.[3] It also marked a shift in the PKK's conceptualisation of the right to self-determination by shifting the demands from independence to democratic citizenship within Turkey (Yeğen, 2016). The second critical development was the European Union's (EU) approval of Turkey's candidate status for full membership, which required Turkey to introduce new reforms, including those related to the Kurdish rights (Ardic, 2019; Yeğen, 2015).

3 To date, Kurds have been attending wide-scale protests every February 15 to demand Öcalan's release.

### *The AKP Era: From the 2000s Onwards*

When the current ruling party, Justice and Development Party (*Adalet ve Kalkınma Partisi*, AKP), first came to power in 2002; it introduced itself as a radical shift from Turkey's illiberal political tradition shaped by military juntas. The current president, Recep Tayyip Erdoğan, came into power as the prime minister in 2003 and had made a name for himself by breaking away from that tradition (Karaveli, 2016). However, throughout the history of the Turkish Republic, there has been the trend of "pursuing a democratic agenda only to the extent to which it promotes the interests of the party" (Kaya and Whiting, 2019, p. 94). The AKP has not fallen far from this general trend. Its reform agenda never aimed fundamental change in the state's positioning towards the citizens (Jongerden, 2018). Seemingly, the reforms were made to move forward with the EU accession negotiations, but that they were more about the AKP's "struggle to conquer the state" (Jongerden, 2018, p. 11).

In parallel to the ambition for breaking away with the past, Erdoğan promised a set of reforms towards democratisation, such as enhancing "the separation of powers, the independence of the judiciary, the freedom of the press, and the rule of law" (Karaveli, 2016, p. 124). As part of this general trend towards democratisation, another vital issue that Erdoğan promised was a change in the state's approach to the Kurdish issue. It is in this context that the AKP launched the "Democratic Opening" in 2005, which continued with secret talks between the Turkish state and the PKK in Oslo, Brussels, and other European countries. What has come to be known as "Oslo Process" was a series of meetings held between 2008–2011 with the representatives of both parties and mediated by several countries, including Norway and the UK (International Crisis Group, 2012; Savran, 2020). These secretly held talks became known to the public only after the minutes of a meeting were leaked through a news agency. The Oslo Process was significant in terms of being the first instance of direct engagement between Turkey and the PKK (Ensaroglu, 2013).

The democratic opening included several legal, political, social, and economic measures to ease the tension between the Kurdish population and the Turkish state, which was among the criteria for EU accession. In the coming months, the government took several social measures such as the establishment of a Kurdish–language TV channel as part of the state-owned Turkish Radio and Television Cooperation. But the most well-known and perhaps most symbolic development was the agreement of the return of 34 PKK members and Kurdish refugees through the Habur crossing on the Turkey-Iraq border. While the Kurdish movement welcomed the returnees with a massive reception rally, the government and the Turkish nationalists reacted angrily (International Crisis Group, 2012; Yeğen, 2015). The process slowed down gradually, and the talks came to an end following the June 2011 parliamentary elections.

In December 2012, Prime Minister Erdogan declared on national television that the government resumed the talks with the PKK again. In January 2013, state delegations and the Peace and Democracy Party[4] took a critical step and announced the start of the peace negotiations in İmralı Island where Öcalan was imprisoned. Despite several pitfalls, this round of negotiations was different from the previous peace efforts, and it raised elevated expectations. First, the government shared the start of the process with the public from the initial stages, which was a long-standing demand of the Kurdish side. This was perceived as a genuine commitment to the peace process since the Oslo Process had been criticised for being held secret (Savran, 2020). Second, several legal and social mechanisms were developed to facilitate the process and gather public support. For example, the government selected 67 people including academics, journalists, politicians, civil society representatives, and artists to form Wise People Committees. These committees were tasked to explain the process in gatherings across the country and discuss the process with the society (Çelik, 2020). Another example is that in June 2014, the Parliament passed the Law to End Terror and Strengthen Social Integration to ensure that the government was authorised to take the necessary steps to move forward the resolution process. It was important in terms of providing a legal basis and guarantee for the process, as Öcalan and the PKK demanded (Yeğen, 2015).

In February 2015, the government delegation and the HDP delegations publicly read the Dolmabahçe Declaration, which listed ten steps to address in the next stages. It was also stated that Öcalan had called the PKK to organise a conference for disarmament in spring (Bianet, 2021). The declaration signified the evolution of the negotiations to a peace agreement (Bor et al., 2021). Both the government representatives and the PKK leadership openly welcomed this move, highlighting the declaration as a historical moment (Bianet, 2021). President Erdoğan made a supportive statement emphasising the significance of the call for disarmament for trust, peace, and stability (Bianet, 2015). However, only a couple of weeks later he stated that he did not approve of the Dolmabahçe Declaration, which gave the first signs of the ending of the peace process (Bor et al., 2021).

## 2.3 Current Political Context: Ongoing Conflict and Authoritarianism

Parliamentary elections in June 2015, the failed military coup d'état in July 2016, and the presidential referendum in April 2017 have been the critical turning points that have shaped Turkey's current authoritarian political

4 The pro-Kurdish BDP was founded in 2008. In 2014, the party decided that its parliamentarians should join the pro-Kurdish HDP which took part in the peace talks after that.

regime (Erensü and Alemdaroğlu, 2018). In the June elections, the left-wing pro-Kurdish, left-wing HDP passed the 10% electoral threshold, becoming the second-largest opposition party in the parliament. A broad base of voters including the Kurds, left-wing activists, LGBTI+ activists, and other minority groups celebrated the HDP's success as a historical moment, and an opportunity to enhance democracy (The Guardian, 2015). With the election results, the Kurdish movement had proved itself as a political power on the national level. The HDP's electoral victory denied the AKP the parliamentary majority it had been holding for a long time. The AKP vote had reduced dramatically, and it implied an end to its hegemony as the dominant party through democratic means (Akkoyunlu and Öktem, 2016).

The election results would require a power-sharing model which would entail Erdoğan asking the opposition to form a coalition or minority government. However, contrary to the optimistic expectations, Erdoğan ignored the democratic conventions and declared early elections for November 2015 while at the same time launching a new phase of war against the PKK (Hakyemez, 2017). Between the June and November elections, the HDP and the pro-Kurdish activists faced an intense period of violence and terror attacks while the Kurdish region experienced the eruption of war between the state security forces and the PKK. The state's military operations against the PKK were accompanied by the government's increasingly nationalist discourse. Using this deliberately created atmosphere of fear and violence, Erdoğan argued that he and his party would be the only way to ensure security and stability (Akkoyunlu and Öktem, 2016; Yılmaz and Turner, 2019). This discourse proved useful and the AKP vote increased again in November elections, providing it with the majority needed to form a single party government once again. It was the first time an election result was ignored since 1950 and describe these repeat elections as the marking point of Turkey's exit from democracy (Akkoyunlu and Öktem, 2016). Summer 2015 also marked the end of the period of the search for a political resolution of the conflict and the Kurdish issue "once again turned into a question of security, order, sovereignty and confrontation of two armed forces" (Yılmaz and Turner, 2019, p. 695).

Following the re-securitisation of the Kurdish issue, the Kurdish movement declared its commitment to self-governance, which was already in development since the 2000s. The self-governance model advocates for breaking down centralised state power and bureaucracy by establishing grassroots organisations and transferring sovereignty to local entities (Küçük and Özselçuk, 2016). Although this model draws on the self-organising communities in the form of assemblies on the level of villages, neighbourhoods, towns, and cities to deal with the daily problems and act politically, Jongerden argues that in the winter of 2015–2016, the PKK over-emphasised the military aspect in the face of the state violence (Jongerden, 2018). The state security forces responded to the self-governance declaration using overwhelming violence to break the barricades and trenches built and dug by the Kurdish militant youth to set up self-governance zones. The winter of 2015–2016 was the peak of the fatality rate in the armed conflict. The rapid escalation of violence and the shift from rural to urban warfare resulted in months-long blanket curfews in the Kurdish region and a heavy military presence of the security and paramilitary forces. The clashes in towns ended up causing the death of many civilians and forced displacement of those whose houses were destroyed by the clashes. According to the United Nations High Commissioner for Human Rights Report on the human rights situation in South-East Turkey:

> Between July 2015 and December 2016, some 2,000 people were reportedly killed in the context of security operations in South-East Turkey. According to information received, this would include close to 800 members of the security forces, and approximately 1,200 local residents, of which an unspecified number may have been involved in violent or non-violent actions against the State.
>
> (UN, 2017)

Following the violent period of clashes, it was in July 2016 that a failed coup d'état took place. The coup attempt marked the beginning of the regime transformation towards authoritarianism. A couple of days after the attempt, the government declared a state of emergency for an initial period of three months, but it was not until the June 2018 elections that the state of emergency was finally abolished. By using the coup and the state of emergency that lasted two years, Erdoğan extended his powers, presenting these changes as nation-saving (Yılmaz and Turner, 2019). The state of emergency enabled the government to target its dissidents, the majority of from the Kurdish movement. The government removed democratically elected mayors in the Kurdish region from office. During this period, hundreds of thousands of civil servants, judges, and security officials were fired based on decrees. Alongside the massive purge in state institutions, several civil society organizations were shut down, including those in the Kurdish region. The repression that targeted civil society increased at that period and played a leading role in shrinking the civic space (Kaya and Öğünç, 2020). Another crucial element of the human rights crackdown was the detention and arrest of Kurdish political figures including the elected mayors, co-chairs, parliamentarians, and human rights activists (Human Rights Watch, 2020).

Erdoğan used this period of suspended freedoms to force the country into a referendum to enable a regime change from a parliamentary system to an executive presidential system (Kaya and Whiting, 2019). A referendum on 16 April 2017 made a constitutional change possible to put a presidential system in place. By expanding the president's powers and reducing those of parliament, this new system was "organized around the supreme power of the

President, erosion of checks and balances and separation of powers" (Yılmaz and Turner, 2019). In the June 2018 elections, Erdoğan was elected as the first president of the new political system. The elections became the last step of the AKP's pursuit of full control of the state and the transformation to authoritarianism (Kaya and Whiting, 2019). However, it must be noted that the authoritarian rule was already a norm in the Kurdish region, and it has gradually turned to a generalised pattern for all over the country since the coup attempt in July 2016. The next section explores one of the key features of the state's presence in the Kurdish region: necropolitics.

## 2.4 Necropolitics in Turkey

So far in this chapter, I have used a chronological lens to give an overview of the Kurdish conflict and the state's approach to the Kurdish issue. From this point on, I move to explore the nature of the state's relation with its Kurdish population by looking at necropolitical violence. This form of violence is central to identifying the organised victim movements discussed in the last section of this chapter. By looking at the necropolitics and the victim movements challenging it, these sections set the scene for Chapter 4's discussion of the Saturday Mothers movement which lies at the centre of my analysis for the role of the organised victims in advancing the transitional justice agenda.

Death has been present in the Turkish state's relation with Kurds in different forms within the context of the armed conflict: enforced disappearances, extrajudicial killings, and torture. Following Mbembe's (2003, p. 39) definition of "the subjugation of life to the power of death", several scholars consider the Turkish state's widespread, systemic, and multidimensional practices towards Kurdish dead bodies as necropolitics (Aydın, 2018; Bargu, 2019; Ozsoy, 2010; Yıldırım, 2021). "The spectacular dimensions of this power to kill and reign over the protocols of burial attest to the systematic elision of the possibilities of collective life and democratic politics in Turkey" (Akıncı, 2017, p. 47). Arguing there is a constant necropolitical undercurrent under Turkey's political regime, Bargu Bargu (2019, p. 213) explains the term "necropolitical violence" as the following:

> those acts that target the dead bodies of those killed in armed conflict, by way of their mutilation, dismemberment, denuding, desecration, dragging and public display, the destruction of local cemeteries and other sacred spaces that are designated for communication with and commemoration of the dead, the delay, interruption or suspension of the conduct of funerary rituals, the imposition of mass or any delay, interruption or suspension of the conduct of funerary rituals, the imposition of mass or anonymous internment, the pressure for clandestine internment and the repression and dispersion of funeral processions for the newly dead.

The burial of killed guerrillas in mass graves, the ban on funeral ceremonies, and the punitive policies towards the families of the dead have been among common state practices. In terms of the Kurdish conflict, sovereign power and the politics of national identity build themselves around the political and symbolic constructions of death and dead bodies (Ozsoy, 2010, p. 13). This was reflected in most of my Kurdish interlocutors' response to my question of the most severe conflict-related victimisation to date. Among them, they highlighted the disappearance and destruction of dead bodies and the disruption of the rituals surrounding death.

The state's necropolitics have shaped the Kurdish political and social space by creating a tradition of resistance. The state's practices around guerrilla funerals, for example, played a significant role in transforming the PKK into a popular movement. As the guerrilla bodies were delivered from the mountains to Kurdish cities and towns in the early 1990s, the process of *serhildan*[5] emerged and spread to the whole region (Ozsoy, 2010). Thus, necropolitics has also shaped the context for organised victim groups and gave emergence to the most systemically organised victims group as a response to the state's politics of death. Section 2.5 explores those groups and Chapter 4 analyses one of them, the Saturday Mothers movement.

### *Extrajudicial Killings*

Enforced disappearances and extrajudicial killings marked Turkey's history of state violence in the 1990s, particularly under the state of emergency rule in the Kurdish region between 1984 and 2012. Following the adoption of a special security strategy in 1993, state security forces employed violent practices such as the destruction, burning down, and evacuation of villages, and the forced displacement of villagers. Enforced disappearances and extrajudicial killings, popularly known as "perpetrator-unknown murders," intensified between 1993 and 1996, becoming one of the most widespread and systematic practices of state violence (Sevimli et al., 2021).

Extrajudicial killings, also known as extralegal or extrajudicial executions, refer to the deliberate killing of individuals by state actors without the sanction of any judicial proceeding (OHCHR, 2021). These acts are typically carried out by government authorities or their agents and are considered serious violations of human rights. In Turkey, extrajudicial killings have been a persistent state practice, particularly in the context of the armed conflict. Throughout the 1990s, Turkish security forces were implicated in numerous extrajudicial killings of Kurdish civilians and suspected PKK members (Human Rights Watch, 2012). These killings were part of a broader

5 *Serhildan* is a Kurdish word meaning uprising or rebellion. It has come to be used to refer to the wide scale Kurdish protests since the 1990s.

strategy to suppress Kurdish political and cultural identity, often carried out with impunity and without accountability (Amnesty International, 1992). The targeted Kurdish individuals included activists, politicians, journalists, and ordinary civilians advocating for Kurdish rights. Especially during the 1990s, state security forces and far-right paramilitary also frequently targeted left-wing dissidents including leftist activists, politicians, and journalists through extrajudicial killings. They were part of a wider campaign to eliminate political opposition and dissent (Human Rights Watch, 2012).

### *Enforced Disappearances*

Enforced disappearances, while related, differ from extrajudicial killings in that they involve the abduction or detention of individuals by state agents, followed by a refusal to acknowledge the person's fate or whereabouts (OHCHR, 2021). This practice aims to remove individuals from the protection of the law and places them outside the reach of judicial oversight. Following the 1980 military coup and throughout the 1990s, enforced disappearances evolved into a systematic state policy targeting Kurds and other dissidents (İHD, 2024) with many activists and civilians disappearing after being taken into custody by security forces (Human Rights Watch, 2012). The key distinction lies in the state's denial of the individual's detention in enforced disappearances, whereas extrajudicial killings involve the direct and deliberate taking of life without legal process (Amnesty International, 1993).

Those who were disappeared in 1990s were mostly allegedly linked to the PKK, therefore mostly Kurds living on the geographical and social margins (Göral, 2021). Even though the exact numbers are not known (İHD, 2007) and therefore thought to be much higher, human rights organisations identified that 1388 people were forcibly disappeared between 1980–2001 (İHD, 2022). In 2011, the Turkish Medical Association set up an investigation committee to investigate the mass graves. They paid a study visit to districts and villages of Bitlis, Siirt, Batman, and Diyarbakir, the areas that had the most mass graves. They shared the findings in a press conference and stated that 114 mass graves are reported to contain the bones of 1,469 people and that the bones of 171 people have been found in 26 mass graves. They added that the real scale of the phenomenon is much larger, and they believe there are thousands of unidentified bodies buried in hundreds of mass graves in a vast geography from Hakkari to Tunceli (Türk Tabipleri Birliği, 2011). Similarly, in 2022, the Human Rights Association Diyarbakir branch's Commission of Enforced Disappearance noted that between 1980–2001, and predominantly in the 1990s, the state's armed forces and paramilitary forces forcibly disappeared 1388 individuals, but they know the real numbers are much higher (İHD Diyarbakır, 2022).

In Turkey and elsewhere, enforced disappearances have been used to silence political opposition and impose terror and silence over the broader society (Duhaime, 2023; Kovras, 2017a). States use them as "a systematic method of oppression in many countries, and particularly affected by this practice are minority, indigenous, ethnic or other groups of people" (Sarkin and Baranowska, 2018, p. 13). Enforced disappearance create the fear that anyone could fall into that unknown place (Göral et al., 2013). The relatives of the disappeared are exposed to the fear of being disappeared, killed, imprisoned, or losing other relatives if they push the topic too hard. Kovras (2017a) provides the example of an Argentinian case, where relatives, friends, and neighbours feared for their own safety and distanced themselves from the families of the disappeared. After the disappeared person, the immediate family members are among the first targets of enforced disappearance and "it intimidates, demobilizes, depoliticizes, and ultimately reduces individuals to passivity with the threat of disappearance" (Bargu, 2014, p. 10).

The International Convention for the Protection of All Persons from Enforced Disappearance (CED) (2006) defines enforced disappearances as:

> [T]he arrest, detention, abduction or any other form of deprivation of liberty by agents of the State or by persons or groups of persons acting with the authorization, support or acquiescence of the State, followed by a refusal to acknowledge the deprivation of liberty or by concealment of the fate or whereabouts of the disappeared person, which place such a person outside the protection of the law.

Enforced disappearance is recognised as one of the few crimes that are continuous (CED art. 8, 2006) which continues until the state acknowledges the detention and release information on the fate about the disappeared person. Even in "the unexplained absence of victims," there is a visibility that all atrocities need for creating a political effect (Humphrey, 2002, p. 26). This form of visibility entails the terror and fear created due to the act of disappearance, and the political effect extends to families and the wider community. According to the CED (art. 24(1)), anyone who has been directly harmed by an enforced disappearance is recognised as a victim of the crime, including the family members of the disappeared. As victims, they have the right to know the truth about the violation and the whereabouts of their loved ones.

In Turkey, relatives of the disappeared either directly witnessed the act of enforced disappearance or have suffered the direct outcomes of the act (Göral et al., 2013). One of my interlocutors, a Diyarbakır-based lawyer, argued that enforced disappearance served multiple objectives. The first was to physically destroy the targeted person, to neutralise and annihilate them. The second was to spread the fear to those who stayed behind and the wider society, conveying the message that this kind of destiny awaits them, too (Interview no:16, 2020).

### *The Aftermath of Enforced Disappearance*

Fear is a determining factor in what happens in the immediate aftermath of the disappearance. Especially in the initial period, the families believe and hope that the disappeared might be alive and refrain from engaging too much with the judicial or law enforcement bodies, thinking that any mistake can cause the death of the loved one (Alpkaya, 1995). Until the 2000s, the cases against the perpetrators of enforced disappearance had not faced any criminal proceedings. Families' fear of the consequences has played a role in that (Işık, 2020). An Istanbul-based lawyer who has been following the enforced disappearance cases highlights that the hesitation to search for the whereabouts of the disappeared still burden the families creating a sense of guilt:

> There is the burden of the fact that they could not search adequately because they were afraid. For example, you file a letter six times, and they say we are going to take you as well if you come for the seventh time. 'I'll get your other child; I'll get your husband. Don't search for your son.' Some dare to continue to search; some don't. Those who don't continue to live with that feeling for their entire life.
>
> (Interview no:3, 2019)

The fear of being criminalised and punished continues to haunt the present. As a Diyarbakır-based lawyer with close ties to the families of the disappeared states, the war continues, and the trauma of the past is yet to be overcome:

> The painful, horrifying acts of the past take space in people's memory. And because the past has not been dealt with, those people, could not yet enter the psychology of calling someone to account. People still think they might be punished in all sorts of ways. Even if it isn't enforced disappearances, they think they might face custody, arrest, and other serious rights violations. Or they think they might face several other problems such as civil death, getting fired from their job and economic violence.
>
> (Interview no:15, 2020)

The long-term direct impact of the enforced disappearances on the families is not limited to fear. Most importantly, it also takes the shape of a life-long grief that maintains families' search for truth and justice. When the body of the deceased is not there to bury, families cannot even start the mourning process (Stover and Shigekane, 2004). Those left behind find themselves in "a complicated psychological space" (Hamber, 2009, p. 81) as a result of the political trauma associated with the disappearance. Pauline Boss (2004, 2006) defines this as "ambiguous loss" as a type of loss that lacks clarity and closure, making it particularly challenging to resolve. It refers to situations where there is no clear verification of death or certainty about the loss, leaving individuals in a state of limbo. The disappearance of individuals due to political repression leads to a profound existential uncertainty for the survivors (Hamber, 2009). Both the survivors and the disappeared exist in a symbolically liminal space; that is, both are part of society but removed from society (Hamber, 2009, p. 81).

In Turkey, the experience of ambiguous loss is compounded by the guilt of not performing the ritualistic duties for the disappeared. The prolonged and disrupted grief has mobilised those unable to bury their children (Aydın, 2020). This partly explains the persistent efforts of the families of the disappeared in their pursuit of truth and justice, as I will explore in the following chapters. The following quote from a relative of the disappeared illustrates how the absence of the body remains a deeply painful experience for families throughout their lives:

> If you ask me what is one of the most painful things in the world, I'd say it is to be the relative of a disappeared person. Especially if you can't find your disappeared loved one, you can't even access his corpse, his dead body; that pain can't be described any way. And you carry this pain for your whole life. Especially if you lost your child.
>
> (Interview no:23, 2020)

The aim of spreading fear to the wider society to prevent people from mobilising for Kurdish rights was also a motivation behind extrajudicial killings. The following quote from a relative of an extrajudicially killed Kurdish lawyer in the 1990s shows how the state mentality behind enforced disappearances and extrajudicial killings is similar:

> I assume the purpose is to convey the message to all segments of society 'don't assume you are going to get away with it because you are rich, or that nobody will care about you because you are poor.' Either way, you are going to get killed if you open your mouth.
>
> (Interview no:18, 2020)

### *Impunity*

The aftermath of enforced disappearances constitutes a critical aspect of necropolitics, particularly in terms of impunity. The mechanisms now recognised under transitional justice were developed and implemented during the 1970s and 1980s in response to severe human rights violations in Latin American countries, most notably enforced disappearances. On a global scale, the advocacy and actions of families of the disappeared against impunity, and their pursuit of justice and accountability, have significantly contributed to the foundational principles and practices of transitional justice (Dewhirst and

Kapur, 2015).[6] In Turkey, challenging the impunity associated with enforced disappearances has similarly been a key dimension of grassroots transitional justice efforts.

Widespread human rights violations of the 1990s were mostly conducted by paramilitary groups, unofficially formed and supported by the state (Göral et al., 2013; Işık, 2020). However, none of the perpetrators were prosecuted for enforced disappearances until the early 2000s. The families of the disappeared submitted applications to legal authorities repeatedly, but the response was either inaction or rejection. In fact, since the early days of the Republic, Turkey has used impunity for state crimes as a consistent state policy, implemented to legitimise state violence against marginalised political, religious, and ethnic groups (Dinçer, 2022).[7]

Due to the total impunity that dominated the domestic judiciary in the 1990s, the ECHR became one of the only platforms that the victims of the Kurdish conflict could rely on to seek justice and truth. The hearings in the ECtHR presented the first opportunity to most applicants to be heard publicly in a legal forum (Çali, 2010). According to the Amicus Curia Report on Enforced Disappearance submitted to the Constitutional Court of Turkey, the number of enforced disappearance cases brought to the ECtHR was 118 by 2016. In 78 per cent of the applications, the ECtHR found Turkey responsible for the violation of the right to life and prohibition of torture, ill-treatment, and its failure to conduct an effective investigation, in complete contrast to domestic law. The cases brought to the ECtHR played an essential role in revealing the truth behind the conflict and challenging the state's policies of denial and silence over conflict-related human rights violations (Budak, 2015; Çali, 2010; Jongerden, 2017; Uçarlar, 2015).

As the term 'perpetrator-unknown murders' suggests, impunity prevails in both enforced disappearances and extrajudicial killings, presenting similar challenges in the pursuit of justice. However, the experiences of families differ significantly between these two crimes. For the families of the disappeared, the uncertainty of not knowing the fate or whereabouts of the loved one creates fear and anxiety, as the disappeared are perceived to be in a state between life and death (Göral et al., 2013). Immediately following a disappearance, relatives actively search to prevent the murder of their loved one, but as hope vanishes after a while, although it never completely ceases, their efforts shift to searching for remains. Additionally, for the relatives of the disappeared, the absence of a body and a grave to mourn over impedes the

6 In a 2025 conference on transitional justice in the MENA region, Sebla Arcan (spokesperson of the Saturday Mothers in Istanbul) emphasised this point.

7 **As explored at more length in the coming chapters, 2008 marked a significant breaking point in terms of "the legal struggle against impunity", although none of the legal cases that began from then on reached a meaningful judicial outcome (Göral, 2019, p. 60).**

mourning process, leaving them "suspended in a vacuum between a hopeful wait and the process of mourning" (Göral et al., 2013, p. 71).

### *Attacks on Kurds' Dead Bodies and Cemeteries*

Necropolitics in Turkey does not only operate through killings or disappearances, but also through attacks on funerals, the destruction of cemeteries, and the torture of the bodies of PKK guerrillas. Burying the Kurdish civilians and PKK guerrillas in mass graves and damaging human remains have been sustained state practices in the Kurdish region throughout the course of the armed conflict. Especially in the 1990s, state security forces used to bury the guerrillas' dead bodies in mass graves or even garbage areas, or where the clashes between the security forces and the PKK took place. Within the literature around necropolitics, unmarked graves hold a prominent place in understanding the origins and outcomes of extreme violence, as these types of graves have the purpose of disappearing the memory of violence and maintaining the fear regimes by perplexing the survivors and increasing chaos and anxiety (Ferrandiz and Robben, 2015). Moreover, the state authorities would ban the funeral ceremonies, and the burials could only take place secretly at night (Aydın, 2015).

A substantial number of Kurdish families did not have a proper grave to mourn over their relatives' death either because the body has been disappeared or been buried in unmarked graves. Cultural and religious ceremonies following the death occupy an essential place in the Kurdish region. The mourning process is the most significant debt owed to the dead (Göral et al., 2013). Leaving the families without a grave or preventing them from carrying out their religious duties following the death means targeting a people's values, traditions, and rituals which have been carried out for hundreds if not thousands of years (Göral et al., 2013) and "erasing and stripping them of their identity" (Interview no:14, 2020).

Following a death, the family establishes a special set-up in a house or a dedicated condolence house (*taziye evi*) to accept condolences from the wider community (Ozsoy, 2010). The relatives, neighbours, friends, and acquaintances come to pay respect and offer condolences to the family. Food and tea are offered to visitors, and religious duties are held in the meantime. This process lasts several days, brings the community together with the family, and creates "a daily sharing space, revealing to what extent mourning is introduced into everyday life and how collective it is" (Bostan, 2022a). If it is the death of a political figure, a party member, or a guerrilla, the entire process gains a strong communal and political character. The prominent Kurdish politicians of the city also visit these condolence houses to show their solidarity with the family and the community. Therefore, preventing condolences gatherings isolates the family in their mourning process and targets the interlinking social and political ties that hold the community together.

To emphasise the critical importance of having a grave for families, a Diyarbakır-based civil society member shared with me a story about various families who decided to accept an unowned grave as their own child's grave and visit it regularly (Interview no:16, 2020). By so doing, they can at least carry out their rituals at a certain location at regular intervals. Another example is in the case of guerrilla deaths, where the official bodies give the families someone else's body because the DNA is mixed and then correct it. By that time, the mother has already bonded with that body, connected with the grave, prayed by it, and even watered the plants around it (Interview no:16, 2020). In such cases, the mother experiences a second layer of loss, this time of the grave and site for commemoration.

Preventing the families from receiving the dead body and thus holding proper burials in line with the cultural obligations have been increasing, especially since the end of the ceasefire in summer 2015 (Aydın, 2020). According to the report published by the Mesopotamia Observatory of Justice and Association of Lawyers for Freedom, the Turkish security forces destroyed 18 cemeteries of PKK guerrillas between 17 September 2015 and 4 April 2020 in 11 Kurdish provinces by air bombardments (Nejbir, 2021). Furthermore, in Kurdish cities, gravestones in guerrilla cemeteries were destroyed; the wider area was turned into special security zones, and the families were denied access (Deniz, 2018).

A Diyarbakır-based lawyer addressed the recently increased attacks on the dead guerrilla bodies and noted that she has been dealing a lot with those who cannot receive their loved ones' dead bodies from the Council of Forensic Medicine (ATK, *Adli Tıp Kurumu*). She highlighted that this type of problem has become worse in recent years. Even if the bodies are identified, the families are not allowed to practise their religious duties for the dead. Attending funerals and burial ceremonies during the daytime is often banned, and only a few people can attend at night. State control of the symbolic, communal, and social rituals around death has increased dramatically. As another interlocutor reflected:

> In the past, the state would not intervene in what happens after the family takes the dead body, and the family would do the funeral and mourning as they liked. And this is not about the pandemic. It used to be possible to hold mass funerals in the cemetery, and there was not much intervention. Now, they almost threaten the family in advance. 'You cannot have anyone over from the party. You cannot be crowded.' They only allow first-degree relatives, and they don't really establish condolence settings.
>
> (Interview no:19, 2020)

During the 2013–2015 peace process, PKK members built 13 guerrilla cemeteries in various parts of the Kurdish region and brought together the guerrilla bodies buried elsewhere and reburied them. Reburials have a community-creating function, as burials and reburials create and reorder community by bringing people together in a setting where they eat, drink, gossip and thereby integrate the dead into the same community as living people (Verdery, 1999). Indeed, Kurds began visiting these guerrilla cemeteries regularly and those sites enabled a collective grieving process (Aydın, 2015). Following the collapse of the peace process, however, the security forces attacked most of those cemeteries and carried the remains of the guerrilla bodies to other places without the families' knowledge (Aydın, 2020).

The most notorious incident happened in 2020, when 282 guerrilla bodies that were previously buried in the Xerzan district of Bitlis were found under a sidewalk in Istanbul (Bianet, 2022; Bostan, 2022b). While the state of emergency was still ongoing in 2017, military forces kept attacking Xerzan Cemetery. When the families went to visit their loved ones in December 2017, they found the whole cemetery destroyed by diggers and the bodies taken away without their knowledge. On 24 December 2017, the Bitlis branch of the Human Rights Association conducted an investigation at Xerzan Cemetery and reported that the cemetery had been demolished by construction machinery; the graves were empty, and no bones or other materials belonging to the burials were found (İnsan Hakları Derneği, 2018). The families' search for the whereabouts of their loved ones continued until 20 May 2020, when the Mesapotamia News Agency journalist Erdoğan Alayumat revealed that these bodies had been taken to Istanbul and buried under a pavement in *Kilyos Kimsesizler Mezarligi* (literally, Kilyos Cemetery for people who have no one) (Yeni Ozgur Politika, 2020). It was not even a proper burial, but a pile-up in a grave dug for only 18 people. On the same day that the news broke, the Association of Lawyers for Freedom investigated the cemetery and released a report stating that the manner that the bodies were buried on the pavement of the Istanbul Kilyos Cemetery is clearly against the law and incompatible with human dignity (Özgürlük İçin Hukukçular Derneği, 2019).

This grave violation of human rights created a sharp rift in Kurdish society, directly affecting hundreds of families and their communities who had their loved ones buried in an unlawful and disrespectful manner. Disappearing the bodies and leaving the families with the unknown was an attempt to punish those who had family members in the PKK, and its impact on the families was immense. Hanifi Can from *Anadolu Yakınlarını Kaybeden Ailelerle Yardımlaşma ve Dayanışma Derneği* (ANYAKAY-DER), who had buried the body of his brother Ferhat Can (killed in a clash in 2012 when he was a PKK guerrilla fighter) in Garzan Cemetery after long efforts described his and other families' devastating experience as follows:

> We took my brother from Kilyos to Bitlis, and this is the fourth time we buried him. We want this to be the last time, we don't want him to be dug up again. When I went to pick up my brother, there was also a mother

> who had come to pick up her child's body. The boxes were filled with dirty water. That mother took the bones of her son out of the box, washed, and shrouded them one by one, just like I did with my brother. Taking the bones of your son or brother and washing them is the greatest evil that can be done to a person.
>
> (BBC News, 2020)

Another form that the attack on dead bodies takes is humiliating the dead and the families through the public display of the distorted dead body, which added a new dimension to the state's treatment of the Kurdish dead body. For example, in August 2015, the image of a woman's dead and naked body went viral on social media alongside celebrations over her death. The woman in the images was Ekin Wan, a PKK guerrilla, who had died some days before in the clashes with security forces (Kaos GL, 2015). This public display and exposure of the dead body sparked protests from the Kurdish women's movement, feminists, and peace activists across the country. This type of display of the dead body is similar to what Carney calls "representational politics of death. A normalisation, spectecularisation, and even celebration of death in everyday life, chiefly by means of media" (Carney, 2019, p. 8).

One of my interlocutors stated that she used to witness through the Kurdish media the dead bodies of guerrillas being dragged across the floor in the 1990s, but such cases were not typically shown publicly by the security forces. This has now changed.

> It used to make the news only on Özgür Gündem,[8] but now the gendarmerie intelligence posts videos containing crimes against humanity on social media accounts with fake names. One of my clients identified his child's beheaded body on an anonymous Instagram account. This is the difference. I think that violence is legitimised seriously by the state.
>
> (Interview no:7, 2019)

Just as in the case of enforced disappearances, the destruction of dead bodies and the attacks on funerals deprive the families and the broader community of a decent burial mourning process, leaving them in an ambiguous place of loss.

8 Özgür Gündem was a daily newspaper published between 1992–1994 and 2011–2016 both in Kurdish and Turkish. It has occupied an important space in Kurdish journalism as it widely covered the conflict and was one of the few sources that reflected the Kurdish resistance. For that reason, the newspaper has been subjected to state violence, including enforced disappearances and arrests of its reporters and supporters.

## 2.5 An Overview of Organised Victim Groups

In this section, I provide an overview of organised victims' groups that have mobilised to challenge the Turkish state's practices of necropolitics, setting the stage for a deeper exploration of their contributions to transitional justice and the complexities of victimhood that I examine throughout the book. When discussing organised victims in the context of the Kurdish conflict, my interlocutors most frequently referenced the Saturday Mothers, Peace Mothers, Yakay-der, and Maya-der. These groups emerged primarily in response to enforced disappearances, guerrilla deaths, or both.

Globally, the families of the disappeared have persistently mobilised due to a profound personal need to mourn, coupled with a strong collective and political pursuit of truth and justice (Kovras, 2017b). Among these groups, the Saturday Mothers stand out as one of Turkey's most enduring and visible social movements. Since their first sit-in protest by families of the disappeared and human rights activists in 1995, the Saturday Mothers have demanded truth, accountability, and justice. I explore the evolution, struggles, and significant contributions of the Saturday Mothers to transitional justice in the following chapters.

In this section, I focus on the work of three additional groups—Peace Mothers, Yakay-der, and Maya-der—offering an introduction to their mobilisation efforts and the specific forms of advocacy they undertake. Before delving into the details of each group I clarify my terminological choice regarding victims and victimhood.

### *The Contested Identity of Victimhood in Turkey*

I acknowledge that the term "victim" may not fully capture the intricacies of a complex identity and remains a contested term based on the assumptions it might have passive connotations that strip people of agency and undermine the myriad complex experiences surrounding victimhood (Druliolle and Brett, 2018; De Waardt and Weber, 2019; Saeed, 2016). As I discuss and analyse at length in Chapter 5, the majority of my interlocutors expressed complex and conflicting feelings about the victim label. However, they indicated that it remains the most widely used term, as no viable alternative exists (Interview no:21, 2020; Interview no:23, 2020). Notably, the Saturday Mothers, despite acknowledging the victimisation experience they have gone through, do not identify as victim group, nor do they use this term in their statements (Arcan, personal communication, 28 December 2024). To reflect this, when I specifically discuss the Saturday Mothers, I often refer to them either as the relatives of the disappeared or the movement, rather than attaching the victim label. However, when presenting my analysis against the backdrop of the literature on victims and agency in transitional justice, I use terms such as organised victims, victim groups, or victim movements. These terms allow me to connect the struggles of the Saturday Mothers movement to critical transitional justice scholarship and practice. Such approaches advocate for "a more actor-oriented approach to victim engagement in transitional justice" (Destrooper, 2024, p. 3). Overall, when I use the term victim or victimhood in this book, I refer to a complex political identity that encompasses various positionalities. This nuanced understanding also recognises victims' agency in resisting and challenging the conditions that victimised them, as well as the individual and collective empowerment they achieve in response.

### *Peace Mothers*

In a ceasefire period in 1999, Kurdish women whose family members were detained, arrested, killed, or went to the mountains to join the guerrilla movement founded Peace Mothers to demand peace between the PKK and the Turkish state (Çağlayan, 2020). It became an association in 1999 with headquarters in Diyarbakır, later opening branches in other cities. As their initial slogan "We are mothers, we are sided with peace" highlights, their purpose has been to end the war between the PKK and the Turkish state and reach a peaceful settlement (Aydın, 2018; Göksel, 2018). Forced displacement and state violence in the 1990s shaped the context where Kurdish mothers mobilised across Turkey (Göksel, 2018), giving rise to both Peace Mothers and Saturday Mothers. Not only did the families in these groups witness the violence that loved ones suffered, but they also became targets of violence themselves. Many of them were subjected to police violence several times, detained and arrested, tortured, and labelled as terrorists (Göksel, 2018; Karaman, 2016).

Unlike Saturday Mothers, who came forth specifically due to the enforced disappearances, Peace Mothers emerged as a response to the escalating violence in the Kurdish region (Karaman, 2016). Their struggle has two major pillars: to bring the issue of guerrilla deaths to public space and to build peace (Aydın, 2018). To achieve those goals, they have organised protests across the country, tried to make contact with state officials and government representatives, and organised sit-ins in front of official state buildings. They have attempted to establish a connection with the mothers of Turkish soldiers based on their mutual pain. They also carried out a less visible form of activism, which is pursuing communal peace by taking part in local mediation groups to solve intra-community conflicts (Göksel, 2018). However, one of their most well-known and visible actions was to act as human shields in conflict zones through holding vigils in the mountains and on the border between Turkey and Iraq to stop the military operations. For instance, when the peace process came to an end in 2015, they held peace vigils asking the parties to restart the process.

The Peace Mothers' activism and demands have been aligned with the Kurdish political movement, such as the improved prison conditions for

Öcalan, education in the Kurdish language, the dissolution of village guard systems, and the prosecution of perpetrators (Karaman, 2016). They initiated their wide-scale activities during the ceasefire period that followed the capture of Öcalan in 1999. In parallel to the Kurdish movement, they find the freedom of Öcalan closely interlinked to peace and democracy in Turkey. Thus, over the years they have gotten involved in campaigns for his freedom and against his imprisonment conditions.[9] Most recently in November 2023, Peace Mothers made a public call for the freedom march to end the war, but also to break the isolation in İmralı Island where Öcalan has been imprisoned alongside several other Kurdish prisoners:

> Whatever happens, people must demand the freedom of Abdullah Öcalan, who is imprisoned within four walls with no news. İmralı holds the key that will bring unity and peace among Kurds. We want this key. With this key we will bring freedom, peace, and democracy.
>
> (Yeni Yaşam, 2023)

Creating a shared language of pain and loss out of individual experiences is a founding component of the Peace Mothers' activism (Göksel, 2018). Individual and collective demands are inseparable for the women involved. They not only want the return of their own child, as it will not guarantee the return of all children, but they also demand the complete end of the war. In a way, the Peace Mothers regard themselves as the maternal figures for all guerrillas, whether living or deceased (Karaman, 2016, p. 393). The language of loss does not lead to a victim position, but instead, the mothers' stories end up becoming stories of resistance and rebellion (Göksel, 2018). Göksel defines the form of mothering performed in Peace Mothers as communal and political:

> One mother's story becomes everyone's story, her children become the children of others, and the Peace Mothers become the mothers of all children involved in the conflict, irrespective of ethnic, religious, or class divisions. This is communal and political mothering.
>
> (Göksel, 2018, p. 15)

### *Yakay-Der and Meya-Der*

Yakay-Der (Association for Solidarity and Support for Relatives of Disappeared Persons), founded in 2001 in Istanbul, and Meya-Der (Mesopotamia

9 For more information in Öcalan's imprisonment conditions and the international campaign advocating for his freedom, see International Initiative for Freedom for Öcalan: https://www.freeocalan.org/main

Association of Assistance and Solidarity for Families with Lost Relatives) in 2007 in Diyarbakır, aimed to "shed light on the enforced and involuntary disappearances of those who have been arrested and to give the families of the disappeared the support and solidarity necessary for their struggle for truth and justice" (FEMED, 2017). At the same time, they have been the two prominent organisations dealing with the guerrilla deaths (Can, 2014). Yakay-Der's activities include "conducting all kinds of research, investigations, and legal processes regarding those who are missing, have lost their lives, or have become disabled; and within this framework, to engage in all activities aimed at achieving social peace" (Bianet, 2011a).

Meya-Der's work, on the other hand, was targeted more towards identifying the guerrillas killed during the war with the founding purpose of being in solidarity with the killed guerrillas' families, revealing the identities of the guerrillas who were killed, and registering them in an archive (Aydın, 2018). Their activities included verifying the identity of the killed guerrillas, receiving the bodies, delivering them to the families, arranging the burial ceremonies and condolences activities, initiating the judicial processes, enabling exhumations of mass graves, providing legal training for the families, and organising commemorations. Through these activities, Meya-Der provided the opportunity for a respectful mourning process for those labelled as terrorists by the state Aydın (2018). As mentioned earlier, condolences take up an important space in the burial rituals in Kurdistan. Therefore, Meya-Der is seen almost as a sacred place for the Kurdish society, and it functions as a roof where all the families of the guerrillas get together. It had branches in other Kurdish cities and was instrumental in supporting the families who applied to the ATK to receive the guerrilla bodies (T24, 2016). During the 2015–2016 curfews in the Kurdish region, for example, Meya-Der played a crucial role in assisting families with finding the bodies of their loved ones killed in the clashes and taking care of the funeral arrangements in the face of the security forces' attacks. Both Yakay-Der and Meya-Der were shut down in 2016 by an executive decree under the state of emergency regulation and were re-established under different names.

### *Overlaps between Groups*

Despite separate and differing political agendas and demands, Saturday Mothers, Peace Mothers, Yakay-Der, and Meya-Der have several overlapping purposes, tools and strategies, and activity areas. All these organisations have been instrumental in vocalising the demands for truth and justice for enforced disappearances, raising awareness about mass graves, providing the families with support in their struggle for justice and truth. They engaged with a wide range of activities, including documentation of the deaths and graveyards, justice efforts to bring perpetrators to justice, and bringing together the families of soldiers and guerrillas killed or injured in the armed conflict.

Their activities therefore have not remained limited to the death of their loved ones, but they have also emphasised broader demands such as the peaceful resolution of the armed conflict and truth and justice for all conflict-related human rights violations. For example, in 2011, Yakay-Der was one of the human rights organisations that invited the civil society to the Civil Society Initiative for Truth Commissions alongside. The initiative made a call to civil society and organised meetings to "work together and clarify the functioning and scope of the truth commission that civil society demands" (Truth Justice Memory Center, 2011). In the same year, a delegation consisting of İHD, Meya-Der, Yakay-Der, and Peace Mothers held several meetings with the parliament members, foreign embassies, and the EU Delegation. They expressed their demands for a truth commission to investigate the human rights violations and deal with the past, and for the exhumations in mass graves to be carried out following the Minnesota Protocol (İnsan Hakları Derneği, 2011).[10] Another activity organised in July 2011 by some human rights organisations, including Meya-Der and Yakay-Der, was the Reality of Mass Graves Conference to force the state to take steps and raise awareness in society (Bianet, 2011b). The final declaration of the conference stated the demands in three main categories: state apology from the relatives from the disappeared, a truth commission, and the Minnesota Protocol to be followed in exhumations of mass graves.[11]

A further commonality is the members or activists of these groups. There are individuals who are involved as regular activists or even as the founding members of more than one group. For example, Hasan Karakoç is one of the executives of Ankay-Der (Anatolia Association for Solidarity and Support for Relatives of Disappeared Persons) and a founding member of the Saturday Mothers movement. He expresses the purpose of the newly established Ankay-Der (founded in 2019) as to fill the gap created in the absence of Yakay-Der:

> With Yakay-Der, which used to be active in Istanbul before getting shut down, we had done much archival and documentation work about the disappeared. Now with the newly established Ankay-Der we aim to reveal the fate of our relatives sooner or later by taking over the Yakay-Der's legacy. This legacy gives us strength . . . We expect those who lost their relatives, no matter in what way, to support the association's work in this period.
>
> (Artı Gerçek, 2019)

10 The Minnesota Protocol refers to the UN Manual on the Effective Prevention of Extra-legal, Arbitrary and Summary Executions of 1991. The revised Minnesota Protocol on the Investigation of Potentially Unlawful Death was presented in 2016.

11 Truth commissions have been a central demand of various grassroots actors with regards to dealing with the past.

His speech reflects the overlaps between these groups. Some relatives have been mobilised to search for the body of their loved one who died while fighting in the armed conflict, and some joined one of the groups to seek justice for an extrajudicially killed family member.

## 2.6 Transitional Justice Initiatives in Turkey

While I drew a picture of most systematic human rights violations that led to the emergence of organised victim groups in the previous section, I will now explore the state-led and grassroots responses to those violations. I consider those responses as transitional justice instances that remark on and prove the existence of "transitional justice in non-transitions" (Hansen, 2011).

Various atrocities, military coups, and widespread human rights abuses have marked the history of modern Turkey. Denial and assimilation have been the constituent elements of the Turkish identity, leading to the fear that the foundation of the modern Turkey would be shattered if the atrocities were to be recognised (Cengiz, 2011). As is the case with several other regimes that tend to suppress or censor alternative memories which are not on the official agenda of the state, the political power in Turkey has suppressed alternative memories by using different tools. Several scholars identify Turkey as suffering from social or collective amnesia in terms of mass atrocities (Bakiner, 2013; Üngör, 2014). Göral, however, uses the notion of cultural aphasia, which she thinks to better capture "the memory debate of the contentious histories of Turkey and Kurdistan" (Göral, 2021, p. 90). She refers to the definition that cultural aphasia is "dismembering, a difficulty speaking, a difficulty generating a vocabulary that associates appropriate words and concepts to appropriate things" (Stoler, cited in Bijl, 2012, p. 449).

Turkey has never adopted an official, overarching transitional justice agenda to deal with past atrocities. The combination of state-sponsored amnesia and denial resulted in a deficiency of justice and reconciliation. Since mass atrocities have played a significant role in consolidating the political power of the nation-state in Turkey, the legacy of state-sponsored human rights violations and war crimes still haunts the present (Bakiner, 2013; Mihr, 2017).

Starting from the early 2000s, the social dynamics of forgetting and remembrance began to change due to the popular demands for truth and remembrance, especially around the period between 2005–2015 (Budak, 2015; Kaya, 2015). Demands for truth, justice, and memorialisation gained popularity among grassroots actors, and these demands became more visible with the support of the EU and the ECtHR (Budak, 2015). Some promising official and grassroots efforts took place to deal with the past (Gülsen, 2022). Grassroots movements mobilised to create spaces of truth recovery to break the silence and denial, and to overcome the long-lived impunity for state violence. Their efforts took different shapes, from organising commemorative events, making calls for accountability for past crimes, documenting human rights violations, organising public events to discuss the ways forward for dealing with the past, to establishing an unofficial truth commission.

As I analyse at length in Chapter 7, the civil society-led Truth and Justice Commission for the Diyarbakır Prison (2007) and the prime minister's apology for the Dersim Massacre (2011) were among the critical developments of the period. In addition to those, a group of activists established the temporary Museum of Shame in 2010 as a memorialisation attempt for the human rights violations committed following the 1980 military coup (Bakiner, 2013). Another example was the "I Apologise" Campaign, in which several intellectuals publicly apologised for the "Great Catastrophe" of 1915 in December 2008, referring to the Armenian Genocide, and launched a petition that drew 31,045 signatories by March 2012 (Bakiner, 2013). All these initiatives took place during the ongoing armed conflict and although they were not explicitly framed under the Transitional Justice umbrella, they brought forth key pillars of TJ such as truth-recovery, justice, memorialisation, and guarantees of non-recurrence.

As mentioned earlier, the government made several reforms regarding Kurdish rights in the early 2000s. However, instead of providing space for a plurality of ways to remember the past, the AKP just shifted the foci of the national memory (Bakiner, 2013). A structured transitional justice process grounded in human rights principles for addressing past events was never planned, which ultimately undermined efforts toward democratic consolidation (Mihr, 2017). Condemning certain periods of the past, while resisting calls to commemorate and take responsibility for certain others, was used as a tool to boost political legitimacy. In other words, the AKP neither offered a critical account of the past nor fundamentally challenged the decades of forced amnesia imposed by the previous governments. Those attempts, therefore, were pragmatic manoeuvres without a long-term or genuine commitment to a democratic transition.

As part of the peace process in 2012–2015, the demands for, and interest in, transitional justice reached their highest level, and several discussions took place on different approaches to transitional justice (Budak, 2015). Dealing with the past was seen as a fundamental component of conflict transformation and peacebuilding. Interestingly, neither grassroots actors nor the government introduced or framed these initiatives under a transitional justice umbrella. However, they used a discourse of dealing with the past and the way they explained their goals and aims were quite the same as the key objectives of transitional justice such as truth-recovery, justice, memorialisation, and guarantees of nonrecurrence. These efforts have not turned into a fully-fledged transitional justice process, and they gradually faded away following the collapse of the peace process in 2015 and the changes in the political atmosphere (Gülsen, 2022). Since state violence and human rights violations continue at present, the current context of the ongoing Kurdish conflict and the authoritarian rule makes it even more challenging to address the past.

## 2.7 Conclusion

This chapter began with a detailed examination of the scope and extent of the Kurdish conflict and situated the current dynamics of the Kurdish issue within the broader context of authoritarianism and ongoing armed conflict. I provided an overview of the historical background to the Kurdish conflict by looking at the foundation of modern Turkey. The state's assimilative and punitive approach to the Kurdish identity constituted the root causes of the conflict and put the identity at the centre of the Kurdish resistance. In this chapter, I also demonstrated how the current political context is shaped by the authoritarian rule and the ongoing conflict that has escalated following the collapse of the last peace process in the summer of 2015. Through the re-securitisation of the Kurdish region by months-long curfews and the crackdown on human rights in the entire country under the state of emergency rule, there was a shrinking of civic space. It is within this space that the demands for truth, justice, and accountability for conflict-related human rights violations have been criminalised, silenced, and rendered invisible.

This chapter also contextualised organised victim groups showing that they have mobilised as a response primarily to enforced disappearances, extrajudicial killings, and killings of guerrilla fighters. Alongside solidarity work with other families, they also carried out truth- and justice-seeking activities. There is an immense amount of grassroots work done by victims, those who have been affected by the conflict. Since this book is an attempt to bridge the gap between the empirical data on victims' agency and demands and the transitional justice scholarship, the following chapter unpacks the victim-centred approach to transitional justice. By doing so, it facilitates our understanding of how victims are seen in the transitional justice literature and discusses the complexities around victimhood, which is crucial in designing a transitional justice process that puts victims at the centre. It then turns to the literature on transitional justice in ongoing conflict, aiming to set out the framework to analyse grassroots efforts for transitional justice regarding Turkey's Kurdish conflict.

### Reference List

Akıncı, E.F., 2017. Sacred children, accursed mothers. In S. Brady and L. Mantoan (Eds.), *Performance in a Militarized Culture*. Milton Park, Abingdon, Oxon; New York, NY: Routledge, pp. 47–65. https://doi.org/10.4324/9781315229027-4

Akkoyunlu, K. and Öktem, K., 2016. Existential insecurity and the making of a weak authoritarian regime in Turkey. *Journal of Southeast European and Black Sea Studies*, 16, pp. 505–527. https://doi.org/10.1080/14683857.2016.1253225

Alpkaya, G., 1995. Kayiplar Sorunu Ve Türkiye. *Ankara Üniversitesi SBF Dergisi*, 3.

Amir Hassanpour, J., Sheyholislami, J. and Skutnabb-Kangas, T., 2012. Introduction. Kurdish: Linguicide, resistance and hope. *International Journal of the Sociology of Language*, 2012, pp. 1–18. https://doi.org/10.1515/ijsl-2012–0047

Amnesty International, 1992. *Turkey: Human Rights Violations against Kurds*. Available at: https://www.amnesty.org/en/wp-content/uploads/2021/06/eur440141992en.pdf (Accessed: 20 February 2025).

Amnesty International, 1993. *Disappearances and Extrajudicial Executions: A Summary of Amnesty International's Concerns*. Available at: https://www.amnesty.org/en/wp-content/uploads/2021/06/act330051993en.pdf (Accessed: 20 February 2025).

Ardic, Z., 2019. *Searching for Transitional Justice Mechanisms in the Kurdish Question in Turkey: Addressing Violations of Social, Economic and Cultural Rights*. PhD thesis, University of Sussex.

Artı Gerçek, 2019. *Yakınlarını kaybedenler ANYAKAY-DER'i kurdu*. Available at: https://artigercek.com/index.php/haberler/yakinlari-kaybedilenler-anyakayder-adinda-bir-dernek-kurdu (Accessed: 5 September 2021).

Avci, E.U., 2019. Denial of the Kurdish question in the personal narratives of lay people. *Ethnicities*, 19, pp. 156–173.

Aydın, D., 2015. Yası Tutulmaya Değer Görülmeyen Bedenlerin Süreklileşmiş Yası. *Zan Enstitü*, pp. 1–11.

Aydın, D., 2018. Kürdistan'da Direnişe Dönüşen Yas: Cumartesi Anneleri. *Barış Anneleri ve MEYA-DER*, pp. 1–24.

Aydın, D., 2020. *Ölülerin gücü, devletin hafıza kırımı*. Interviewed by Bekir Avci. Available at: https://birartibir.org/olulerin-gucu-devletin-hafiza-kirimi/ (Accessed: 20 April 2021).

Bakiner, O., 2013. Is Turkey coming to terms with its past? Politics of memory and majoritarian conservatism. *Nationalities Papers*, 41, pp. 691–708. https://doi.org/10.1080/00905992.2013.770732

Bargu, B., 2014. Sovereignty as Erasure. *Qui Parle*, 23, pp. 35–75. https://doi.org/10.5250/quiparle.23.1.0035

Bargu, B., 2019. *Turkey's Necropolitical Laboratory*. Edinburgh: Edinburgh University Press.

Barkey, H. and Kadioglu, D., 2011. The Turkish Constitution and the Kurdish Question. *Carnegie Endowment for International Peace*. Available at: https://carnegieendowment.org/research/2011/08/the-turkish-constitution-and-the-kurdish-question?lang=en (Accessed: 10 march 2025).

BBC News, 2020. "261 PKK'lının cenazeleri Kilyos'ta yol kenarına gömüldü" iddiasıyla ilgili olarak kim ne diyor? *BBC News Türkçe*.

Beşikçi, İ., 1990. *Devletlerarası Sömürge Kürdistan*. Paris: Kürt Enstitüsü.

Bianet, 2011a. *Kayıp Yakınlarıyla Dayanışma Sürüyor*. Available at: https://bianet.org/haber/kayip-yakinlariyla-dayanisma-suruyor-142426 (Accessed: 19 December 2024).

Bianet, 2011b. *Toplu mezarlar gercegi sonuc bildirgesi aciklandi*. Available at: https://m.bianet.org/kurdi/insan-haklari/131740-toplu-mezarlar-gercegi-sonuc-bildirgesi-aciklandi (Accessed: 22 September 2021).

Bianet, 2015. *Erdogan YOK'u ziyaret etti*. Available at: https://bianet.org/bianet/siyaset/162955-erdogan-yok-u-ziyaret-etti (Accessed: 15 July 2021).

Bianet, 2021. *Dolmabahçe Mutabakatı sonrası neler yaşandı*? Available at: https://m.bianet.org/bianet/siyaset/240074-dolmabahce-mutabakati-sonrasi-neler-yasandi (Accessed: 5 April 2021).

Bianet, 2022. *23 yıl sonra kardeşinin kemiklerine kavuştu*. Available at: https://bianet.org/haber/23-yil-sonra-kardesinin-kemiklerine-kavustu-271429 (Accessed: 19 December 2024).

Bijl, P., 2012. Colonial Memory and Forgetting in the Netherlands and Indonesia. *Journal of Genocide Research*, 14(3–4), pp. 441–461.

Bor, G., Daşlı, G. and Alıcı, N., 2021. *From Converging Roads to Narrowing Grounds: The Struggle for Peace by LGBTI+ and Women's Organizations in Turkey*. Available at: https://demos.org.tr/new-research-report-from-converging-roads-to-narrowing-grounds-the-struggle-for-peace-by-lgbti-and-womens-organizations-in-turkey-published/ (Accessed: 14 January 2022).
Boss, P., 2004. Ambiguous loss research, theory, and practice: Reflections after 9/11. *Journal of Marriage and Family*, 66, pp. 551–566.
Boss, P., 2006. *Loss, Trauma, and Resilience: Therapeutic Work with Ambiguous Loss*. New York: W.W. Norton.
Bostan, C., 2022a. *Games of Justice: Ethnographic Inquiries on Space, Subjectivity and Law in Northern Kurdistan*. Doctoral thesis. Lund University, Sociology of Law Department. Available at: https://portal.research.lu.se/en/publications/games-of-justice-ethnographic-inquiries-on-space-subjectivity-and (Accessed: 26 February 2025).
Bostan, C., 2022b. Law and game of truth in the case of Xerzan Cemetery. *Oñati Socio-Legal Series*, 12. https://doi.org/10.35295/osls.iisl/0000-0000-0000-1293
Bozarslan, H., 2008. Cambridge history of Turkey—Kurds and the Turkish state. In R. Kasaba (Ed.), *The Cambridge History of Turkey*. Cambridge: Cambridge University Press (Cambridge History of Turkey), pp. 333–356.
Budak, Y., 2015. Dealing with the past: Transitional justice, ongoing conflict and the Kurdish issue in Turkey. *International Journal of Transitional Justice*, pp. 219–238. https://doi.org/10.1093/ijtj/ijv002
Çağlayan, H., 2020. *Women in the Kurdish Movement: Mothers, Comrades, Goddesses*. Cham: Springer International Publishing. https://doi.org/10.1007/978-3-030-24744-7
Çali, B., 2010. The logics of supranational human rights litigation, official acknowledgment, and human rights reform: The Southeast Turkey cases before the European Court of Human Rights, 1996–2006. *Law and Society Inquiry*, 35, pp. 311–337. https://doi.org/10.1111/j.1747-4469.2010.01187.x
Can, B., 2014. Barış Anneleri. *Toplum ve Kuram Dergisi*, 9, pp. 35–43.
Carney, J., 2019. Projecting 'New Turkey' deflecting the coup: Squares, screens, and publics at Turkey's 'democracy watches.' *Media, Culture and Society*, 41, pp. 138–148. https://doi.org/10.1177/0163443718803254
Çelik, A., 2014. *Savaş ve bellek: doksanların zorla kaybetme fenomeni olarak beyaz Toros*. Paper presented to the conference Vies d'objets souvenirs de guerre, University of Lorraine, 8–9–10 October , 2014.
Çelik, A.B., 2020. Agonistic peace and confronting the past: An analysis of a failed peace process and the role of narratives. *Cooperation and Conflict*. https://doi.org/10.1177/0010836720938401
Cengiz, O.K., 2011. *1915, Dersim, yüzleşme. . .* Available at: http://www.radikal.com.tr/yazarlar/orhan-kemal-cengiz/1915-dersim-yuzlesme-1070158/ (Accessed: 20 December 2018).
Constitution of the Republic of Turkey, 1982. *Government of Turkey*. The official translation published by the Grand National Assembly of Turkey, Department of Laws and Resolutions, May 2019. Available at: https://anayasa.gov.tr/media/7258/anayasa_eng.pdf
Coşkun, V., Derince, Ş. and Uçarlar, N., 2013. Scar of tongue: Consequences of the ban on the use of mother tongue in education and experiences of Kurdish students in Turkey. *DISA Publications*, 12, pp. 355–357. https://doi.org/10.1007/s10993-012-9251-x
de Waardt, M. and Weber, S., 2019. Beyond victims' mere presence: An empirical analysis of victim participation in transitional justice in Colombia. *Journal of Human Rights Practice*, 11(1), pp. 209–228.

Deniz, Ö., 2018. Nekro-politika, yerinden edilen kemikler ve direnişe dönüşen yas (II). *Gazete Karınca*. Available at: https://gazetekarinca.com/2018/01/nekro-politika-yerinden-edilen-kemikler-direnise-donusen-yas-ii-oyku-deniz (Accessed: 7 June 2021).

Derince, M.Ş., 2013. A break or continuity? Turkey's politics of Kurdish language in the new millennium. *Dialectical Anthropology*, 37, pp. 145–152. https://doi.org/10.1007/s10624-013-9303-4

Destrooper, T., 2024. *Generations of Victim Engagement: Towards an Encompassing Analytical Framework for Understanding Victims' Roles in Transitional Justice Processes*. New York: Opinio Juris.

Dewhirst, P. and Kapur, A., 2015. *The Disappeared and Invisible: Revealing the Enduring Impact of Enforced Disappearance on Women*. International Centre for Transitional Justice. Available at: https://www.zotero.org/nisanalc/search/disappearance/titleCreatorYear/items/DJGB2SMN/attachment/HZFG87BJ/reader

Dinçer, H., 2022. Reconfiguration of the Regime of Impunity and Authoritarian Statecraft in Turkey. In International Research Group on Authoritarianism and Counterstrategies (Eds.), *Global Authoritarianism: Perspectives and Contestations from the South*. Bielefeld: transcript Verlag, pp. 119–138.

Druliolle, V. and Brett, R., 2018. Introduction: Understanding the construction of victimhood and the evolving role of victims in transitional justice and peacebuilding. In V. Druliolle and R. Brett (Eds.), *The Politics of Victimhood in Post-Conflict Societies*. Cham: Springer International Publishing, pp. 1–22.

Duhaime, B., 2023. Enforced disappearances in the contemporary world. In *Psychoanalytic, Psychosocial, and Human Rights Perspectives on Enforced Disappearance*. Routledge.

Ensaroglu, Y., 2013. Turkey's Kurdish question and the peace process. *Insight Turkey*, 15(2), pp. 7–17.

Erensü, S. and Alemdaroğlu, A., 2018. Dialectics of reform and repression: Unpacking Turkey's authoritarian turn. *Review of Middle East Studies*, 52, pp. 16–28. https://doi.org/10.1017/rms.2018.8

FEMED, 2017. *Abusive Closure of Two Turkish Member Associations Yakay-der and Meya-der*. Available at: https://www.disparitions-euromed.org/en/content/press-release-abusive-closure-two-turkish-member-associations-yakay-der-and-meya-der (Accessed: 9 November 2021).

Ferrandiz, F. and Robben, A.C.G.M., 2015. Introduction. In F. Ferrandiz and A.C.G.M. Robben (Eds.), *Necropolitics: Mass Graves and Exhumations in the Age of Human Rights*. Philadelphia: University of Pennsylvania Press, pp. 1–38.

Göksel, N., 2018. Losing the one, caring for the all: The activism of the peace mothers in Turkey. *Social Sciences*, 7, p. 174. https://doi.org/10.3390/socsci7100174

Göral, Ö.S., 2019. Any hopes for truth? A comparative analysis of enforced disappearances and the missing in the Middle East, North Africa and the Caucasus. *Truth Justice Memory Center = Hakikat, Adalet ve Hafiza Calismalari Dernegi Yayinlari*, Istanbul.

Göral, O.S., 2021. Memory as experience in times of perpetual violence: The challenge of Saturday Mothers vis-à-vis cultural aphasia. *Kurdish Studies*, 9, pp. 77–95. https://doi.org/10.33182/ks.v9i1.569

Göral, Ö.S. and Benlisoy, F., 2024. Sosyalistlerin büyük sınavı: Irkçılıkla mücadele. *11 Express*. Available at: https://birartibir.org/sosyalistlerin-buyuk-sinavi-irkcilikla-mucadele/ (Accessed: 19 December 2024).

Göral, Ö.S., Işık, A. and Kaya, Ö., 2013. *The Unspoken Truth: Enforced Disappearances*. Truth Justice Memory Center.

Gülsen, E., 2022. *Restorative role of public memorials and memorialization after the periods of violence and oppression: The case of Turkey*. PhD thesis, Middle East Technical University.
Gunes, C., 2013. Explaining the PKK's mobilization of the Kurds in Turkey: Hegemony, myth and violence. *Ethnopolitics*, 12, pp. 247–267. https://doi.org/10.1080/17449057.2012.707422
Hakyemez, S., 2017. Inhabiting the margins: Middle eastern minorities revisited. Margins of the archive: Torture, heroism, and the ordinary in prison No. 5, Turkey. *Anthropological Quarterly*, 90, pp. 107–138.
Hamber, B., 2009. *Transforming Societies after Political Violence. Truth, Reconciliation, and Mental Health*. Springer. https://doi.org/10.1007/978-0-387-89427-0
Hansen, T.O., 2011. Transitional justice: Toward a differentiated theory. *Oregon Review of International Law*, 13, pp. 1–46. https://doi.org/10.2307/840816
Human Rights Watch, 1990. *Destroying Ethnic Identity: The Kurds of Turkey*. Available at: https://www.hrw.org/reports/pdfs/t/turkey/turkey907.pdf (Accessed: 19 December 2024).
Human Rights Watch, 2012. *Time for Justice: Ending Impunity for Killings and Disappearances in 1990s Turkey*. Available at: https://www.hrw.org/report/2012/09/03/time-justice/ending-impunity-killings-and-disappearances-1990s-turkey (Accessed: 20 February 2025).
Human Rights Watch, 2020. *Turkey: Kurdish Mayors' Removal Violates Voters' Rights*. Available at: https://www.hrw.org/news/2020/02/07/turkey-kurdish-mayors-removal-violates-voters-rights (Accessed: 22 September 2021).
Humphrey, M., 2002. *The Politics of Trauma and Reconciliation*. Routledge. https://doi.org/10.2298/TEM1001009H
İnsan Hakları Derneği, 2007. *Kayıpları Unutmadık*. Available at: https://www.ihd.org.tr/wp-content/uploads/2007/11/kayiplari_unutmadik.pdf
İnsan Hakları Derneği, 2011. *Toplu mezarlar BM Minesota Prokolune gore acilsin hakikat komisyonu kurulsun*. Available at: https://www.ihd.org.tr/toplu-mezarlar-bm-minesota-prokolune-gore-acilsin-hakikat-komisyonu-kurulsun/ (Accessed: 12 May 2021).
İnsan Hakları Derneği, 2018. Bitlis İli Tatvan İlçesi Yukarıölek Köyü Yakınlarındaki Mezarlığın (279 Mezar) Ortadan Kaldırılmasına Dair Rapor. *İnsan Hakları Derneği*.
İnsan Hakları Derneği, 2022. Available at: https://ihddiyarbakir.org/tr/post/24581/uluslararasi-gozaltinda-kayiplara-karsi-mucad
İnsan Hakları Derneği, Diyarbakır, 2022. *Uluslararası Gözaltında Kayıplara Karşı Mücadele Haftası: Zorla kaybetme insanlığa karşı işlenmiş bir suçtur*. Available at: https://ihddiyarbakir.org/tr/post/24581/uluslararasi-gozaltinda-kayiplara-karsi-mucad (Accessed: 19 December 2024).
International Crisis Group, 2012. Turkey: The PKK and a Kurdish settlement. *International Crisis Group Europe Report*, 11 September, pp. 1–42.
Interview no:3, Interview by Author, 2019.
Interview no:7, Interview by Author, 2019.
Interview no:14, Interview by Author, 2020.
Interview no:15, Interview by Author, 2020.
Interview no:16, Interview by Author, 2020.
Interview no:18, Interview by Author, 2020.
Interview no:19, Interview by Author, 2020.
Interview no:21, Interview by Author, 2020.
Interview no:23, Interview by Author, 2020.
Işık, A., 2020. *The Emergence, Transformation and Functions of Paramilitary Groups in Northern Kurdistan (Eastern Turkey) in the 1990s*. PhD thesis, Utrecht University.

Jongerden, J., 2017. Looking beyond the state: Transitional justice and the Kurdish issue in Turkey. *Ethnic and Racial Studies*, 0, pp. 1–18. https://doi.org/10.1080/01419870.2017.1330486

Jongerden, J., 2018. Conquering the state and subordinating society under AKP rule: A Kurdish perspective on the development of a new autocracy in Turkey. *Journal of Balkan and Near Eastern Studies*, 0, pp. 1–14. https://doi.org/10.1080/19448953.2018.1497751

Jongerden, J. and Akkaya, A.H., 2015. Kurds and the PKK. *Wiley Blackwell Encyclopedia of Race, Ethnicity, and Nationalism*, pp. 1–5. https://doi.org/10.1002/9781118663202.wberen026

Kaos, G.L., 2015. *Ekin Wan'in bedeni ve savasta cinsel siddet*. Available at: https://kaosgl.org/haber/ekin-wanrsquoin-bedeni-ve-savasta-cinsel-siddet (Accessed: 12 February 2022).

Karaman, E.R., 2016. Remember, S/he was here once: Mothers call for justice and Peace in Turkey. *Journal of Middle East Women's Studies*, 12, pp. 382–410. https://doi.org/10.1215/15525864–3637576

Karaveli, H., 2016. Erdogan's journey: Conservatism and authoritarianism in Turkey. *Foreign Affairs*, 95, pp. 121–130.

Kaya, D.G., 2015. Coming to terms with the past: Rewriting history through a therapeutic public discourse in Turkey. *International Journal of Middle East Studies*, 47, pp. 681–700. https://doi.org/10.1017/S0020743815000938

Kaya, Ö. and Öğünç, P., 2020. *Satranç, Saklambaç ve İnat Zor Zamanlarda Sivil Toplum*. Anadolu Kültür. Available at: https://www.anadolukultur.org/_FILES/Contents/1539/akcivilsocietyreport_en.pdf?v=20250508141616 (Accessed: 21 March 2025).

Kaya, Z.N. and Whiting, M., 2019. *The HDP, the AKP and the Battle for Turkish Democracy*. https://doi.org/10.1080/19448953.2018.1497751

Kovras, I., 2017a. The daughters of Antigone in Latin America. In *Grassroots Activism and the Evolution of Transitional Justice*. Cambridge University Press, pp. 61–83. https://doi.org/10.1017/9781316711262.003

Kovras, I., 2017b. *Grassroots Activism and the Evolution of Transitional Justice: The Families of the Disappeared*. 1st ed. Cambridge University Press. https://doi.org/10.1017/9781316711262

Küçük, B. and Özselçuk, C., 2016. The Rojava experience: Possibilities and challenges of building a democratic life. *South Atlantic Quarterly*, 115, pp. 184–196. https://doi.org/10.1215/00382876–3425013

Kurban, D., 2020. *Limits of Supranational Justice: The European Court of Human Rights and Turkey's Kurdish Conflict*. Cambridge: Cambridge University Press. https://doi.org/10.1017/9781108776585

Mbembe, A., 2003. Necropolitics, translated by Libby Meintjes. *Public Culture*, 15(1), pp. 11–40.

McDowall, D., 2007. *A Modern History of the Kurds*. Revised ed. London: I.B. Tauris.

Mihr, A., 2017. Regime consolidation through transitional justice in Europe: The cases of Germany, Spain and Turkey. *International Journal of Transitional Justice*. https://doi.org/10.1093/ijtj/ijx003

Mohammed, S.J. and Romano, D., 2023. The Kurdish conflict in Turkey: The central role of identity recognition (or lack thereof). *Ethnopolitics*, 0, pp. 1–18. https://doi.org/10.1080/17449057.2023.2275229

Nejbir, D.A., 2021. *Applying Humanitarian Law: A Review of the Legal Status of the Turkey—Kurdistan Workers' Party (PKK) Conflict*. https://doi.org/10.1163/18781527-bja10026

OHCHR, 2021. *Fact Sheet No. 11: Extrajudicial, Summary or Arbitrary Executions*. Available at: https://www.ohchr.org/Documents/Publications/FactSheet11rev.1en.pdf (Accessed: 20 February 2025).

Özgürlük İçin Hukukçular Derneği, 2019. KİLYOS MEZARLIĞI GÖZLEM RAPORU. Available at: https://ozgurlukicinhukukcular.org/tr/detay/kilyos-mezarligi-gozlem-raporu

Ozsoy, H., 2010. *Between gift and taboo: Death and negotiation of national identity and sovereignty in the Kurdish conflict in Turkey*. PhD thesis, University of Texas.

Personal communication with Sebla Arcan, 28 December 2024.

Saeed, H., 2016. Victims and victimhood: Individuals of inaction or active agents of change? Reflections on fieldwork in Afghanistan. *International Journal of Transitional Justice*, 10(1), pp. 168–178.

Sarkin, J. and Baranowska, G., 2018. Why enforced disappearances are perpetrated against groups as state policy: Overlaps and interconnections between disappearances and genocide. *Católica Law Review*, 2(3), pp. 11–50. https://doi.org/10.34632/catolicalawreview.2018.9098

Savran, A., 2020. The peace process between Turkey and the Kurdistan Workers' Party, 2009–2015. *Journal of Balkan and Near Eastern Studies*, 22(6), pp. 777–792.

Sevimli, E.A., Kiliç, E., Zeren, G., Gebeş, M. and Zıngıl, Ö., 2021. *1990'lı Yıllardaki Ağır İnsan Hakları İhlallerinde Cezasızlık Sorunu: Kovuşturma Süreci*. Available at: https://hakikatadalethafiza.org/sites/default/files/2022-12/cezasizlik_kovusturmasureci.pdf (Accessed: 18 March 2025).

Stover, E. and Shigekane, R., 2004. Exhumation of mass graves: Balancing legal and humanitarian needs. In E. Stover and H.M. Weinstein (Eds.), *My Neighbor, My Enemy: Justice and Community in the Aftermath of Mass Atrocity*. Cambridge: Cambridge University Press, pp. 85–103. https://doi.org/10.1017/CBO9780511720352.007

T24, 2016. *İşte il il kapatılan derneklerin listesi*. Available at: https://t24.com.tr/haber/iste-il-il-kapatilan-derneklerin-listesi,370409 (Accessed: 8 April 2021).

The Guardian, 2015. *Turkey Election: Ruling Party Loses Majority as Pro-Kurdish HDP Gains Seats*. Available at: https://www.theguardian.com/world/2015/jun/07/turkey-election-preliminary-results-erdogan-akp-party (Accessed: 30 September 2021).

Truth Justice Memory Centre, 2011. *Hakikat komisyonlari icin sivil toplum toplantisi*. Available at: https://hakikatadalethafiza.org/hakikat-komisyonlari-icin-sivil-toplum-toplantisi/ (Accessed: 11 December 2021).

Türk Tabipleri Birliği, 2011. *Türkiye, büyük çaplı bir "toplu mezarlar" gerçekliği ile yüz yüzedir*. Available at: https://www.ttb.org.tr/haberarsiv_goster.php?Guid=66c241a6-9232-11e7-b66d-1540034f819c (Accessed: 19 December 2024).

Türkiye Büyük Millet Meclisi, 2013. *Terör ve Şiddet Olayları Kapsamında Yaşam Hakkı İhlallerini İnceleme Raporu*. Ankara: TBMM İnsan Haklarını İnceleme Komisyonu.

Uçarlar, N., 2015. *Nothing in Its Right Place. Demands of Justice and Coming to Terms with the Past in the Post-Conflict Period*. DİSA Publications.

Üngör, U.Ü., 2014. Lost in commemoration: The Armenian genocide in memory and identity. *Patterns of Prejudice*, 48, pp. 147–166. https://doi.org/10.1080/0031322X.2014.902210

United Nations, 2006. *International Convention for the Protection of All Persons from Enforced Disappearance*. CED.

United Nations, 2017. *Report on the human rights situation in South-East Turkey*. Geneva: Office of the United Nations High Commissioner for Human Rights.

Üstündağ, N., 2019. Mother, politician, and guerilla: The emergence of a new political imagination in Kurdistan through women's bodies and speech. *Differences*, 30, pp. 115–145. https://doi.org/10.1215/10407391

Verdery, K., 1999. *The Political Lives of Dead Bodies: Reburial and Postsocialist Change*. Columbia University Press.

Yarkın, G., 2022. Turkish racism against Kurds: Colonial violence, racist slurs and mob attacks. *The Commentaries*, 2, pp. 77–90. https://doi.org/10.33182/tc.v2i1.2218

Yavuz, M., 2001. Five stages of the construction of Kurdish nationalism in Turkey. *Nationalism and Ethnic Politics*, 7(3), pp. 1–24.

Yeğen, M., 1996. The Turkish state discourse and the exclusion of Kurdish identity. *Middle Eastern Studies*, 32, pp. 216–229. https://doi.org/10.1080/00263209608701112

Yeğen, M., 1999. The Kurdish question in Turkish state discourse. *Journal of Contemporary History*, 34, pp. 555–568.

Yeğen, M., 2015. The Kurdish peace process in Turkey: Genesis, evolution and prospects. *Global Turkey in Europe*, Working Paper, 11.

Yeğen, M., 2016. Armed struggle to peace negotiations: Independent Kurdistan to democratic autonomy, or the PKK in context. *Middle East Critique*, 25(1), pp. 1–19. https://doi.org/10.1080/19436149.2016.1218162

Yeni Ozgur Politika, 2020. *261 cenaze kaldırımın altında*. Available at: https://www.ozgurpolitika.com/haberi-261-cenaze-kaldirimin-altinda-583 (Accessed: 19 December 2024).

Yeni Yaşam, 2023. *Barış Anneleri: Herkes 'Özgürlük Yürüyüşü'ne katılmalı*. Available at: https://yeniyasamgazetesi5.com/baris-anneleri-herkes-ozgurluk-yuruyusune-katilmali/ (Accessed: 19 December 2024).

Yıldırım, U., 2021. Spaced-out states: Decolonizing trauma in a war-torn middle eastern city. *Current Anthropology*, 62, pp. 717–740. https://doi.org/10.1086/718206

Yılmaz, Z. and Turner, B.S., 2019. Turkey's deepening authoritarianism and the fall of electoral democracy. *British Journal of Middle Eastern Studies*, 46, pp. 691–698. https://doi.org/10.1080/13530194.2019.1642662

Zeydanlıoğlu, W., 2008. The White Turkish man's burden: Orientalism, Kemalism and the Kurds in Turkey. In *Neo-Colonial Mentalities in Contemporary Europe: Language and Discourse in the Construction of Identities*. Newcastle: Cambridge Scholars Publishing, pp. 155–174.

Zeydanlioğlu, W., 2012. Turkey's Kurdish language policy. *International Journal of the Sociology of Language*, pp. 99–125. https://doi.org/10.1515/ijsl-2012–0051

Zürcher, E.J., 2017. *Turkey: A Modern History*. 4th ed. London: I.B. Tauris.

Chapter 3

# Victimhood and Transitional Justice in Ongoing Conflicts

## 3.1 Introduction

This book brings together two key evolving areas in the scholarship of transitional justice: victims in transitional justice and transitional justice in ongoing conflicts. Drawing on these areas, this chapter dives deep into the key concepts underpinning this book. This research understands and conceptualises conflict-affected communities (victims, survivors, or any other way that may identify) as political actors. Although victims' participation in transitional justice processes has been researched for some time, victims as political actors have only gained momentum more recently. In an endeavour to move beyond the narrow interpretations of victims' centrality in transitional justice, the first part of the chapter discusses victims' agency and complex political victims extensively. Following an overview of how victims are usually seen in transitional justice theory and practice, either as victims of individual violations in need of healing or as passive individuals lacking agency, I discuss the complexities of victim and perpetrator categories. By identifying the key debates around victims and victimhood in transitional justice, this first part lays the groundwork to understand organised victims' contribution to transitional justice as well as the complexities and construction of victimhood in Turkey, which I will discuss in later chapters.

The potentials and implications of using transitional justice mechanisms during an ongoing conflict is also a growing area of inquiry. While there is much more recent interest paid to this area, there is still a need for more empirical research on what this could look like in reality. For this reason, the second part of the chapter identifies the gaps in transitional justice research regarding this specific area and investigates the arguments for using transitional justice in the absence of a peace process or conflict transformation. Drawing on the recent scholarship on transitional justice in ongoing conflicts in specific and in aparadigmatic transitions in general, this second part helps situate transitional justice efforts in Turkey.

DOI: 10.4324/9781003432579-3

## 3.2 Victims in Transitional Justice

### *How is Victimhood Defined?*

In transitioning societies, victimhood is socially, politically, legally, subjectively, and technically constructed and produced (Hearty, 2018; Saeed, 2016). Who the victims to be consulted are and whose expectations and demands are to be taken into consideration is a challenging question, especially in deeply divided societies. The victimhood status often determines who is entitled to benefits and rights (Álvarez Berastegi and Hearty, 2019; Moffett, 2016; Saeed, 2016; Sajjad, 2016). The legal, political, and sociological significance of defining who qualifies as a victim becomes especially critical in post-conflict or transitional settings, where victimhood stems from political violence or ethnic conflict. This is due to the magnitude of past abuses, its strong connection to wider ethnopolitical struggles, and the strategic use of the terms "victim" and "perpetrator" for political purposes (Lawther, 2024).

While transitional processes are designed, the decision of which victim groups will be consulted or get involved might seriously affect the result of the entire process and might even cause further inequalities or conflict among the victim groups. Nevertheless, although identifying the victims lies at the heart of most efforts to design transitional justice measures, it is hard to provide a clear-cut definition of the term victim (Brett and Druliolle, 2018; de Waardt, 2016). Victimhood is not a universal category. It is defined by human rights law and determined by the mandates of the transitional justice mechanisms (Humphrey, 2003). Hearty notes that "one might legitimately ask whether the victim centeredness involves *all* victims or only some victims, and if the latter, what, and who, is it that determines which victims will be included and which victims will be excluded" (Hearty, 2018, p. 889).

Having been harmed is a necessary but insufficient condition to be classified as a victim, because "social norms and customs, developed in politics, law and culture, partly shape the selection of those who will be allocated victim status" (Huyse, 2003). Victims are defined by what happened to them and how it is articulated in law, rather than what and how they experience the process, which might neglect their agency (Robins, 2017). For example, as is the case with the Compensation Law[1] in Turkey and the Act on Victims of Terrorism in the Basque country, laws might articulate the victims as only the victims of terrorism (Berastegi, 2016; Kurban, 2012). In this case, the fact that the state does not associate itself with terrorism means that only those who have been victimised by the acts of the armed groups will be entitled to rights. This draws a clear distinction within victim groups, favouring some of

1 See Chapter 5 for more information on the victimhood category implied in Turkey's 2004 Compensation Law.

them over others. Victimhood, therefore, becomes a political field where the struggles about the meanings of the past take place (Hearty, 2018; McEvoy et al., 2017).

### *What Does Structural Violence Have to Do with It?*

Interpreting victimhood according to their victimisers or the harms makes the issue unrelated to victims themselves, creating a clear hierarchical approach to harms in transitional justice processes, often leaving structural violence insufficiently addressed (Hearty, 2018). This applies to both legal measures such as reparations and the non-judicial mechanisms such as truth commissions. With respect to reparations, because the budget is often limited there must be a selectivity to decide which loss will be materially compensated. The Compensation Law in Turkey, for instance, has been critiqued for not including non-pecuniary damages (Budak, 2015). With regards to truth commissions, the South African Truth and Reconciliation Commission (TRC) is an accurate example where the narrow definition of victimhood only recognised the harm caused by gross human violations. This meant that deserving access to the TRC excluded structural violence. Many victims, as a result, did not have the space to benefit from the TRC.[2] As Hamber notes:

> Rather, the TRC chose to define victims narrowly, that is, as the direct victims of gross human rights violations such as murder, torture, abduction and disappearances. From this perspective, the TRC failed sufficiently to make the link between the structural violations of apartheid (for example, systematic poverty or inequality in access to services) and the direct human rights violations suffered by those who testified.
>
> (Hamber, 2002, p. 66)

The narrow interpretation of victimhood reflects a common phenomenon in transitional justice, which, like the liberal peace paradigm, puts greater emphasis on acts than it puts on chronic structural violence and social relations (Gready and Robin, 2014). Emphasising mostly single violent acts detaches these acts from the historical and social context in which the violence was shaped (Baines, 2015). This aligns with the critiques to the TRC.

2 According to the Act that set up the Truth and Reconciliation Commission, "gross violation of human rights" means the violation of human rights through (a) the killing, abduction, torture or severe ill-treatment of any person; or (b) any attempt, conspiracy, incitement, instigation, command or procurement to commit an act referred to in paragraph (a), which emanated from conflicts of the past and which was committed during the period 1 March 1960 to the cut-off date within or outside the Republic, and the commission of which was advised, planned, directed, commanded or ordered, by any person acting with a political motive" (Promotion of National Unity and Reconciliation Act, 1995, p. 3).

For example, Mamdani (1996 cited in Moon, 2009) argues that "Consequently, the TRC's account of the past excluded a proper accounting of the insidious structural violence of apartheid: in particular of the race, education, and pass laws, of which many thousands more people were victims than of party-political violence". However, Du Toit claims that it would not be realistic to expect a TRC to focus on structural violence comprehensively (Du Toit, 2018). If the TRC had not individualised the crimes, reminded the personal responsibility of perpetrators, and emphasised the personal dignity of victims, it would have the unrealistic task of dealing with millions of participants. For this reason, although it operated within a limited mandate, the TRC managed to serve social justice in three ways (Du Toit, 2018). First, in the final report, structural violence was officially recognised with a great emphasis on social, economic, and political context, such as the impact of poor living conditions on the emotional wellbeing of the victims (Hamber, 2009). Second, several reparation tools were recommended to compensate for the damages that the victims suffered under apartheid. And third, by emphasising victims' personal dignity, structural violence was challenged.

As the TRC example shows, defining victimhood solely based on the harm leads to the inclusion of only some parts of victims. In an endeavour to challenge this, Álvarez Berastegi and Hearty (2019) propose the context-based model as a new lens to see political victimhood. They consider the victim identity as a complex social process which is influenced by the particularities of each context. Their proposed model therefore requires situating each victim in a complex framework that is shaped by the unique features of each conflict context. While doing so, they put the suffering of victims at the centre and recognise that their needs depend on the specific circumstances of their victimisation. Since in this model the purpose is "to progressively avoid the label 'victims of . . .' and empower victims solely as 'victims'" this approach would not allow space for political manipulation that a hierarchical approach to victimhood would create (Álvarez Berastegi and Hearty, 2019).

## *Therapeutic Approaches to Victimhood and Transitional Justice*

This section elaborates critically on the dominant therapeutic approach to victims in mainstream transitional justice practice and scholarship. It has been widely acknowledged that transitional justice should address the psycho-social needs of the victims and survivors (Kizilhan and Neumann, 2020). Indeed, transitional justice has adopted an emotional healing-based language; emotions and emotional recovery are now central pillars to transitional justice discourse and practice (Karstedt, 2016). This approach views victims as harmed and traumatised by individual violations, which has two key implications for post-conflict responses: 1) The over-emphasis on the conflict's psycho-social impact and victims' emotional recovery and 2) the obscuring of wider political context and structural violence.

Although it was evident that wars had a concrete psychological impact on military personnel, it was not until the Vietnam War that a set of identifiable symptoms was defined as post-traumatic stress disorder (PTSD) (Moon, 2009). As a result of defining trauma as a psychological category that results from wars, the therapeutic discourse has been on the rise in post-conflict reconciliation processes (Moon, 2009). The 1990s marked a significant shift from individual combatants to the entire communities who were traumatised by combat. This shift took place in parallel to the developments in the scholarship on war, the most dominant was Kaldor's theory of new wars suggesting that contemporary wars do not only take place between combatants, but they also involve civilians and violence have a greater impact on them (Kaldor, 2013).

According to the therapeutic discourse in transitional justice responses to violent pasts, trauma is not only an outcome of the conflict but also a reason for recurrence of violence, and therefore the post-war order should have the capacity to address and heal trauma (Moon, 2009). In exploring the contradictions between individual psychological processes and national processes such as truth commissions, Hamber and Wilson use the notion of "psychologizing the nation" (Hamber and Wilson, 2002, p. 36). They refer to a procedure that wrongly implies that the individual and national ways to deal with the past are almost identical and that are homogenous entities. Similarly, Moon suggests (2009) that interpreting political violence from a pathological viewpoint is based on the illusion of a unitary entity which shares the same psychological pathologies as individuals. She notes the following:

> This discourse intimately connects the assumptions normally applied to individual intrapsychic healing to national governance. In this context, we can understand postconflict reconciliation as a strategy of trauma management writ large in which the nation appears as the subject of war trauma, thus appearing amenable to therapeutic intervention.
>
> (Moon, 2009, p. 84)

Taking the psychological health of victims into account is undoubtedly important in repairing the harm. Adopting a systematic approach and embedding mental health experts into transitional justice mechanisms, alongside training practitioners to address trauma and fostering community-based support systems, can address unresolved psychological harm that undermines reconciliation and societal healing (International Center for Transitional Justice, 2024). However, by putting too much emphasis on individual processes they often obscure the social and political roots of the conflict (Moon, 2009). Both trauma and PTSD have been shorthand concepts that often fail to capture the complexities of the particular context in which the violence takes place (Hamber, 2015). Hamber argues that the PTSD diagnosis serves to pathologise a socio-political reality and it obscures the structural categories connected to long-term marginalisation of victims, such as poverty, inequality, gender, and ethnicity (Hamber, 2015). In exemplifying this, Moon argues that the TRC is an example of this, which adopted a therapeutic approach to deal with the whole society as an individual and addressed the individual victims and perpetrators instead of shedding a light on the wider context that made the human rights violations possible at the first place (Moon, 2009).

In parallel to the lack of attention to the context, another risk is that PTSD might equate different experiences of violence as if they all require the same treatment or result in the same consequences (Hamber, 2015). Hamber addresses the disrupting effect of extreme political traumatisation on the meaning systems and notes that each incident refers to a particular set of meanings which, therefore, has specific political, social, and cultural impacts (Hamber 2009, 2015). Political traumatisation is strongly linked to the context and healing is more likely when it provides a broader framework to the harms that happened. The ways of interpretation of the traumatic event by the individual and the community are as important as the event itself, therefore, they need to be addressed (Hamber, 2009). Removing the individual from the context does not allow enough space to explore the attachment that one might have to it. In a similar vein, Robins argues that "imposing the frame of trauma on victims implies a diagnosis of post-traumatic stress disorder and a consequent need for 'therapy', in contrast to potentially more relevant and local understandings of how they might respond to the impact of victimisation" (Robins, 2017, p. 48).

Despite the centrality of healing and emotional recovery in the debates on the impact and process of transitional justice, there is not enough empirical evidence to theorise whether transitional justice is and should be able to deliver healing and recovery for victims (Hamber, 2009; Karstedt, 2016; Stauffer, 2013). Truth commissions, for instance, have been discussed as one of the most important mechanisms to deliver emotional recovery because of the tendency to assume that truth-telling will bring healing to victims (Porter, 2015). However, several scholars indicate that revealing or sharing hurts (especially publicly) is not necessarily useful for emotional healing or recovery (Du Toit, 2018; Hamber, 2009; Karstedt, 2016). In fact, there is evidence that victims and survivors experience an increase in the symptoms of trauma such as anxiety, fear, and stress following the recalling and retelling of the traumatic experience (Clark, 2010; Karstedt, 2016; Porter, 2015; Stauffer, 2013). Giving testimony for a truth commission might leave some victims feeling more vulnerable and can cause distress among some (Becker, 2004; Hamber, 2009). It may also come with emotional pain for some victims and thus might be experienced as neither therapeutic nor empowering (Byrne, 2004). Testifying can create a spontaneous, emotional initial relief. However, this is unlikely to be sustained without long-term socio-affective support.

The lack of socio-affective responses may be a contributory factor to the prevalent feelings of anger and disappointment among many victim-witnesses (Mendeloff, 2009, p. 605). What type of response is given in the aftermath of the emotion-sharing plays a greater role than the act of expressing the emotion (Karstedt, 2016). Therefore, truth commissions' impact is also dependent on how political trauma is dealt with by the community and the society. Therefore, a combination of cognitive responses to reframe the violent events and help to understand the causes and socio-affective responses to support the victims will achieve the best results in terms of healing (Karstedt, 2016). As Gallagher et al., 2012) note about the need to be mindful of the wider context:

> In summary, violence and dealing with its mental health legacy means that we need to understand violence in context and address it not only individually, but socially and politically. Although it is extremely important to focus on the victims and survivors of the conflict, we need to simultaneously move beyond this narrow focus and consider the wider society.

Hamber (2009) suggests that the expected outcome of a truth commission should not be therapeutic through testifying but should only aim to have some therapeutic benefits and at least not have a negative impact on the emotional recovery of victims. Truth commissions have the potential to contribute to healing, but only if they are supported by other means that will deliver socio-economic recovery, justice, accountability, and reparations. The consequences of testifying cannot be evaluated in isolation from the outer context. If truth is revealed to a sufficient extent, then truth commissions might provide a framework for narratives. This would then allow individuals to put their own experience in a framework that makes sense personally and explain the traumatic event in accordance with that framework.

## 3.3 Complexities of Victim and Perpetrator Categories

One of the other key topics in relation to victims in transitional justice lies in the complexities of defining the categories of victims and perpetrators. By emphasising the need for a nuanced understanding of victims, this section sets the scene for the discussion on the construction and complexities of victimhood in Turkey's Kurdish conflict (Chapter 5). Victimhood is argued to be a relational category that is usually defined by the innocence, purity, lack of responsibility, the absence of guilt, and moral superiority of the victim over the perpetrator guilt (Bouris, 2007). Victims are associated with innocence, purity, and moral superiority while perpetrators are associated with blame, guilt, and moral inferiority (Hearty, 2018; Moffett, 2014). These characteristics are overly emphasised because once actors' positions are simplified, policymaking becomes easier (Bouris, 2007). Christie defines the ideal victim status as "a sort of public status of the same type and level of abstraction as that for example of a "hero" or a "traitor" (Christie, 1986, p. 18). Western criminology, from which the political and social construction of victimhood takes its roots, considers victim as an oppositional category to perpetrator. According to this understanding, the true victim is the innocent victim (McEvoy and McConnachie, 2012). The innocence that is attributed to victims legitimises their claim to rights and enables them to be entitled to resources and assistance. Cole acknowledges that "victimization should be addressed without recourse to matters of innocence, character, resilience or agency. And we must question and resist the impulse to delete the term "victim" from our political vocabulary" (Cole, 2016, p. 271).

As pointed out by numerous scholars, the assumed binary of evil and guilty perpetrator and the innocent and blameless victim is problematic (Baines, 2015; Bouris, 2007; Hearty, 2015; McEvoy and McConnachie, 2012; Moffett, 2016). The binary categorisation often leads to the depoliticisation of the question of responsibility while at the same time blurring the complexity of responsibility. The ideal victim is in a passive position with no political agency, while the perpetrator has infinite agency that should be brought under control (McEvoy and McConnachie, 2012). Innocence signifies the non-combatant status of the victim and the absence of wrongdoing, and moral superiority is often associated with righteousness (Bouris, 2007). However, this simplistic understanding does not provide a tool to capture the complex realities of conflicts where people go through different phases of being victims, victimisers, perpetrators, and bystanders (Porter, 2015). Since human beings are more complex than we could explain with two binary categories, there is a whole set of dynamics and factors that stem from socio-political settings. In the light of these complexities, the only way to have a realistic picture of what is needed from transitional justice is to be conscious of the distinct roles of individuals.

Moreover, the discourse of the ideal victim takes any culpability and responsibility from the good, passive, blameless, innocent victim who has been harmed by the bad, guilty, evil perpetrator who holds the responsibility (Hearty, 2018). Human rights discourse often presents victims and perpetrators as two distinct and homogeneous categories (Borer, 2003). However, in reality, individuals can have complex identities and therefore it is difficult to draw purely separate categories for victims and perpetrators, especially in those conflict settings where there are many individuals who have been on both sides of these categories. It would therefore be simplistic to refer to two distinct blocks of victims and perpetrators (McEvoy and McConnachie, 2012; Moffett, 2016).

Baines uses the life story of a Ugandan woman, Sara, to demonstrate that an individual can be in situations where they have been victimised and at the same time be in a place where others have been victimised (Baines, 2015). Sara was abducted by the Lord's Resistance Army (LRA) as a child and then sexually abused by the LRA. She had also experienced violence in her family before she was recruited. As an adult, she faces many challenges in her own community and is neglected by society because she was part of the LRA. Therefore, she played a role in the victimisation of others, but she was also victimised first by her family, then by the LRA, and finally by society. Baines argues that Sara's story is an example of how victimisation goes beyond the singular acts of extreme violence and can be caused by several reasons such as poverty, marginalisation, abuse, and neglect. This points to the importance of recognising diffuse responsibility in contexts of mass violence and the need to be aware of the complicity of different parties to the conflict. As Baines notes: "In this framework, 'victim' and 'perpetrator' are blurred, and the community is both subject to the same overt and structural violence as Sara and complicit in her suffering" (Baines, 2015, p. 327). Moving beyond the victim-perpetrator binary and recognising diffuse responsibility also allows us to acknowledge the political agency of victims, which in turn allows transitional justice scholarship to focus on social relations. This new focus, Baines argues, will help us to see the limitations of transitional justice mechanisms based on the premise of punishing the perpetrator and rescuing the victim (Baines, 2015).

Hansen notes that the field of transitional justice has been expanding both vertically and horizontally (Hansen, 2014). The vertical expansion refers to both internationalisation and localisation of transitional justice, with the involvement of a more diverse set of actors such as international actors, civil society, and local communities. Horizontal expansion, on the other hand, refers to the new contexts to which transitional justice applies. It includes the use of transitional measures in conflict settings without a fundamental political transition. Similarly, Engstrom points to the expansion of transitional justice both in terms of its normative ambitions and the geography to which it applies (Engstrom, 2013). The next section explores this type of expansion with a special focus on transitional justice when there is an ongoing conflict and in the absence of a political will to transition.

## 3.4 Victims' Agency

Victims' agency is another concept that draws significant attention in the literature on the role of victims in transitional justice (Mendez, 2016). Robins defines agency "primarily as the autonomy of the subject, both as individual and community: the sense in which victims are in control of their own destiny and are agents in processes to address their needs" (Robins, 2017). Likewise, Shepherd considers the key aspect of agency as "the idea of autonomy (literally 'self law'), the capacity to act independently of external constraints or coercion". Björkdahl and Selimovic argue that when the agents employ agency with the purpose of challenging existing norms, power relations, and inequalities as well as claiming their rights, they exercise a form of critical agency (Björkdahl and Selimovic, 2015).

In transitional contexts, agency is particularly important, because the victims of the conflicts usually have been victimised and marginalised long before direct violence starts. They are often subject to discrimination based on poverty, ethnicity, and gender, and excluded from political power (Robins, 2017). Emphasising the agency of victims has the potential to challenge existing power relations. These power relations often enable and reproduce conflict and tend to persist in the post-conflict period. A fundamental transformation of the conflict is only possible if these power relations are recognised and challenged (Parlevliet, 2010). Otherwise, elite groups are likely to define and implement transitional justice mechanisms on behalf of victims and reproduce the same power hierarchies in transitional periods. Gready and Robins note that:

> Typically, those most affected by violations have little or no opportunity to impact upon the goals of the process or the nature of particular mechanisms. Furthermore, privileging discourse that is often alien to victims, such as the predominantly legal discourses of transitional justice, can empower elites and outsiders at the expense of victims, particularly the most disempowered, who have both the greatest need for and least access to the language of rights. This is an articulation of the fact that in a state where only elites know what rights are, they can become something that is largely claimed on behalf of victims rather than by victims themselves.
>
> (Gready and Robin, 2014, p. 343)

## 3.5 Political Agency and Agency as Resistance

Baines discusses the political agency available to wartime victims and the notion of agency in complicity and responsibility after violence by looking at the story of Sara, as explained earlier (Baines, 2015). She presents a narrative that draws on four significant moments in Sara's life, marked by transformation and reflection periods (Baines, 2015). These moments are when she verbally confronts her oppressors/perpetrators and draws attention to the harm they cause. The first one is when she confronts her father, then the old LRA commander who sexually abused her, then the rebels who tried to kill her and her child, and finally her husband, who gave her no food. Baines considers these moments of confrontation with those who hold the power as "a particular form of politics practiced by subordinate groups in settings of extreme violence, which might be understood as a negotiation over the value of a human life". The concept of political agency refers to the assertion of one's "personhood in relation to others who would treat her otherwise" Baines, 2015, p. 328). According to this definition, "Sara is a political agent in the sense that she asserts her personhood in relation to others who would treat her otherwise, contesting their actions and forcing them to recognise their complicity and responsibility" (Baines, 2015, p. 328). Victims may be vulnerable, but it does not strip them of their capacity to go beyond coping and survival strategies.

In her book *Complex Political Victims*, Bouris discusses the ways in which the political victims exercise their agency, how they act in a way that will challenge their victimisation, and how we understand political victims as possessing agency (Bouris, 2007). She argues that the agency of political victims derives from several roles that they might take up during the peacebuilding process in the aftermath of the conflict. Like Baines, Bouris indicates that the agency comes from victims' capacity to render visible and challenge the discourses that oppress them (Bouris, 2007). In parallel to how Baines sees Sara's resistance to her oppressors as the realisation of her agency, Bouris also sees the agency in relation to resistance to the oppressing discourse and practices. She refers to Foucault's concept of technologies of self, which is related to the subjectivation of one's self as resistance to politically attributed identity and involves both ethical principles and behavioural practices (Foucault, 1988 cited in Bouris, 2007).

As Foucault argues, challenging the attributed roles by the dominant, oppressive power is itself resistance and is the actualisation of one's agency. "Victim" is such a role that is ascribed by the dominant power. Self-care (including bodily care), contemplation, and self-reflection enable the subjectivation and a create a new experience of self (Foucault, 1988 cited in Bouris, 2007). In this understanding, subjectivation practises might become political resistance as well:

> The practice of the care of the self has much political resonance and importance as well; it is the rejection of the politically ascribed identity, the rejection, in this case, of the identity enabling victimisation and the identity of the ideal victim.
>
> (Bouris, 2007, p. 122)

This is how victims might exercise political agency: by creating different identities for themselves that are challenging the ascribed ones.

In this regard, exercising agency does not need to be altering the physical conditions that victimise the victim. Challenging the discourse or making it visible is also way to exercise agency. This is how political victims contribute to peacebuilding by rejecting and resisting the discourse that enabled the victimisation (Bouris, 2007). Although it might not bring an end to oppression or the war, it still challenges the setting that enables the oppression to happen and allows victims to go beyond their victim position. Bouris claims that:

> by insisting upon practices of self-subjectivation, by refusing to accept transcendental identities that emerge from a narrow political space, victims are challenging the very legitimacy upon which their victimisation

> is premised and articulating an alternate and nuanced role for their own participation in the peacebuilding process.
>
> (Bouris, 2007, p. 123)

This argument is in tune with Baines, according to whom Sara contested the way that her humanness is denied and led others to face their responsibility and complicity:

> Recognition of victim agency (such as the ways Sara contested those relationships that would harm her or fail her as a person) also reveals the spaces in which power is challenged. Sara's response to each of the offences named in her life story illustrates the concept of political agency advanced here.
>
> (Baines, 2015, p. 327)

Therefore, agency is relational and politically situated. In their article discussing gendered agency, Björkdahl and Selimovic similarly argue that "the agentive subject is always situated" and that locating agency in space allows us to see the hidden and diverse spaces in which agency is exercised (Björkdahl and Selimovic, 2015, p. 171). This is crucial to see the critical agents that might be situated outside the formal and informal structures and listen to their voices that are silent or silenced.

Transitional justice contexts tend to underestimate and undervalue the political agency of victims or fail to fully capture their experiences as political actors (Baines, 2015; Sajjad, 2016). Transitional justice practice is usually carried out from an externally driven top-down approach and fails to recognise local agency when it comes to key issues (Sharp, 2013). However, the transitional justice literature has increasingly paid more attention to informal, locally owned, bottom-up processes. The next section focuses on one approach within this field: the victim-centred approach, which recognises victim agency as central to transitional justice processes.

## 3.6 Victim-Centred Approach to Transitional Justice

In the initial stages of transitional justice responses to mass abuses and violent conflicts, victims did not have much impact on state-led transitional justice mechanisms (Robins, 2017). Over time, transitional justice practice and scholarship have evolved from the initial state-centric approach to a more victim-centred one (Álvarez Berastegi and Hearty, 2019; Karstedt, 2016). There is now a universal recognition of and commitment, at least in principle, to the centrality of victims in transitional justice processes. The importance of the involvement of victims' experiences and their roles in justice and accountability processes are widely accepted. According to Robins' (2012) definition, a victim-centred approach means to have a transitional justice process that emerges directly out of the needs of the victims as expressed by the victims themselves and it has the potential to challenge the elite-led approach of most transitional justice processes.

What is key to a victim-centred transitional justice process is that the victims are not only the participants of the implementation or the passive recipients of a transitional justice process, but they are rather active agents of peace and transitional justice processes' design, management, analysis, and evaluation (Lundy and McGovern, 2008; Mendez, 2016). Thus, "securing popular access to and participation in all aspects of transitional justice processes (design, implementation, evaluation), and encouraging culturally resonant mechanisms that resist global models" can be very useful in challenging local and international exclusion mechanisms and power relations (Gready and Robin, 2014, p. 349).

Despite a widespread discourse arguing the victim-centredness of transitional justice, a more mainstream view that "victims are passive or apolitical" is still reflected in current transitional justice mechanisms (Brett and Druliolle, 2018, p. 2). For example, victims' right to truth, to justice, and to reparations are considered as key elemes in present transitional justice practice and scholarship (Hearty, 2018). Yet, the victims-centred advocacy and the agency of victims as a political force are yet to be fully acknowledged and victims as political actors mark an absence in transitional justice literature (García-Godos, 2016; Robins, 2017; Sajjad, 2016). The populations who were affected by the conflict are not usually consulted to determine the transitional justice process or encouraged to engage because the transitional justice practice is still state-centric, especially the main mechanisms such as truth commissions (Gready and Robin, 2014; Lambourne, 2009).

The failure to recognise the agency of victims as political actors makes the design of transitional justice process even more relevant. This brings us back to the question of the design process of transitional justice, which is usually led and shaped by elites, international professionals, and donors rather than local movements that include victims (Gready and Robin, 2014). Looking at what victims need to fulfil their demands for justice is only possible if the victims are consulted from the beginning about their understanding of justice. However, that consultation process tends to remain superficial in most contexts (Robins, 2012). Regarding the decisions about the type of transitional justice method that will be employed in a particular context, Lambourne argues that the needs of all the participants should be reflected:

> In determining the specific path to take in any particular transitional justice context, it is critical to take into account the needs, expectations and experiences of conflict participants—the perpetrators, victims, survivors and other members of society directly affected by the violence, who are intimately involved in the peacebuilding process.
>
> (Lambourne, 2009)

The state-centricity of transitional justice mechanisms results in an ongoing tension between what victims perceive as their needs and demands and what is offered to them by transitional justice practices that prioritise the needs of a liberal state (Robins, 2017). Remote and short-lived transitional justice institutions end up having less impact on victims than the social economic and political conditions that shape everyday life (Robins, 2017, p. 46).

An empirical study conducted with the families of victims of serious harms in Timor Leste illustrates that the needs and expectations that victims express are in contrast with what transitional justice mechanisms offer them (Robins, 2012). In reviewing a report that asked for victims' views of the transition in Nepal, Robins indicates that "the vast majority of the victims prioritised the daily struggle of surviving, a task made more difficult by victimhood, over judicial process" (Robins, 2009, p. 325). In other words, a majority of victims believe that compensation is more important than prosecutions and that basic needs are a higher priority than the judicial process. However, basic needs and economic and social rights are not on the priority list of human rights agencies in the transitional agenda in Nepal, although they are among the top priorities of victims. In parallel to Nepal, the families of missing persons in Timor Leste are in favour of economic support as their most immediate needs (Robins, 2012). In both contexts, the daily struggle of surviving is a more important priority for victims than the prosecution of the perpetrators, yet this is not reflected in the respective transitional justice processes.

One of the problems that contributes to this ongoing tension is the remoteness and detachment of transitional justice mechanisms from the communities they are intended to serve (Robins, 2017). This includes both the physical distance and abstract, as in a lack of understanding of social context/background surrounding the victims and a broader acknowledgement of how mass violence impacts the populations. The dominance of a narrow legalistic approach plays an important part in it, for which transitional justice scholarship, policy, and practice have long been criticised (McEvoy, 2007; Robins, 2017). The law is isolated from victims' social context, contributing further to the detachment of transitional justice practice from them (Robins, 2017). Even though prosecutions are not the only forms of redress, and they are usually only one of several different demands of victims, prosecutions are still privileged over other forms (Huyse, 2003; Robins, 2017). This "prevalence of legalism" in general and the "primacy of prosecution" might overlook the diversity of ways in which violence is experienced and often fails to capture the full complexity of post-conflict contexts (Robins, 2017). This detachment can be observed in Northern Ireland, Sierra Leone, and Rwanda, where transitional justice is understood to belong to formal mechanisms and institutions which are distant from the conflict-affected communities (McEvoy, 2007). Justice delivery is still seen mainly as the state's prerogative, which is often an obstacle against local ownership and undermines the accountability towards whom transitional justice is claimed to serve (McEvoy, 2007).

A victim-centred approach has to understand the different social and symbolic implications of violent events for the impacted populations, as it means that there are different versions of justice that will be meaningful to individuals (Porter, 2015; Robins, 2012). To deliver and ensure a sustainable peace which recognises the needs and interests of local constituents over the interests and politics of international community, the meanings and implications of different components of justice need to be understood (Visoka and Bolton, 2011). What the victims expect from justice might vary in a range of measures from prosecutions to reconciliation, official apology to truth recovery. It might and often does include a combination of different methods which are both addressing the truth-recovery needs and retributive justice (Gready and Robin, 2014). For this reason, hybrid approaches that combine internationally or nationally led trials, reparations, amnesty, truth commissions, and more traditional community-based and localised approaches are sometimes chosen to respond to different needs of the victims in a way that builds on contextual and cultural approaches (Clark, 2010; Gready and Robin, 2014; Lambourne, 2009). Gacaca courts in Rwanda and Fambul Tok in Sierra Leone are examples of these hybrid approaches which operated alongside criminal prosecutions and used traditional, cultural, localised resources for community-level healing (Ingelaere, 2007).

However, there are certain difficulties and challenges to hybrid approaches. Gacaca, for instance, was internally hybrid due to its combination of legal and non-legal objectives (healing, forgiveness, clearing the backlog of genocide cases, etc.) and methods. Some objectives of Gacaca are compatible with each other, such as forgiveness, healing, reconciliation, and peace. Yet, the pursuit of hybrid and sometimes conflicting objectives simultaneously, such as truth and healing, retributive/deterrent justice, and restorative justice/reconciliation, is a difficult job. Truth-telling, for example, does not necessarily lead to healing and it might even further traumatise the victims, which might hamper the reconciliation (Clark, 2010). Failing to carefully reflect on how different mechanisms might complement each other therefore carries certain risks (Du Toit, 2018). Transitional justice mechanisms usually tend to be analysed in isolation from one another. However, if multiple mechanisms are not linked together, there is not a realistic picture of how transitional justice works. For instance, the persecution of individual criminals is not capable of delivering justice for widespread systematic injustices and inequalities. Likewise, reparations cannot address the social injustices or structural inequalities themselves. Truth-telling processes are not necessarily healing, and they can have the adverse effect if they are not supported by other mechanisms. Traditional, community-based processes also run the risk of reinforcing gender roles if there is insufficient attention paid to gender policy (Du Toit, 2018). These challenges point at a crucial need while designing transitional justice processes. One needs to give utmost care and thought to how different mechanisms can be interlinked in a way that will avoid the risks and maximise the benefit for victims. This should be done in partnership with victims' groups so that their demands and visions for transitional justice are reflected in the transitional justice design.

As victims' groups are not a homogenous group, the issue of their engagement in the design process is a complex one. Victim groups contribute to justice in proportion to their capacity to organise (Méndez, 2016). First of all, not all victim groups have the same level of access to policymakers or practitioners. Secondly, they are usually not equal in terms of the resources available to them. For instance, the literacy level of a particular victim group and the language in which they are fluent are important factors that determine their ability to lobby and reach the relevant networks for their cases to be heard (Shepherd, 2015). Some victim groups might be working with more established NGOs with national and international contacts, while some others might be relying on voluntary work and local support. This plays a certain role while practitioners are trying to reach some representatives of victim groups to consult (Crocker, 1998). The time limit of these processes and the urgency to establish the mechanisms might make it even harder to map the victim groups and ensure the participation of all of them. All these reasons give way to a situation where victims and survivors are detached from, or outside of, transitional justice.

## 3.7 Transitional Justice in Ongoing Conflicts

The mechanisms of transitional justice were originally developed for post-conflict or post-authoritarian settings, and transitional justice interventions were initially typically conceived as coming "after evil" (Bevernage, 2015; Meister, n.d.). Although transitional justice mechanisms have been predominantly used in post-peace-agreement contexts where the physical violence has officially ended, the expansion of transitional justice has now become a topic of interest in the literature. While transitional justice mechanisms are assumed to apply in transitional periods, the possibilities to implement transitional justice in the absence of a clear-cut transition, when there is no peace process and the conflict is still ongoing, and where the society is deeply conflicted have started to be analysed (Ní Aoláin and Campbell, 2005). Several authors suggest that transitional justice is no longer connected to an exclusive period and being increasingly used during ongoing conflicts or widespread human rights abuses (Engstrom, 2013; Hansen, 2017; Quinn, 2014). For example, Engstrom indicates that the attempts to deal with a violent past after a war-to-peace transition are being replaced by the attempts to seek for accountability for atrocities even before the armed conflict is resolved by a political settlement (Engstrom, 2013). Sarkin proposes that the scope of transitional justice should expand in a way that goes beyond post-transition and post-crisis periods and that there is no need for transitional justice to wait to deal with human rights violations until they have happened, or the conflict has come to an end (Sarkin, 2016). More recently, with a growing number of transitional justice contexts of limited political change, ongoing conflict, or democratic setback, such as Sudan, Egypt, DRC, Bahrain, Syria, or Libya, the area of transitional justice has expanded to include aparadigmatic cases of transitional justice in contexts of ongoing violence and authoritarianism (Aboueldahab, 2018; Destrooper et al., 2023).

In a parallel endeavour to explore the centrality of transition in transitional justice, Quinn deals with the question of how far transition can be stretched (Quinn, 2014). She suggests that it is crucial to understand what transition means and what it entails to deal with the question of the extent of transitional justice more meaningfully. Similarly, Sarkin asks if transition needs to occur for transitional justice to be implemented and explores whether "a focus on dealing with the present or the immediate past is outside of what is envisaged as possible within a transitional justice framework" (Sarkin, 2016, p. 294).

It has been argued that transitional justice has the potential to facilitate the ending of a conflict by transforming social relations in protracted conflicts, where the violence is very much penetrated into daily lives of people (Van Nievelt, 2016). In the countries where there is no transition, even limited attempts could be beneficial for peaceful transformation (Hansen, 2014). Transitional justice can promote dialogue, assist with reconciliation, promote social cohesion and nation building, provide redress, and achieve guarantees of non-repetition, which would ultimately bring about peace (Sarkin, 2016). However, there is a need to focus more on the root causes of the conflict so that a wider array of transitional justice tools could be benefited to secure a more peaceful future.

Revising the normative transitional justice framework, Hansen makes a distinction between different contexts based on the presence of a transition (Hansen, 2011). He analyses the variations in transitional justice cases in fundamental political transitions and in non-transitions. He makes further distinction within these two categories. Within the category of "transitional justice in non-transitions", he defines a sub-category of "transitional justice in deeply conflicted societies" (Hansen, 2011, p. 23). Colombia, Kenya, Sudan, and Uganda are among the countries where several transitional justice tools have been placed in fragile and deeply conflicted societies in the absence of a fundamental political transition. Drawing on the Colombian transitional justice process that launched in 2005 in the absence of a peace process, Hansen demonstrates that even in the absence of a transition, some amount of justice could be achieved while seeking to limit the armed conflict (Hansen, 2011). As there have been several transitional justice initiatives without a fundamental political transformation or regime change, I argue that Turkey fits this model. In Chapter 7, I discuss it at length.

Sarkin points out that although justice during conflict is an understudied area, both governments and the oppositional forces use justice processes during conflicts for varied reasons (Sarkin, 2016). While governments often prosecute their opponents as a way of dealing with them or for the purpose of intimidation, oppositional forces do so to a much more limited extent. The cases that are brought against the perpetrators of human rights violations might prepare the groundwork for the transition that will take place at a later stage. Even if those cases end up serving the impunity, they are still important in the sense that they bring the issue to the attention of the public and in some cases gather the international community's attention as well. As governments do not want their role to be recognised or to be held accountable, they are usually not in favour of transitional justice processes during a conflict. Therefore, ongoing human rights monitoring and reporting by local and international actors is key to the success of judicial processes during conflict (Sarkin, 2016).

Mainstream transitional justice literature, however, does not fully capture the settings where there have been distinct phases and levels of transition, and where the conflict and widespread human rights abuses have never come to an end. At the same time, questions remain as to the applicability of the transitional justice framework in such cases (Sriram, 2007). Hansen highlights this need for "a differentiated framework for understanding and evaluating the highly diverse set of cases where attempts to deal with a legacy of violence or repression are conceptualised as transitional justice" (Hansen, 2014, p. 111). The opportunities that transitional justice might offer for the transformation of conflicts in the absence of an institutional willingness have not been adequately studied. There is, therefore, a need for a nuanced approach to analyse the prospects, challenges, and opportunities that might arise when transitional justice is applied in conflicted societies.

## 3.8 Conclusion

This chapter has provided a conceptual overview of two key areas in which this book is situated. The first part of the chapter explored the victims' centrality in transitional justice. It has set forth that despite the victim-centred approach having gained momentum in policy and practice, victims' political agency is still undermined. In parallel to the victim-centred approach that guided this research, I have highlighted that victims' political agency needs to be acknowledged to challenge top-down and elite-driven transitional justice tendencies. In the second part of the chapter, I reviewed the currently growing body of literature on transitional justice in non-transitions, specifically examining ongoing conflict settings. I elaborated on the argument that transitional justice can transform social relations in conflict settings where violence penetrated everyday lives and therefore, it can facilitate conflict transformation. The following chapter turns towards the Saturday Mothers movement and unpacks how organised victim movements can become strong political actors in the context of transitional justice in non-transitional settings.

## Reference List

Aboueldahab, N., 2018. *Writing Atrocities: Syrian Civil Society and Transitional Justice*. Brookings Doha Center. Available at: https://www.brookings.edu/articles/writing-atrocities-syrian-civil-society-and-transitional-justice/ (Accessed: 22 February 2025).

Álvarez Berastegi, A. and Hearty, K., 2019. A context-based model for framing political victimhood: Experiences from Northern Ireland and the Basque Country. *International Review of Victimology*, 25, pp. 19–36. https://doi.org/10.1177/0269758018782237

Baines, E.K., 2015. "Today, I Want to Speak Out the Truth": Victim agency, responsibility, and transitional justice. *International Political Sociology*, 9, pp. 316–332. https://doi.org/10.1111/ips.12100

Becker, D., 2004. Dealing with the consequences of organised violence in trauma work. In A. Austin, M. Fischer, and N. Ropers (Eds.), *Transforming Ethnopolitical Conflict: The Berghof Handbook*. Wiesbaden: VS Verlag für Sozialwissenschaften, pp. 403–420. https://doi.org/10.1007/978-3-663-05642-3_19

Berastegi, A.A., 2016. *Exploring Transitional Justice in Democratic States: The Definition of Victims in Northern Ireland and the Basque Country*. Dissertation submitted in partial satisfaction of the requirements for the degree Doctor of Philosophy in Transitional Justice Tab.

Bevernage, B., 2015. The past is evil/evil is past: On retrospective politics, philosophy of history, and temporal Manichaeism. *History and Theory*. https://doi.org/10.1111/hith.10763

Björkdahl, A. and Selimovic, J.M., 2015. Gendering agency in transitional justice. *Security Dialogue*, 46, pp. 165–182. https://doi.org/10.1177/0967010614552547

Borer, T.A., 2003. A taxonomy of victims and perpetrators: Human rights and reconciliation in South Africa. *Human Rights Quarterly*, 25, pp. 1088–1116. https://doi.org/10.1353/hrq.2003.0039

Bouris, E., 2007. *Complex Political Victims*. 1st ed. Boulder, CO: Lynne Rienner Publishers.

Brett, R. and Druliolle, V., 2018. *The Politics of Victimhood in Post-conflict Societies*. https://doi.org/10.1007/978-3-319-70202-5

Budak, Y., 2015. Dealing with the past: Transitional justice, ongoing conflict and the Kurdish issue in Turkey. *International Journal of Transitional Justice*, pp. 219–238. https://doi.org/10.1093/ijtj/ijv002

Byrne, C.C., 2004. Benefit or burden: Victims' reflections on TRC participation. *Peace and Conflict: Journal of Peace Psychology*, 10, pp. 237–256. https://doi.org/10.1207/s15327949pac1003_2

Christie, N., 1986. The ideal victim. In E.A. Fattah (Ed.), *From Crime Policy to Victim Policy: Reorienting the Justice System*. London: Palgrave Macmillan UK, pp. 17–30. https://doi.org/10.1007/978-1-349-08305-3_2

Clark, P., 2010. *The Gacaca Courts, Post-Genocide Justice and Reconciliation in Rwanda: Justice without Lawyers*. Cambridge Studies in Law and Society. Cambridge: Cambridge University Press. https://doi.org/10.1017/CBO9780511761584

Cole, A., 2016. All of us are vulnerable, but some are more vulnerable than others: The political ambiguity of vulnerability studies, an ambivalent critique. *Critical Horizons*, 17, pp. 260–277. https://doi.org/10.1080/14409917.2016.1153896

Crocker, D.A., 1998. Transitional justice and international civil society: Toward a normative framework. *Constellations*, 5, pp. 492–517. https://doi.org/10.1111/1467–8675.00110

de Waardt, M., 2016. Naming and shaming victims: The semantics of victimhood. *International Journal of Transitional Justice*, 10, pp. 432–450. https://doi.org/10.1093/ijtj/ijw011

Destrooper, T., Engbo Gissel, L. and Bree Carlson, K. (Eds.), 2023. *Transitional Justice in Aparadigmatic Contexts: Accountability, Recognition, and Disruption*. Routledge.
Du Toit, F., 2018. *When Political Transitions Work: Reconciliation as Interdependence*. https://doi.org/10.1093/ia/iiaa065
Engstrom, P., 2013. Transitional justice and ongoing conflict. In C.L. Sriram, J. Garcia-Godos, J. Herman and O. Martin-Ortega (Eds.), *Transitional Justice and Peacebuilding on the Ground: Victims and Ex-Combatants*. New York: Routledge, pp. 41–61.
Gallagher, E., Hamber, B. and Joy, E., 2012. Perspectives and possibilities: Mental health in post-agreement Northern Ireland. *Shared Space: Research Journal of Peace, Conflict and Community Relations in Northern Ireland*, 13, pp. 63–78.
García-Godos, J., 2016. Victims in focus. *International Journal of Transitional Justice*, 10, pp. 350–358. https://doi.org/10.1093/ijtj/ijv038
Gready, P. and Robin, S., 2014. From transitional to transformative justice: A new Agenda for practice. *International Journal of Transitional Justice*. https://doi.org/10.1093/ijtj/iju013
Hamber, B., 2002. "Ere their story die": Truth, justice and reconciliation in South Africa. *Race and Class*, 44, pp. 61–79. https://doi.org/10.1177/0306396802044001587
Hamber, B., 2009. *Transforming Societies after Political Violence. Truth, Reconciliation, and Mental Health*. Springer. https://doi.org/10.1007/978-0-387-89427-0
Hamber, B., 2015. Dealing with painful memories and violent pasts: Towards a framework for contextual understanding. In *Transforming War-Related Identities*. Berghof Foundation.
Hamber, B. and Wilson, R.A., 2002. Symbolic closure through memory, reparation and revenge in post-conflict societies. *Journal of Human Rights*, 1, pp. 35–53. https://doi.org/10.1080/14754830110111553
Hansen, T.O., 2011. Transitional justice: Toward a differentiated theory. *Oregon Review of International Law*, 13, pp. 1–46. https://doi.org/10.2307/840816
Hansen, T.O., 2014. The vertical and horizontal expansion of transitional justice: Explanations and implications for a contested field. In *Transitional Justice Theories*. Routledge, pp. 117–136.
Hansen, T.O., 2017. The time and space of transitional justice. In C. Lawther, L. Moffett, and D. Jacobs (Eds.), *Research Handbook on Transitional Justice*. UK: Edward Elgar Publishing, pp. 34–51.
Hearty, K., 2015. Legislating hierarchies of victimhood and perpetrators: The civil service (Special Advisers) Act (Northern Ireland) 2013 and the meta-conflict. *Social and Legal Studies*, 25, pp. 333–353. https://doi.org/10.1177/0964663915614887
Hearty, K., 2018. Victims of human rights abuses in transitional justice: Hierarchies, perpetrators and the struggle for peace. *International Journal of Human Rights*, 22, pp. 888–909. https://doi.org/10.1080/13642987.2018.1485656
Humphrey, M., 2003. From victim to victimhood: Truth commissions and trials as rituals of political transition and individual healing. *Australian Journal of Anthropology*, 14, pp. 171–187. https://doi.org/10.1111/j.1835-9310.2003.tb00229.x
Huyse, L., 2003. Victims. In D. Bloomfield, T. Barnes, and L. Huyse (Eds.), *Reconciliation after Violent Conflict: A Handbook*. Stockholm: International Institute for Democracy and Electoral Assistance, pp. 54–66.
Ingelaere, B., 2007. *Does the truth pass across the fire without burning? Transitional Justice and its Discontents in Rwanda's Gacaca Courts*. University of Antwerp, Institute of Development Policy (IOB).
International Center for Transitional Justice, 2024. *'The Search for People's Well-Being': Mainstreaming a Psychosocial Approach to Transitional Justice*. International Center for Transitional Justice.

Kaldor, M., 2013. In defence of new wars. *Stability: International Journal of Security and Development*, 2, p. 4. https://doi.org/10.5334/sta.at

Karstedt, S., 2016. The emotion dynamics of transitional justice: An emotion sharing perspective. *Emotion Review*, 8, pp. 50–55. https://doi.org/10.1177/1754073915601214

Kizilhan, J.I. and Neumann, J., 2020. The significance of justice in the psychotherapeutic treatment of traumatized people after war and crises. *Frontiers in Psychiatry*, 11. https://doi.org/10.3389/fpsyt.2020.00540

Kurban, D., 2012. Reparations and displacement in Turkey. Lessons learned from the compensation law. In *Case Studies on Transitional Justice and Displacement*. ICTJ, pp. 1–13.

Lambourne, W., 2009. Transitional justice and peacebuilding after mass violence. *International Journal of Transitional Justice*, 3, pp. 28–48. https://doi.org/10.1093/ijtj/ijn037

Lawther, C., 2024. Constructing victimhood: Beyond innocence and guilt in transitional justice. In *Constructing Victimhood*. Oxford: Oxford University Press, pp. 1–25. https://doi.org/10.1093/9780191938634.003.0001

Lundy, P. and McGovern, M., 2008. Whose justice? Rethinking transitional justice from the bottom up. *Journal of Law and Society*. https://doi.org/10.1111/j.1467-6478.2008.00438.x

McEvoy, K., 2007. Beyond legalism: Towards a thicker understanding of transitional justice. *Journal of Law and Society*, 34, pp. 411–440. https://doi.org/10.1111/j.1467-6478.2007.00399.x

McEvoy, K., Dudai, R. and Lawther, C., 2017. Criminology and transitional justice. In A. Leibling, S. Maruna, and L. McAra (Eds.), *The Oxford Handbook of Criminology*. Oxford: Oxford University Press, pp. 391–416.

McEvoy, K. and McConnachie, K., 2012. Victimology in transitional justice: Victimhood, innocence and hierarchy. *European Journal of Criminology*, 9, pp. 527–538. https://doi.org/10.1177/1477370812454204

Meister, R., n.d. *After Evil: A Politics of Human Rights*. Columbia University Press.

Mendeloff, D., 2009. Trauma and vengeance: Assessing the psychological and emotional effects of post-conflict justice. *Human Rights Quarterly*, 31, pp. 592–623. https://doi.org/10.1353/hrq.0.0100

Méndez, J.E., 2016. Victims as protagonists in transitional justice. *International Journal of Transitional Justice*, 10, pp. 1–5. https://doi.org/10.1093/ijtj/ijv037

Moffett, L., 2014. Navigating complex identities of victim-perpetrators in reparation mechanisms. *SSRN Electronic Journal*, 25, pp. 1–23. https://doi.org/10.2139/ssrn.2494759

Moffett, L., 2016. Reparations for 'Guilty Victims': Navigating complex identities of victim–perpetrators in reparation mechanisms. *International Journal of Transitional Justice*, pp. 146–167. https://doi.org/10.1093/ijtj/ijv030

Moon, C., 2009. Healing past violence: Traumatic assumptions and therapeutic interventions in war and reconciliation. *Journal of Human Rights*, 8(1), pp. 71–91. https://doi.org/10.1080/14754830902717726

Ní Aoláin, F. and Campbell, C., 2005. The paradox of transition in conflicted democracies. *Human Rights Quarterly*, 27, pp. 172–213. https://doi.org/10.1353/hrq.2005.0001

Parlevliet, M., 2010. Rethinking conflict transformation from a human rights perspective. *Berghof Handbook Dialogue Series*, 2010, pp. 15–46.

Porter, E.J., 2015. *Connecting Peace, Justice & Reconciliation*. Boulder, CO: Lynne Rienner Publishers.

Quinn, J.R., 2014. Whiter the transition of transitional justice. *Interdisciplinary Journal of Human Rights*. https://doi.org/10.3366/ajicl.2011.0005

Republic of South Africa, 1995. *Promotion of National Unity and Reconciliation Act*. Avalilable at: https://www.gov.za/sites/default/files/gcis_document/201409/act34of1995.pdf (Accessed 2 April 2025).

Robins, S., 2009. Whose voices? Understanding victims' needs in transition: Nepali voices: Perceptions of truth, justice, reconciliation, reparations and the transition in Nepal: By the International Centre for Transitional Justice and the Advocacy Forum, March 2008. *Journal of Human Rights Practice*, 1, pp. 320–331. https://doi.org/10.1093/jhuman/hup006

Robins, S., 2012. Challenging the therapeutic ethic: A victim-centred evaluation of transitional justice process in Timor-Leste. *International Journal of Transitional Justice*, 6, pp. 83–105. https://doi.org/10.1093/ijtj/ijr034

Robins, S., 2017. Failing victims? The limits of transitional justice in addressing the needs of victims of violations. *Human Rights International Legal Discourse*, 11, pp. 41–58.

Saeed, H., 2016. Victims and victimhood: Individuals of inaction or active agents of change? Reflections on fieldwork in Afghanistan. *International Journal of Transitional Justice*, 10, pp. 168–178. https://doi.org/10.1093/ijtj/ijv032

Sajjad, T., 2016. Heavy hands, helping hands, holding hands: The politics of exclusion in victims' networks. *International Journal of Transitional Justice*, 42, pp. 25–45. https://doi.org/10.1093/ijtj/ijv033

Sarkin, J., 2016. Refocusing transitional justice to focus not only on the past, but also to concentrate on ongoing conflicts and enduring human rights crises. *Journal of International Humanitarian Legal Studies*, 7, pp. 294–329. https://doi.org/10.1163/18781527-00702002

Sharp, D.N., 2013. Beyond the post-conflict checklist: Linking peacebuilding and transitional justice through the lens of critique. *Chicago Journal of International Law*, 14, pp. 165.

Shepherd, L.J., 2015. Constructing civil society: Gender, power and legitimacy in United Nations peacebuilding discourse. *European Journal of International Relations*, 21, pp. 887–910. https://doi.org/10.1177/1354066115569319

Sriram, C.L., 2007. Justice as peace? Liberal peacebuilding and strategies of transitional justice. *Global Society*. https://doi.org/10.1080/13600820701562843

Stauffer, J., 2013. Speaking truth to reconciliation: Political transition, recovery, and the work of time. *Humanity*, 4, pp. 27–48. https://doi.org/10.1353/hum.2013.0007

Van Nievelt, M.A., 2016. Transitional justice in ongoing conflict: Colombia's integrative approach to peace and justice. *Cornell International Affairs Review*, 11(2), pp. 1–20.

Visoka, G. and Bolton, G., 2011. The complex nature and implications of international engagement after Kosovo's independence. *Civil Wars*, 13, pp. 189–214. https://doi.org/10.1080/13698249.2011.576158

Chapter 4

# Understanding the Saturday Mothers Movement

## 4.1 Introduction

In Chapter 2, I set out the context that led to diverse forms of victimhood during the Kurdish Conflict. This same context also gave rise to grassroots mobilisation, resulting in long-lasting movements through the exercise of political agency. Among these, the relatives of the disappeared stand out as the most visible and systematically organised victim movement advancing the goals of transitional justice in Turkey. Encouraged by the families of the disappeared and human rights activists, the Saturday Mothers began mobilising in 1995 to protest against enforced disappearances. Over time, they transformed into a significant social movement demanding truth, justice, accountability, and recognition.

This chapter delves into the Saturday Mothers movement to understand how relatives of the disappeared have built one of the most enduring social movements despite an unfavourable social and political climate. I analyse a range of factors that have enabled their decades-long struggle. The chapter is divided into three main sections. The first section describes the context in which the Saturday Mothers movement emerged, evolved, and expanded to new cities and participants. The next section discusses the transformation of individual grief into collective mobilisation. Finally, I conclude by examining the tools and strategies adopted by the Saturday Mothers movement that enhanced their legitimacy and credibility, ultimately contributing to their sustainability.

## 4.2 Emergence, Evolution, and Expansion of the Saturday Mothers Movement

### *Beginning*

On 21 March 1995, Hasan Ocak, a 30-year-old teacher known for his socialist identity, left his home in Istanbul and was never heard from again (Duvar, 2022). His family searched tirelessly for 55 days with no assistance from the police, who denied any record of Hasan's detention despite witnesses'

DOI: 10.4324/9781003432579-4

accounts. Eventually, on 17 May 1995, Hasan Ocak's family and the Human Rights Association (*İnsan Haklari Dernegi*, İHD) found Hasan's tortured body in an unmarked grave.

Hasan Ocak's disappearance, along with that of Rıdvan Karakoç, whose family also discovered his body, led to a press statement at Galatasaray Square. This press statement prompted the need for activist groups to act against enforced disappearances. Inspired by the impactful protests in Argentina, Chile, and Guatemala, families of the disappeared, along with women human rights activists and feminists, called for regular silent gatherings demanding justice and accountability for enforced disappearances (Karakuş, 2022; Mater, 2014). Although the Kurds were the primary target, left-wing activists from other ethnic groups were also forcibly disappeared. Consequently, the Saturday Mothers have included families from a diverse range of ethnic backgrounds (Karaman, 2023; Sezer Şanlı, 2018). They describe themselves as follows:

> As the Saturday Mothers, known to the public, we are the families of people who were taken into custody by security forces in various parts of Turkey—from Edirne to Kars, from Istanbul to Hakkari, from Izmir to Diyarbakır, and from Ankara to Adana—whose existence was denied and who were never heard from again, as well as human rights defenders standing in solidarity with them.
>
> (Saturday Mothers, 2021)

### *Context of Social Mobilisation*

The Saturday Mothers movement emerged in a context of vibrant social and political movements. A group of activists, primarily led by the mothers of prisoners, was campaigning against human rights violations in prisons in the aftermath of the 1980 military coup.[1] Through "petitions to the parliament and to political parties, waiting outside the prisons, organizing demonstrations in public space, showing the blood-stained laundry of their children in prison, and going on hunger strikes" they were protesting inhumane prison conditions (Ahiska, 2020). Nimet Tanrıkulu,[2] a feminist human rights

1 For a detailed account of the prisoners' mothers' campaigns and actions at the time, see Orhan, 2008.

2 At the time of writing the book, she has been imprisoned since November 2024. See Amnesty International's call for her release: https://www.amnesty.org/en/documents/eur44/8960/2025/en/

defender involved in the Saturday Mothers movement since the beginning, provides insights into this background:

> Women and men of our generation experienced torture and death due to the 1980 military coup. Together with the coups, which are the heaviest of atrocity politics, we also witnessed disappearances in custody. However, we could not pursue justice for those disappearances of the 12 September [1980], much like they could not [go after] the 1915 disappearances.[3] Exactly for this reason, we were only a handful when we sat down in front of that grandiose door of Galatasaray High School on 25 May 1995, but we had felt as strong as that door.
>
> (Tanrıkulu, 2014)

A broader human rights movement was also active at the time, organised mostly by women. For example, the "Don't Touch My Friend" (*Arkadaşıma Dokunma*) campaign emerged, led largely by non-Kurdish feminists opposing racism, nationalism, and state violence against Kurds.[4] Ayşe Günaysu (2014b, para. 2), an activist involved in that campaign and later in Saturday sit-ins, describes those activists as "a group of women who knew each other through the feminist movement and human rights struggle". She recounts the period as follows:

> Our revolt against the war, increasing Kurd-phobia, racism, and nationalism and our urge to do something to raise a voice from the Turkish part of the society had brought us together. Feminists were already politically quite active for a while.
>
> (Günaysu, 2014b, para. 3)

Being aware of their privileged status as non-Kurds, they took on the responsibility to take an active stance against state violence against Kurds.[5] To make their stance publicly known, they issued a press statement in March 1994 on a left-wing newspaper to declared that "We, women who are not Kurdish, are ashamed of the privilege our identity cards grant us".[6] This prior

3 Many people, including İHD activists, consider the 1915 Armenian Genocide as the origin of the Turkish state's enforced disappearance practices and argue for the need for an official acknowledgement of the genocide.

4 This slogan was initially used in the anti-racist movements of Belgium, France, Holland, and Germany in early 1980s. The same slogan was then used in different political campaigns in Turkey.

5 Most women activists of that period have continued to take part in feminist peace activism.

6 It is not uncommon in other countries for feminists and women activists to take the lead to act against state violence and get involved in peace activism. There are other examples of women activists from the privileged nationalities/ethnicities taking

experience of mobilisation enabled them to take an active role in starting the Saturday sit-ins.

This vibrant context of human rights and feminist activism laid the groundwork for the first Saturday Mothers sit-in on 27 May 1995. Around 30 individuals, including the families of Hasan Ocak, Rıdvan Karakoç, Kenan Bilgin, Hasan Gülünay, and Hüseyin Toraman, gathered at Galatasaray Square, claiming that their loved ones were detained through extra judicial procedures and disappeared (Pişkin, 2018). Most were affiliated with the İHD (Arcan, 2022). With this first sit-in, the "kind of loss that cannot be certified in and by law, but that is 'overwhelmingly present,' has provided the significant connection among a wide range of agents who started the political performance of the Saturday Mothers in 1995" (Ahiska, 2020, p. 136). The sit-ins expanded as more families and human rights activists found out about them each week and some families started traveling from other cities to join them (Göker, 2013).

### *Evolution*

The Saturday Mothers movement evolved in both scope and strategy over the years, shaped by ongoing state repression and the persistent efforts of its organisers. Initially, a core group of activists, many of whom were women from the Don't Touch My Friend campaign, played a critical role in drafting press statements and coordinating weekly actions (Karakuş, 2022). This work was carried out in close collaboration with the İHD Commission Against Enforced Disappearances Under Custody (İHD Commission), which became the organisational backbone of the movement.

The Human Rights Association (İHD) was founded in 1986 as a result of the efforts of relatives of political prisoners against gross human rights violations in prisons, and in alliance with intellectuals and human rights advocates (Toker Kılınç et al., 2021). Human rights violations in prisons were the primary concern in the first days of the İHD, which brought the Diyarbakır Prison to their attention, and ultimately the Kurdish issue in the 1990s (Interview no:11, 2019).[7] This made the İHD the first civil society organisation that documented the human rights violations in the Kurdish region (Interview no:7, 2019).

Mothers' activism played a particularly influential role in founding the İHD (Ahiska, 2020; Orhan, 2008). The organic connection between the İHD

responsibility to stand against violence in the name of their nations. For instance, a similar position is seen in the Serbian Women in Black activists when they stood against their own state's war in Bosnia and Kosovo during the collapse of former Yugoslavia.

7 Diyarbakır Prison is known for severe human rights violations including systematic sexualised torture and ill-treatment committed against thousands of Kurdish political prisoners in the aftermath of the 1980 military coup. See Chapter 7 for more information.

and mothers of the disappeared became a defining characteristic of the movement. A long-standing member of the İHD described this intergenerational collaboration:

> When the İHD was first established, it consisted primarily of lawyers, doctors, academics, prisoner rights advocates. In the mid 90s, families of the disappeared and political party members got involved as well. In the 2000s, their children got involved, hence this constant interaction and connection . . . For example, the İHD lawyers have followed the court cases of some families since the 1990s. Some of those family members have become members or directors of the İHD.
>
> (Interview no:15, 2020)

The İHD Commission has played a pivotal role in coordinating the movement's activities. Each week, they oversee essential organisational and practical tasks, such as determining which disappeared individual to commemorate, locating and preparing photographs, writing press statements, and assigning speakers to share the stories of the disappeared (Bianet, 2023). It consists of both relatives of the disappeared and activists who have been part of the movement for many years. Beyond the sit-in, the İHD Commission also takes care of linking family members with media outlets when there is an interview request (Interview no:21, 2020).

### *A 10-Year Break*

Despite its growing visibility, the Saturday Mothers have faced increasing police violence and repression starting from its early stages. While the sit-ins began as small gatherings, the number of participants had increased when police attempted to intervene in the sit-ins in the third month. Since there were several media outlets following the sit-in on that day, the protesters released a press statement as a response to police intervention. From that point on, silent sit-ins started to include a press statement (Karakuş, 2022). In 1998, the families and activists were surrounded by a heavy police presence. As of 15 August 1998 (week 170), the police started dispersing the sit-ins every Saturday, taking mothers into custody on a weekly basis. Younger activists wanted the mothers to take a pause for a while and continue on their own, but the mothers refused to do so. However, by March 1999, the participation had decreased dramatically. After 200 consequent weeks of Saturday sit-ins, the group made a collective decision to suspend the sit-ins on 13 March 1999 (week 200) (Göker, 2013; Sezer Şanlı, 2020). An activist recalled the decision-making process:

> It was decided to continue. But some of us started to break apart from the group. Some of our friends said in our meetings with all sincerity and

> honesty that they were so afraid and that they did not want to encounter the police, did not want to be taken into custody.
>
> (Günaysu, 2014a, para. 25)

Despite the suspension, the movement had already achieved significant gains during its first 200 weeks. Orhan explains these gains as follows: First, the number of disappearances reduced over the four years Saturday Mothers held their vigils. While there were 68 cases of enforced disappearances when they began in 1996, this number had declined to nine in 1998. Second, they raised a prominent level of public awareness on the issue of disappearances in Turkey. Due to media coverage, many people had also found out about brutal police violence against mothers. Third, by using the photographs of their disappeared loved ones and sharing their unique stories, the mothers represented their children as individuals with distinct stories rather than numbers (Orhan, 2008). The Saturday Mothers did not abandon their struggle in the absence of sit-ins. They continued advocating for justice through national and international platforms, keeping the memory of the disappeared alive (Karaman, 2023).

### *Resumption of Sit-ins in 2009*

A decade later, the Saturday Mothers resumed their sit-ins on 31 January 2009 in response to the Ergenekon trials—a series of legal proceedings targeting individuals tied to the Turkish deep state (discussed in Chapter 6). The trials were presented by the government as "the legal fight against the remnants of the deep state" (Karaman, 2016). Some of the defendants were implicated in the enforced disappearances of the 1990s, which motivated the mothers to restart protesting (Sezer Şanlı, 2020). In a press statement, explaining their decision to resume the sit-ins, the İHD declared:

> We, the Saturday Mothers and human rights advocates, restarted our sit-ins on 31 January 2009 on Galatasaray Square after a 10-year break because of the confessions made by official authorities; the discovery of the bones of our children and loved ones disappeared in custody in acid wells, streams, holes; and because some of the names prosecuted in Ergenekon trials are among the perpetrators of our disappeared relatives.
>
> (T24, 2010)

The decade-long break did not weaken the campaign against the disappearances (Günaysu, 2014a). Remarkably, the gatherings began to attract even larger crowds (Interview no:10, 2019). In this post-2009 phase, although demands for uncovering about the whereabouts of the disappeared were still present, the sit-ins also began to focus more on tangible demands around accountability and justice and on ensuring the prosecution of the perpetrators

(Göker, 2013; Göral, 2019; Sezer Şanlı, 2018). In that period, the Saturday Mothers also became a prominent voice in broader human rights advocacy, linking their struggle to issues such as state violence and impunity. From that point on, the movement has demanded (İHD, 2018):

- The state should recognise its responsibility in the crime of enforced disappearance.
- The fate of those who disappeared in custody should be revealed, and their remains should be returned to their families.
- End the impunity protecting the perpetrators and those responsible for enforced disappearances, and ensure justice is served.
- Implement legal regulations to prevent and prosecute the crime of enforced disappearance, recognising it as a crime against humanity, and ensure that no one is ever forcibly disappeared again.
- Turkey should sign, ratify, and implement without any reservations the international convention prepared by the United Nations for the protection of all persons from enforced disappearance.
- Turkey should become a party to other international conventions, protocols, and statutes that prohibit impunity.

In more recent years, the movement has faced significant challenges regarding the sit-ins. The district governor banned their gatherings in Galatasaray Square on the 700th week in August 2018, citing security concerns. This prohibition led to judicial harassment and police violence with mothers and activists getting into detentions during their attempts to assemble (Frontline Defenders, 2021; Saturday Mothers, 2023; Tosun, 2024). In November 2023, following legal appeals and public pressure, the ban was partially lifted, allowing up to ten participants to hold vigils in the square. Despite this concession, restrictions remain, and the group continues to advocate for the full restoration of their right to peaceful assembly (Al Jazeera, 2024).

### *Expansion to the Kurdish Cities*

It was after the resumption of the gatherings in 2009 when, through a "boomerang effect", the Saturday sit-ins expanded to the Kurdish cities of Batman, Diyarbakır, the Cizre district of Şırnak, and Yüksekova district of Hakkari (Daşlı, 2024; Göral, 2021, p. 10). Under the name Saturday Mothers, or the Kurdish equivalent, *Dayikên Şemiyê,* relatives of the disappeared in these cities adopted the same gathering format as their counterparts in Istanbul.

There is an X (formerly Twitter) account of Saturday Mothers and the İHD Commission, which is called *Cumartesi Anneleri* (Saturday Mothers). This account is managed by the group in Istanbul to share the news about their weekly sit-ins, making announcements, and sharing updates on legal cases. The account also frequently circulates the news about Saturday actions in Kurdish cities by retweeting the local İHD branches, demonstrating the vibrant and constant interaction and coordination among actions in different cities.

While the group in Istanbul has consistently referred to itself as Saturday Mothers/People, gatherings in Kurdish cities are often described as 'relatives of the disappeared'. Those in the Kurdish region, announce their Saturday gatherings as *Kayıplar Bulunsun Failler Yargılansın* (Find the Disappeared and Prosecute the Perpetrators) actions of the relatives of the disappeared.

This distinction in terminology appears to have emerged organically rather than as a deliberate strategy. A Diyarbakır-based lawyer with extensive experience representing families of the disappeared explained:

> The structure in Istanbul is a little different. There are people from various segments. Here it has a narrower circle, a narrower area . . . Because Istanbul is a metropolitan city, there are people from different ethnicities who lead and participate in the gatherings. But, here, it is a space where mostly Kurds attend and lead.
>
> (Interview no:19, 2020)

This localised dynamic also shapes the composition of the gatherings. In Istanbul, the sit-ins bring together a heterogeneous crowd—relatives of the disappeared, human rights defenders, feminist activists, and political figures. In contrast, as scholar Göral notes, the gatherings in Cizre and other Kurdish cities are far more homogeneous, consisting predominantly of the wives and mothers of the disappeared:

> Cizre's Saturday Mothers are and always have been quite different from the protesters in Istanbul. In the metropolis, there is a heterogeneous crowd comprised of relatives of the disappeared, human rights defenders, activists, and politicians, whereas the crowd is much more homogeneous in the predominantly Kurdish city, comprising mainly of wives and mothers of the disappeared.
>
> (Göral, 2021, p. 84)

The sit-ins in Istanbul have been more visible and widely known, and supported by a broader range of people than those in other cities. This visibility has been amplified by the presence of well-known figures such as artists, journalists, and politicians, as well as by extensive media coverage, documentaries, and songs dedicated to the movement.[8] However, the gatherings in

8 See for example: *33 Yıllık Direniş Berfo Ana,* 2013 by Veysi Altay; *Bıraktığın Yerden*, 2019 by Volkan Güney Eker; *Katarsis*, 2020 by Zelal Buldan for documentaries; and *Cumartesi Türküsü*, 1997, Sezen Aksu; *Beni Bul Anne*, 1995, Ahmet Kaya; 2012, Selda Bağcan;

Diyarbakır, Batman, and Cizre face significant obstacles in achieving similar levels of recognition, especially outside the Kurdish region. Notably, there are fewer scholarly sources on the relatives of the disappeared in the Kurdish region. One of my interlocutors, part of the Istanbul group, reflects on the additional challenges faced in Diyarbakır:

> I have a huge admiration for the people gathering there, especially in Diyarbakır. Because although we gather in Istanbul, and get subjected to violence, faced with problems, their problems tend to be a lot heavier: death threats, heavier stuff, surveillance, etc. Because, you know, as you go towards the east and southeast Anatolia, the already non-existing law starts to cease existing completely.
>
> (Interview no:21, 2020)

Increased securitisation and militarisation in the Kurdish region since 2015–2016 have further limited media access, reducing the visibility of these gatherings. Few media outlets cover the sit-ins outside Istanbul, and those unfamiliar with the movement often remain unaware of actions taking place in Diyarbakır or Batman.

In all three of these cities, the groups were banned from holding gatherings in their regular spots, a symbol and key strategy for the movement. On 25 August 2018 (week 700), the district governor banned the Saturday Mothers' sit-ins at Galatasaray Square, citing security concerns. The square, which had served as the movement's symbolic and physical heart, became inaccessible. To continue the protests despite the ban, the group began reading their press statements in front of the nearby İHD Istanbul branch. However, mothers and activists remained determined to reclaim Galatasaray Square. They suspended their signature sit-in format until they were back to where the sit-ins belong: Galatasaray Square (Tosun, 2024). Each week, a core team of mothers and activists persistently tried to walk to Galatasaray Square. Not only was this prevented by police, but members were sometimes even taken into custody.

Just days after the ban in Istanbul on 1 September 2018, authorities prohibited gatherings at Koşuyolu Park in Diyarbakır. It was where the families and the activists gathered for the disappeared in front of the Right to Life monument. Similarly, gatherings were banned on Gulistan Avenue in Batman, where families had held weekly protests for over 400 weeks in front of the Human Rights statue.

In response to these bans, families and activists shifted their gatherings to the local İHD branches. the families and the activists resumed the gatherings

2014 by Sansar Salvo, 2018 by Ceylan Ertem and the relatives of the disappeared for the 700th week of Saturday sit-ins; *Benim Annem Cumartesi* (My Mother is Saturday), 2009, Bandista, and most recently Benim Annem Cumartesi, 2024, Teoman for songs.

in the local İHD branches. During the Covid-19 pandemic in 2020–2021, the gatherings moved online in Istanbul and Diyarbakır, and paused for a couple of months in Batman. While this adaptation ensured continuity, it marked a significant shift from the movement's signature sit-in format in public spaces until these key sites were accessible again.

## 4.3 From Individual Grief to Collective Mobilisation: Politicised Motherhood and Feminist Activism

### *The Role of Women Activists*

Feminist scholarship has consistently shown that political violence often redefines power relations and gender hierarchies, enabling women to exercise new forms of political agency and leadership (Björkdahl and Selimovic, 2015; Ni Aolain et al., 2011; O'Rourke, 2012). In contexts of political violence, women have been at the forefront of resistance movements, using civil resistance and public protests to claim space and amplify their voices (Berry, 2018; Zulver, 2022). This dynamic has been particularly evident in the Saturday Mothers movement, where women—as mothers, sisters, daughters, and activists—have played a central role in advancing the struggle against enforced disappearances.

Feminist activists involved in the early days of the movement described how decisions were reached through dialogue and consensus, rather than hierarchical imposition. Ahıska defines this feminine mode of doing politics as one that "is open to interaction and solidarity with others, sharing the traces of shared trauma—a mode that enables contact with loss in its multiple forms and temporalities" (Ahiska, 2020, p. 139). In a well-known feminist newspaper of the time, *Pazartesi,* the cover pages would be dedicated to a group of women in Galatasaray Square and their way of doing politics. Koçali, an activist involved in both the Do Not Touch My Friend campaign and Saturday gatherings wrote in the *Pazartesi* newspaper on women's unique way of doing politics: "Nobody imposes what they think right in the decision-making processes. They only try to convince. Instead of re-telling the same idea for hours repeatedly, they easily say 'I agree'" (Koçali, 1996). In the same issue, Karakuş discusses why it is predominantly the women activists who revolted against the state violence against the Kurds. She explains that in terms of its purpose, the Do Not Touch My Friend campaign did not have to be a women-only group, and men's involvement was not rejected in principle. However, none of the women made any efforts to include men, she notes:

> On the contrary, we were worried that if men got involved, the group's activities and chats would not have been as joyful and easy. As the women from Do Not Touch My Friend, we felt the matter of being Galatasaray People against the disappearances in our hearts and minds and got together with other women working for human rights. To materialise the proposal

> that emerged in another platform and to ensure its continuity, we made our best effort with belief and pleasure.
>
> (Karakuş, 1996)

### *The Shaping of 'Saturday Mothers'*

The group brought together a diverse set of participants. They had not come together as mothers, wives, or simply as female relatives, but as a group of human rights defenders, feminists, left-wing activists, and the relatives of the disappeared of different generations (Arcan, 2022). Therefore, they deliberately identified as Saturday People to reflect this varied participation. The starting point was an urgent action taken by a diverse group of people who were concerned about the disappearances and wanted to react collectively. For example, they initially signed press releases as Saturday People and emphasised this in interviews. Mothers, specifically, came to be at the group's heart and acted as the driving force (Interview no:15, 2020; Interview no:21, 2020; Interview no:23, 2020).

Towards the end of the first year of the Galatasaray sit-ins, the movement became known as Saturday Mothers in Turkey and internationally. The media insisted on the name Saturday Mothers (Göker, 2013, p. 112) emphasising the motherly pain and the motherhood identity and "every newspaper article and book used the term Saturday Mothers to describe the sit-ins" and that "the reporters insisted on making interviews exclusively with the mothers" (Can, 2014, p. 176). The name Saturday Mothers was quickly and widely embraced (Pişkin, 2018). This shift was partly due to powerful connotations of the image of mothers searching for their children, and because of the earlier internationally well-known experiences such as the Plaza de Mayo Mothers (Can, 2014). Günaysu, part of the first group, confirms this position:

> We did not call ourselves Saturday Mothers. Because there were not only mothers. There were male and female relatives of the disappeared. But the press called the people in the sit-ins 'Saturday Mothers' and the public adopted this name, being taken by its sentimentality. We clarified it a few times in interviews, but we could not prevent it.
>
> (Günaysu, 2014a, para. 10)

Currently, the names Saturday Mothers and Saturday People are used interchangeably or together as Saturday Mothers/People. Sebla Arcan, a member of the İHD Commission, explained how they ended up identifying as Saturday Mothers/Saturday People:

> The media insisted to refer to us as the Saturday Mothers and the public embraced this description. Despite us, in fact, we were started to be called

> as Saturday Mothers. We realised that there was no point in continuing to insist. Therefore, we decided to introduce ourselves as Saturday Mothers/Saturday People and signed the statements accordingly.
>
> (Arcan, 2022)

Tanrıkulu, one of the initial activists and ongoing members, asserted that Saturday Mothers/Saturday People began to be used together to avoid being associated solely with motherhood:

> Because the naming Saturday Mothers somehow became permanent, we tried to get out of the "motherhood" label by using Saturday Mothers/Saturday People. I will not go into the details of the "motherhood" debate in this piece, but it is already problematic to sum up the relatives of the disappeared under the title "Saturday Mothers". First and foremost, among the relatives of the disappeared, were there not spouses, partners, fathers, children, siblings, and comrades alongside mothers?
>
> (Tanrıkulu, 2014)

Saturday Mothers usually refers to the mothers, whereas Saturday People is used to refer to the broader network of family members and activists who regularly attend the meetings and support their cause (Interview no:21, Interview no:23).

While I was conducting this research, I found out that there is a public perception that the movement identified as Saturday Mothers from the beginning due to a shared motherhood experience. This perception is particularly interesting because the initial participants did not see it as a mothers' movement and insisted on the name Saturday People (Göral, 2021). The responses of my interlocutors who belong to a younger generation suggest that different activists have their own assumptions about the group's name evolution. Two activist leaders, for example, believe that the name Saturday People became more popular as the protests expanded and attracted new supporters. In line with this, they consider that the movement emerged primarily as a motherhood-based movement and should maintain this essence. An activist leader, a relative of the disappeared, described the evolution:

> Because it has always been Saturday Mothers. Saturday People was never used. But if you ask me, and although I haven't discussed this with anyone, there was probably a decision to start using Saturday People. To include our supporters a little bit more . . . Because of this [increased support], of course, it turned into something more inclusive than Saturday Mothers, into Saturday People . . . But in essence, those who are leading this are still the Saturday Mothers.
>
> (Interview no:23, 2020)

Another activist leader made a clear distinction. According to him, everyone who supports the mothers, attends the gatherings, and spreads the mothers' message are Saturday People, including himself. These people have diverse identities in terms of gender, political affiliation, profession, ethnicity, and age. This support varies from regularly attending the sit-ins to conveying the Saturday Mothers' messages on social media. Saturday Mothers, however, refers to very specifically to the mothers who lost their children and go on the square. This highlights that mothers are at the core of the movement:

> All our supporters are Saturday People. Those who mention us on social media or in a café, or those who hold our photos on the squares are all Saturday Mothers. They are our supports, in its true sense. But the mothers, who lost their children, are Saturday Mothers.
>
> (Interview no:21, 2020)

Another interlocutor shared that the mothers are at the heart of the moment; Saturday Mothers evolved to Saturday People organically as the mothers aged or passed away, and younger relatives took over (Interview no:18, 2020). The intergenerational aspect is significant, as several founding members and key figures have died or are too old to attend gatherings. My interlocutor noted that despite this, the term Saturday Mothers should be preserved to maintain the movement's strength and focus:

> Unfortunately, after 25 years, the mothers got old, and their participation got a bit more difficult. It is passed on to the second generation, and with this second generation and those who support this demonstration, it turned into an expanded demonstration. That is why it is referred to as Saturday People, but if you ask my personal opinion, I am in favour of continuing to use Saturday Mothers.
>
> (Interview no:23, 2020)

My interviews demonstrate a shared understanding that mothers have always been the essence of the movement. Motherhood, despite the initial claims to be a diverse group and not limited to a motherhood movement, appear to have played a pivotal role in broadening support for the movement. An emphasis on motherhood has helped the groups to gain legitimacy, visibility, and credibility. One interlocutor reflected that the power and success of the movement comes from the mothers' central position:

> My mom is a Saturday mother; I am a Saturday person. But I think the reason why this spirit spreads so beautifully is the mother phenomenon, the fact that the mothers are in it. Because of that, and because I believe it is a lot more visible, I also call them Saturday Mothers.
>
> (Interview no:21, 2020)

The same interlocutor indicated that this growing support is significant, with new people joining every week increasing their motivation and morale. Yet, she believes that the term "Saturday Mothers" should be maintained to preserve the strength in the discourse because the movement was started by mothers:

> This is an incredibly beautiful support, but because this is a type of demonstration that mothers initiated, that mothers look for their own children or husbands, I think as a discourse, Saturday Mothers is more appropriate. Because when you say Saturday People, it loses that thing, I mean, the essence of the matter dissolves a little bit. It is as if that first connotation gets lost. [The connotation] of Saturday Mothers from generation to generation . . . I mean, what will people understand when you say Saturday Mothers in ten, twenty years from now? [It is] like the mothers of Plaza de Mayo.
>
> (Interview no:23, 2020)

This understanding highlights the fear of shifting from the mothers' experiences to something broader, potentially losing focus on their cause.

## *The Role of Mothers*

Although the movement did not originate solely from a common motherhood experience, mothers indeed became the group's heart and driving force (Interview no:15, 2020; Interview no:21, 2020; Interview no:23, 2020). Despite the variety of actors involved, all decisions are informed by mothers' priorities (Tanrıkulu, 2014). The İHD Commission also plays more of a facilitatory role than a decision-making role to "take the burdens from the mothers" and "to make sure that they can ask for the fates of their children and their minds focus only on that" (Interview no: 21, 2020).

To understand this better, I asked my interlocutors about how key decisions are made. It was brought to my attention, for example, that when there is a need to decide about a central issue, such as how to proceed when Galatasaray Square is banned, İHD Commission summons the elderly of the group, including the mothers and other members who have been part of the movement for a long time. After the square was banned on week 700 in August 2018, the first decision was to keep trying every week to access the square despite knowing they would face police violence and potentially detention. After trying for ten weeks, violence reached an intolerable level and to protect the elderly, the İHD Commission summoned and consulted the elderly of the group. The decision then was made to gather in front of the İHD Istanbul office. The families decided not to carry out the sit-ins until they had a clearer idea of how and when they would reach Galatasaray Square. As the sitting format is an important symbolic gesture, it would only be meaningful if it was linked to another symbolic component of the gatherings, namely the square itself.

> They [families] said that whenever we know more about Galatasaray, whenever we determine what path to follow to go to Galatasaray, then we will sit again. That's how we made the decision. Mothers are always the determining factor for us. [The İHD] Commission consists only of the volunteers who work to spread their work and make sure that it reaches to more people.
>
> (Interview no:21, 2020)

A similar process took place in Diyarbakır where mothers are seen as the pioneers of the movement and the decisions are made in consultation with them. In parallel to the İHD Commission against Enforced Disappearances in İstanbul, there is an İHD commission to investigate the enforced disappearances and unsolved political murders in Diyarbakır. When it was banned to hold gatherings in Koşuyolu Park in Diyarbakır in September 2018, as an İHD lawyer recalls, the Commission organised a meeting with the families. Based on the families' preferences, İHD organised the gatherings inside the building for a while, and then they moved it in front of the building, in such a way that the İHD emblem is visible. A lawyer working with the relatives of the disappeared reminded us that "Therefore, when we are making a decision, we are only a part of the decision, the real decision makers are the relatives of the disappeared" (Interview no:15, 2020).

Due to patriarchal gender norms, global narratives often construct women as ideal victims (Cohen, 2018; Schwöbel-Patel, 2018). Christie (1986) defines the ideal victim as "a person or category of individuals, who, when hit by crime, most readily are given the complete and legitimate status of being a victim" (p. 18). At the same time, motherhood and a mother's suffering are universally understood experiences across societies and contexts (Laqueur, 2002). In many cultures, mothers are the prototypical figures of mourning since they are perceived as the primary caregivers and nurturers, making their grief and mourning more visible. Especially in contexts of mass violence, such as genocide or systematic killings, mothers often become prominent public figures as they take on the task of mourning and remembering the deceased. Their public expressions of grief serve as powerful reminders of the humanity and individuality of the victims. Moreover, witnessing a mother's grief evokes not only sympathy for her suffering but also a deep, personal fear, as it forces parents to confront the painful possibility that they too could experience such profound loss (Wright, 2016).

Maternal activism, in terms of "women's deployment of the mother identity in their campaigns for economic, social, and political change" (Orozco Mendoza, 2016, p. 1), serves "as the archetype of a universal ethic of care and love in search of rightful retribution" (Orozco Mendoza, 2016, p. 2). In multiple countries in Latin America and the Middle East with political violence, mothers have been at the forefront of social justice struggles (Orozco Mendoza, 2016). In these cases, motherhood provided them with moral authority to resist injustices and advocate for political change. Especially in contexts marked by state repression, taking collective action through the shared motherhood identity can garner moral authority and public sympathy and can serve as an effective tool for social and political change (Bouvard, 1994; Helms, 2013). Motherhood identity, therefore, can be leveraged to challenge oppressive regimes and bring public attention to human rights and justice issues. This type of maternal activism has been exemplified most notably in The Mothers of the Plaza de Mayo in Argentina, the mothers of femicide and disappeared women in Ciudad Juárez and Chihuahua, Mexico, and the Mothers for Peace in Palestine (Orozco Mendoza, 2016). The Saturday Mothers are another such example.

Mothers in the Saturday Mothers movement have played a prominent role because of their relative advantage in navigating repressive contexts, in relation to how they are perceived externally as ideal victims. The notion of mothers as innocent victims searching for their children developed over time, and motherhood provided a strong basis for wider society to empathize with their pain and support their cause (Interview no:15, 2020; Interview no:21, 2020; Interview no:23, 2020). This allowed the group to tap into powerful connotations of the image of mothers searching for their children, a globally recognised image thanks to the Argentinian Mothers of Plaza de Mayo (Can, 2014, p. 140). Baydar and Ivegen (2006, p. 696) note:

> [T]he name Saturday Mothers domesticates the sittings, renders them safe and harmless in the eye of the public. It turns public attention away from the political content of the protest to the private realm of emotions. That is, possible political outrage is instead channelled toward private sentiments toward a mother who lost her child.

Drawing on dominant ideas of victimhood based around innocence, purity, lack of responsibility, absence of guilt, and moral superiority can be a crucial factor in legitimising claims and accessing resources and support (Bouris, 2007, p. 39). Motherhood, as a universally understood experience with the potential to trigger widespread emotional responses, has been key to creating strong relatability and legitimacy, linking the private and the public realm (Baydar and Ivegen, 2006). By translating their individual suffering into collective mobilisation and therefore politicising their motherhood experience, the Saturday mothers have redefined traditional understandings of motherhood.[9]

9 For a thorough analysis of the construction of motherhood as a form of political agency, see Karaman, 2016.

By doing so, they have also managed to reach out to a wide network of activists from various professional, ethnic, and political backgrounds who are now dedicated participants of the Saturday Mothers/People movement. In the following section, I delve into the tools and strategies they have employed to enhance their visibility and secure broader support, offering deeper insights into their collective mobilisation.

## 4.4 Tools and Strategies Employed

### *Independence from Political Groups*

From the outset, the Saturday Mothers movement agreed on the principle of independence. They have been an independent movement free from political groups, organisation, and parties (Interview no:23, 2020). This principle of independence has been crucial in preserving the movement's strong and credible image and ensuring legitimacy in the eyes of the public. They aimed at preserving Galatasaray Square as a dedicated space solely for the stories of enforced disappearances (Can, 2014). By focusing on mothers' experiences and the stories of enforced disappearances, they avoided being co-opted for political gains. An early member explains:

> Our principle was independence. Apart from the disappearances under custody, and their photos, there shouldn't have been any [political] organisation banner, poster or slogan. We would kindly request it every time. Only by doing so, could the struggle preserve its realness, genuineness, and inclusiveness. Our persuasiveness in the eye of public was so important to us. We were only calling out for the disappearances under custody. We were trying to explain that the disappearances were too big human rights violations to instrumentalise for political interests with pragmatic approaches.
>
> (Günaysu, 2014a, para. 12)

The emphasis on independence has also helped the movement counter attempts to criminalise and discredit their struggle. When organised victim groups hold a strong political profile with wider demands than their own suffering, they may be targeted by suspicious claims (Brett and Druliolle, 2018). These demands may wrongly be interpreted as these groups are not mobilising for legitimate motives, and they have a hidden agenda implying that they are not 'innocent victims'. The group has remained conscious of the risks of being perceived as politically aligned and thus remained committed to independence. An activist-leader explained:

> We don't accept to get affiliated to any political entity, movement, or anything. When there is such demand, as there was a couple of years ago,

> we do not accept it. There were some incidents happening (I won't name them) when they asked us to include it into Saturday Mothers' press statement. But we didn't. Because then the Saturday Mothers would have been deviated from its own purpose. It would have gone towards another direction and then the state would have said: "so you don't get together for this, you have a different purpose." It is not that we were afraid. Our thing is to search for the disappeared. It is a prominent position, important space, important movement. We can't associate it with something else, we should not, because it would mean disrespecting our own struggle.
>
> (Interview no:23, 2020)

Maintaining independence from political groups has been a crucial factor in keeping the movement united and fostering diverse participation. The Saturday Mothers, especially the group gathering in Istanbul, is heterogeneous in terms of identity and political affiliation. Their strong commitment to a shared goal of justice and determination to resist external influences have been key to sustaining the movement over many years. The following statement highlights this point:

> We are an independent group that has been active for 25 years under the umbrella of the Human Rights Association, with no affiliation to any political party, institution, or organisation, and committed to maintaining an equal distance from all political parties. We are people from diverse worldviews, ethnicities, and faiths, united around the demand for justice. In fact, we represent all the colours of Turkey in its sociological reality.
>
> (Saturday Mothers, 2021)

Across the world, mothers are often seen as politically neutral, and therefore relating to, and empathising with, the mothers' suffering is easier for society. An activist leader described how the consistent public display of mothers' pain without shifting their focus away from mothers' demands helped garner support and empathy for the movement's cause:

> It has been accepted in the public opinion that the demands of Saturday Mothers are rightful. These are mothers, they are searching for their children or want their children's bodies to be returned. Since it is a very fair demand, honestly, the only thing they can do is to shut down Galatasaray Square, nothing else.
>
> (Interview no:23, 2020)

Especially in countries like Turkey, Chile, and Argentina, where opposition is violently oppressed, the assumed neutrality grants mothers a certain level of ease when sharing their anger and pain publicly. The Turkish government has tried to undermine the Saturday Mothers by labelling them as terrorists or the families of terrorists (Karaman, 2016). Having a strong emphasis on motherhood has helped legitimise their struggle and counter criminalisation attempts by the state to some extent (Karaman, 2016). At least initially, the focus on the mothers' loss, grief, and pain, along with the public perception of their activism as ideal victims, facilitated their access to public forums that would otherwise have been inaccessible (Şimga and Göker, 2021, p. 5). However, they have repeatedly encountered police violence and judicial harassment, demonstrating that the protection associated with motherhood has been ultimately ineffective.

Society's over-emphasis of motherhood as a category of innocence, moral superiority, and attributed political neutrality can have problematic implications. It risks creating binary and hierarchical categories within victimhood, privileging 'ideal victims' (who deserve to be heard, seen, and taken seriously) over others (whose demands could be rendered invisible as they do not conform to the ideal victim perceptions whose pain may not be as easily relatable). This emphasis may overlook and even criminalise 'complex political victims' who do not fit this role and render their demands unfair and invisible.

In parallel to the discussions in Chapter 3 about how victimhood is socially, politically, legally, and subjectively constructed (Hearty, 2018; Saeed, 2016), Breen-Smyth (2018) discusses who defines victimhood. She argues that among others, the media decides who are the legitimate victims and, therefore, whose suffering should be grieved. In the Saturday Mothers case, as well, media played a key role in the beginning of marking a social movement of a variety of actors as a motherhood movement, fostering the understanding that mothers are legitimate victims, and their loss is grievable.[10] The way in which the victim status is defined at a particular context and time grants certain victims access to rights, support, and benefits and while excluding others who do not conform to that status. As a result, the risk is to exclude families, victims, survivors, and activists whose positionalities (for example, due to the political, social, or ethnic components of their complex identities) do not grant them a relatability and empathy the same way that the mothers' positionalities do.

Another implication of the society's overemphasis on motherhood is that the support given to the Saturday Mothers does not necessarily address and challenge the political conditions that enabled their victimisation. For example, popular musicians have released songs for the Saturday Mothers, contributing to their message's wider dissemination (see Section 4.2). However, this support has rarely translated into a broader message against state violence. One recent example is the famous rock singer Teoman's cover of *Benim Annem Cumartesi* (My Mother is Saturday) for the 1000th sit-in.

10 For a detailed discussion on the concept of grievable, see Butler, 2009.

Teoman, who identifies as apolitical, explained why he could not say no to this invitation:

> As you know, I am distant from politics, it is a field I do not like. I define myself as above politics, on the side of conscience, not political parties. The invitation to perform this song came to me from the Saturday Mothers. I sensed the negative reactions that might come, but I didn't think for a moment to refuse this offer . . . If I had refused, I would have had to live with a lifelong remorse of conscience.
>
> (Duvar, 2024)

This quote shows that he sees mothers' struggle as relating to conscious and therefore beyond and above politics. It proves the usefulness of strategic use of the motherhood category in reaching a wider audience, however, also signals the risk of depoliticising their struggle.

Despite the careful decision to remain independent from any political groups, the Saturday Mothers movement has taken a strong political stance on broader political issues such as the peaceful resolution of the Kurdish Conflict, the recognition of Armenian Genocide, and various forms of state violence (De Clippel, 2022). Similar to Madres de Plaza de Mayo, whose demands for truth and justice regarding disappearances expanded to encompass broader human rights and socio-political issues in Argentina and beyond (Bosco, 2006), the Saturday Mothers have also been vocal in addressing formal political processes. Notably, they have become important actors in the peacebuilding scene with elaborate visions of peace going beyond "just the absence of war but also [include] the freedoms of expression and interpersonal harmony that foster social justice" (Karaman, 2016; Interview no:15, 2020; Interview no:19, 2020). For example, in their first gathering of 2016, a couple of months after the peace process collapsed, they wished for 2016 to bring peace and called on the state to end its war policies:

> Stop your war policies that lead to the killing of unborn babies, children, women and the elderly under the pretext of neutralising armed people. Stop your policies that leave dead bodies on the streets for days and prevent them from being buried.
>
> (Bianet, 2016b)

A lawyer and human rights advocate with extensive experience working with the Saturday Mothers in Diyarbakır explained how their political struggle includes demands for peace:

> In fact, in the political sense, they really lead a peace struggle. This is how I perceive it. They always speak as political subjects and [they say] that the resolution is still possible. And yes "our relatives lost their loves, yes we

> experienced enormous pain, it is impossible to describe it, we experience irreparable things, but there is really a solution to that". They fight for that resolution to take place. This is how I see it. It is a social movement that demands accountability and coming to terms with the past but at the same time a movement that leads a struggle for peace.
>
> (Interview no:15, 2020)

When the Saturday Mothers address broader political issues, they do so within the framework of their own cause. This approach is consistent with their commitment to independence and ensures they remain solely focused on their struggle. When they criticise other forms of state violence, they usually frame it in relation to their quest for justice. In their weekly press statements, they often refer to various political developments, drawing links between past atrocities and current ones, and broadening the demand for justice. For example, they ask about the fate of Armenian intellectuals deported from Istanbul in 1915, highlighting both the unofficial start of the Armenian Genocide and the origins of Turkey's practice of enforced disappearance (Ahiska, 2020). When curfews were imposed in the Kurdish region in 2015 and 2016, in almost every sit-in, the Saturday Mothers called on state authorities to end violence. For instance, the sit-in on 30 January 2016 was dedicated to Kemal Mübariz, who had disappeared in 1994 in Cizre (Bianet, 2016a). At the time of the sit-in, Cizre was under curfew, the security forces were committing gross human rights violations. The statement asked for justice for Kemal Mübariz and for the human rights violations in Cizre to stop. The following quote from the press statement shows how they drew links between their cause and the wider struggle against continuing state violence:

> In today's Cizre, the children, grandchildren of those whose houses were set on fire, who were slaughtered, who were disappeared in the 90s are forced to live in an atrocity atmosphere where law and humanity are suspended. The dead bodies in Cizre are kept on streets, the wounded are abandoned to death. Those in charge of protecting everyone's right to life without looking into who they are, are making society watch the slow death of the wounded who are stranded in a basement in Cizre by preventing medical intervention.
>
> (Bianet, 2016b)

Another example is one I observed in person, from the last Saturday of 2024, when the press statement began with a call for the release of journalists who had been imprisoned just a few days earlier. They highlighted the unlawful imprisonment of these journalists, noting that under normal circumstances, they would have been there to report the sit-ins.

### *The Format of the Gatherings: Silence and Non-Violence in Galatasaray Square*

The carefully chosen format of Saturday gatherings is one of the key tools that ensured the Saturday Mothers movement would have a unique identity. After discussing various formats at the beginning, such as using music or walking around the square, the activists decided to hold a weekly half an hour sit-in without any slogans, placards, or organisation signatures. That way, anybody could participate in the gatherings regardless of their ethnic, political, or cultural identities (De Clippel, 2022). Silence (except the press statement), non-violence, and the place of the sit-ins have been the hallmarks of this format.

This format would serve the purpose of a constant action that has a well-defined framework and a demand, where people could join individually and feel like a part of it (Karakuş, 2023). In the *Pazartesi* newspaper, Nadire Mater, one of the first Saturday People, explains how they came up with the format. After finding out about Hasan Ocak's death, those who felt enraged came together with the families of the disappeared:

> Since human rights violations in Turkey were similar to those around the world, the methods of struggle should have been similar too. We thought we would look at the protests, those who drew most attention about disappearances, such as what Argentinian, Chilean, Guatemalan women did. Being in a place periodically and keeping the issue alive constantly is a useful method. It is something that would not carry any group's name or label, and that any one passer-by could say "I should be with them too." We said: let's sit down silently.
>
> (Interview no:21, 2020)

Every Saturday, the sit-in starts at noon with a silent sit-in in Galatasaray Square, except for the period where the square was banned. Each week is dedicated to the memory of one forcibly disappeared person. The family members share their testimonies of the disappearance. Information is provided about the legal developments on the case. To determine the disappeared person who will be commemorated each week, İHD Commission research who was disappeared or extrajudicially killed around the date of the gathering. As my interlocutor who was part of the İHD commission at the time explained:

> Unfortunately, in our region, there are enough disappearances to fit in every week. Especially in our mothers' archives, there are enough people to commemorate every week. Presently, there are already more than 500 families that we are in constant contact with. I mean, even if we wanted to do it every day, we could always find someone to commemorate.
>
> (Interview no:21, 2020)

In each sit-in, Saturday Mothers hold up red carnations and the photographs of the disappeared in silence without using any slogans or applause. In front of the mothers, there is a large banner on the floor reading "Perpetrators Are Known Where Are the Disappeared? (*Failler Belli Kayıplar Nerede?*)". The only time that the silence is interrupted is when the press statement is read to detail the case of the disappeared person and vocalise the truth and justice demands. The entire process takes around 30 minutes.

Silence is a careful choice as it represents a peaceful way of searching for the disappeared, without creating inconvenience for the public (Amnesty International, 1998). As one of my interlocutors clarified, the use it is as an important strategy to help protect the movement from potential police violence because it symbolises non-violence:

> In fact, they could not really touch us, or say much about us. Because we hold a silent protest. For example, there is no slogan, no applause, no shouting or anything like that. There is only sitting. Ten minutes, fifteen minutes, twenty minutes . . . however long it takes. Depending on whose anniversary that week is, their family speaks to provide a statement. After that, everyone silently finishes and leaves.
>
> (Interview no:23, 2020)

A major component of the format is the use of non-violent means with the purpose of communicating a clear and socially relatable goal with which people can easily empathise. The same interlocutor considers that non-violence enhances the Saturday Mothers' credibility and protects them from the government's criminalisation efforts:

> I am truly clear on this matter, and I like this style of the Saturday Mothers very much. They made themselves untouchable with this protest format. Not shouting any slogans, not shouting out, not destroying around. Do you see what I mean? Only expressing their demands. And we've seen this: violence does not always open a path. In fact, this type of protests conveys much stronger messages, can have a much more transformative role.
>
> (Interview no:23, 2020)

The deliberate choice of the place of the sit-ins, therefore, is another key aspect of the format. One of the reasons why the Saturday Mothers hold such a unique place in Turkey's opposition history is that the protestors integrated with Galatasaray Square, which has become a symbol of opposition inextricably bound to the Saturday Mothers' struggle over the years (Can, 2014; Sezer Şanlı, 2020). Galatasaray Square is one of the most centrally located spots in Istanbul with a unique position in the city's cultural, social, political, and economic life. Located on the pedestrian İstiklal Street in the Beyoğlu district, one of Istanbul's most vibrant commercial and touristic regions, it is a vivid gathering area for many intellectuals and social organisations.

By choosing such a busy and publicly visible place, Saturday People aimed to receive more visibility from a diverse audience and have some protection from police violence (Can, 2022; Kocabıçak, 2003). Indeed, "the time and place chosen for the action have contributed to the popularization and agenda of the Saturday Mothers" (Kaya and Acar, 2023, p. 134).

The reason they chose holding their actions in front of the Galatasaray High School on İstiklal Street primarily because it "is a crowded, central place, accommodating diverse people" (Kocabıçak, 2003, p. 77). The transportation facilities also played an important role, because İstiklal Street is reachable by one vehicle from almost all locations in Istanbul, and Galatasaray Square is easily accessible from multiple points as it is on the crossroads. Another critical aspect of the square is its closeness to Galatasaray Post Office, which became the point where Saturday People would send letters to the prime minister, president, and parliamentarians (Kocabıçak, 2003). Moreover, "the labyrinthine web of roads leading to Istiklal Street" enabled the participants of the gatherings to remain anonymous while they used these roads to arrive and leave their meeting point on Galatasaray Square (Baydar and Ivegen, 2006, p. 699).

As a central crossroads for people from diverse backgrounds, the square provides the opportunity for random passersby to engage with the mothers and learn about their struggles (Baydar and Ivegen, 2006). It increases their visibility by ensuring the sit-ins reach a wide variety of audiences who could have otherwise remained oblivious to the issue of enforced disappearances. The Square now holds a symbolic and material significance for Saturday Mothers, "to testify to the life and disappearance of a person and to the injustices that befell them" (Can, 2014, p. 153).

The specific sit-in format is closely tied to Galatasaray Square. Following the ban on the square, the Saturday Mothers began reading their press statements in the narrow street where the İHD İstanbul office is located. However, they never considered or embraced it as their protest place (Tosun, 2024). Routinely, they met in front of the İHD office for 29 years every Saturday before moving to Galatasaray Square to start the protest. They did the same after the ban, although this time they were blocked by police and not able to reach the square. Even during the period they were forced to stay away from Galatasaray Square, it remained their true gathering place. One of my interlocutors elucidated that they have not even used the sit-in format while reading the press statement in front of the İHD office, as it does not hold the same symbolic meaning as Galatasaray Square:

> Of course, ever since, since week 700, we have not sat down anywhere. We don't want to embrace where we are. For us, there is only one place to sit, and that is in front of Galatasaray High School. That is why we have never sat anywhere else. We carry out our protests only by standing with the photos, until we return to Galatasaray.
>
> (Interview no:21, 2020)

The third unique aspect of the protest format is the way mothers are situated at sit-ins. Mothers are lined up in front of the crowd, at the forefront of the gatherings, immediately in front of the press, and if a mother stays at the back, she is brought to the front next to the other mothers (Can, 2014). The choice of keeping mothers at the centre and most visible point of the sit-ins strengthens the political message that these sit-ins are motivated by the mothers' experiences of loss. This physical position of the mothers in sit-ins reflects a complex choice of emphasising the centrality of the mothers' experiences as discussed. The publicity of the locations chosen for the sit-ins and the heightened visibility of the protest format was hoped to offer protection from state violence, although this has not been always the case (Can, 2022).

## 4.5 Global Connections

There are several commonalities that Saturday Mothers share with other movements, both in terms of the tools and strategies used. They drew on experiences from various parts of the world, mostly by women activists linking to an increasingly recognised universality in strategies albeit with a unique aspect in each context. One of them is the model of the Argentinian Madres and Abuelas de Plaza de Mayo who created a new form of protest through the peculiar combination of politics, family, and gender in the public realm (Göral, 2021). Symbolic gestures such as giving the front place to the families in sit-ins and restating the names of the responsible political authorities and the perpetrators are familiar in this form of protest (Göral, 2021). The Plaza de Mayo Mothers' struggle was so influential that other human rights organisations in other parts of the world adopted some of their symbols such as silent vigils, black and white photos, and headscarves (Kovras, 2017). Alongside mothers and other relatives in Kashmir and the Tiananmen Mothers in China, Saturday Mothers are among those who took inspiration from Plaza de Mayo Mothers and adopted some of their symbolism (Dewhirst and Kapur, 2015). However, they also created their specific methods, as Rosa Tarlovsky de Roisinblit, one of the Plaza de Mayo grandmothers who attended a sit-in Galatasaray Square, noted:

> It wasn't just the mothers there, on Saturdays everyone marched together; mothers, siblings, cousins, uncles, children were all together. They had their own methods. They were putting photographs of their relatives on the ground, lighting candles. We shared our experience with them, and we would be happy if they adapted something useful from our experience to their own struggle.
>
> (Õztürk, 2014)

Another example is the feminist organisation Women in Black in Serbia, which has been holding silent protests in Republic Square, the most central location in Belgrade, to protest war and militarism. Similarly to Saturday Mothers, their key methods are silence, wearing black, and using their bodies as a means for protest. They were inspired by other women's organisations such as the Argentinian mothers, the white mothers in South Africa, and the Israeli Women in Black (Daşlı et al., 2017). Another example is the Mothers Front, formed in Sri Lanka in 1984 as a response to the disappearance of thousands of Tamil men by the state (De Alwis, 2009). The membership of the group reached approximately 20,000 members in a short while and became a grassroots movement (De Alwis, 2009). Putting motherhood at the centre, the Mothers Front held pictures of the disappeared relatives in the protests and called on the authorities for investigations. Their first large action was a day-long silent protest in which over 500 mothers attended. Throughout the years, they organised marches, protests, and petitions (Whetstone, 2020). As the examples demonstrate, Saturday Mothers keyed into the increasingly recognised symbolism of the international context. This increased their local and international visibility and legitimacy, and again accounts for why the media and activists chose to focus on motherhood as a key defining identity feature.

The legitimacy gained through the motherhood identity is common to other movements as well. For instance, Mothers Front in Sri Lanka insisted that they were merely mothers wanting the return of their children and that they were not political, which forced the state to renew its counter practices (de Alwis, 1997). In a similar vein, the Argentinian mothers carefully highlighted that they were simply mothers searching for their children, free from political motivations (Kovras, 2017). The mobilisation of the Plaza de Mayo Mothers spoke to the national and international audience because mothers are seen as socially legitimate actors (Kovras, 2017).

However, the Saturday Mothers movement differs from other motherhood movements around the world in the sense that they have always consisted of a diverse network of families and activities, as opposed to a mothers-only group. Galatasaray gatherings were not like the mothers' demonstrations in Plaza de Mayo, and the mothers were not even the majority of the relatives of the disappeared, but only one part of the group (Karakuş, 2022). Argentinian mothers were not accompanied by other members of the public, due to the police intervention and the fear created by the military rule (Baydar and Ivegen, 2006). The active members of other movements based on a motherhood identity often remain limited to female relatives of the disappeared. As was shown with the Saturday Mothers/People discussion, this has been different in Turkey.

## 4.6 Conclusion

The Saturday Mothers have emerged as strategic political actors amid violence and repression, who link their struggle to wider visions of change. Having made sense of their victimisation in political terms, the Saturday Mothers/People have been the most systematically organised victim group in Turkey. Faced with a context of impunity, denial, and limited political change, they have particularly emphasised the need for justice and truth regarding enforced disappearances. Turning the private political and politicising and collectivising motherhood have been significant tools to access political spaces and gain support and legitimacy. The carefully chosen sit-in format has been a powerful tool for consolidating the movement's struggle, increasing its recognisability, reclaiming public space, and enacting resistance.

While reviewing the literature on victims in transitional justice in Chapter 3, I focused on the complexities of victimhood and perpetrator categories. The binary understanding of these categories is based on an ideal victim figure who is innocent, blameless, and morally superior. It draws on an unrealistic and unnuanced view of victims as a homogenous group, and risks creating hierarchies within different victim groups. Mothers' resistance and political determination have played a pivotal role in the Saturday Mothers' long-lasting mobilisation which created awareness of enforced disappearances (see Chapter 6). Yet, society's over-emphasis on the motherhood category and motherly pain, instead of the political context of mothers' mobilisation, runs the risk of silencing other victims whose identities or experiences could be deemed less legitimate. As I elaborate more in the next chapters, a nuanced understanding of the construction and complexities of victimhood is imperative to have an inclusive transitional justice process that responds to the demands of a broad range of victims. Deriving from this need, with the next chapter, the book moves from the specific case of Saturday Mothers towards a wider discussion about the construction and complexities of victimhood in the Kurdish conflict.

## Reference List


Ahiska, M., 2020. Memory as encounter: The Saturday Mothers in Turkey. In A.G. Altınay, M.J. Contreras, M. Hirsch, J. Howard, B. Karaca, and A. Solomon (Eds.), *Women Mobilizing Memory*. Columbia University Press, pp. 133–151. https://doi.org/10.7312/alti19184-009.

Al Jazeera, 2023. *Turkey's Saturday Mothers Allowed to Hold Vigil for First Time since 2018*. Available at: https://www.aljazeera.com/news/2023/11/11/turkeys-saturday-mothers-allowed-to-hold-vigil-for-first-time-since-2018 (Accessed: 17 November 2024).

Amnesty International, 1998. *TURKEY: Listen to the Saturday Mothers*. Available at: https://www.amnesty.org/en/wp-content/uploads/2021/06/eur440171998en.pdf (Accessed: 23 December 2024).

Arcan, S., 2022. Sebla Arcan ile "Niçin Kayıplar Mücadelesi?". *İnsan Hakları Okulu*. Available at: https://www.insanhaklariokulu.org/sebla-arcan-ile-nicin-kayiplar-mucadelesi-youtube-kanalimizda/ (Accessed: 24 February 2025).

Baydar, G. and Ivegen, B., 2006. Territories, identities, and thresholds: The Saturday Mothers phenomenon in İstanbul. *Signs*, 31, pp. 689–715. https://doi.org/10.1086/498986.

Berry, M.E., 2018. *War, Women, and Power: From Violence to Mobilization in Rwanda and Bosnia-Herzegovina*. Cambridge: Cambridge University Press.
Bianet, 2016a. *90'larda Katledilenlerin Çocukları Şimdi Yine Cizre'de Vahşeti Yaşıyor*. Available at: https://bianet.org/haber/90-larda-katledilenlerin-cocuklari-simdi-yine-cizre-de-vahseti-yasiyor-171649 (Accessed: 8 July 2024).
Bianet, 2016b. *Cumartesi Anneleri: 2016 Barış Yılı Olsun*. Available at: https://bianet.org/haber/cumartesi-anneleri-2016-baris-yili-olsun-170729 (Accessed: 23 December 2024).
Bianet, 2023. *Kuruluş ve mücadelesiyle İnsan Hakları Derneği*. Available at: https://bianet.org/haber/kurulus-ve-mucadelesiyle-insan-haklari-dernegi-287501 (Accessed: 10 May 2024).
Björkdahl, A. and Selimovic, J.M., 2015. Gendering agency in transitional justice. *Security Dialogue*, 46, pp. 165–182. https://doi.org/10.1177/0967010614552547.
Bosco, F.J., 2006. The Madres de Plaza de Mayo and three decades of human rights' activism: Embeddedness, emotions, and social movements. *Annals of the Association of American Geographers*, 96, pp. 342–365. https://doi.org/10.1111/j.1467–8306.2006.00481.x.
Bouris, E., 2007. *Complex Political Victims*. 1st ed. Boulder, CO: Lynne Rienner Publishers.
Bouvard, M.G., 1994. *Revolutionizing Motherhood: The Mothers of the Plaza de Mayo*. Wilmington, DE: Scholarly Resources Inc.
Breen-Smyth, M., 2018. Suffering, victims and survivors in the Northern Ireland conflict: Definitions, policies, and politics. In P. Terhoeven (Ed.), *Victimhood and Acknowledgement*. De Gruyter, pp. 39–58. https://doi.org/10.1515/9783110581508-003.
Brett, R. and Druliolle, V., 2018. *The Politics of Victimhood in Post-conflict Societies*. https://doi.org/10.1007/978-3-319-70202-5.
Butler, J.P., 2009. *Frames of War: When Is Life Grievable?* Verso Books.
Can, B., 2014. *Making: The Cases of Torture and Enforced Disappearances in Post-1980 Turkey*. PhD thesis, University of Pennsylvania.
Can, B., 2022. How does a protest last? Rituals of visibility, disappearances under custody, and the Saturday Mothers in Turkey. *American Anthropologist*. https://doi.org/10.1111/aman.13749.
Christie, N., 1986. The ideal victim. In E.A. Fattah (Ed.), *From Crime Policy to Victim Policy: Reorienting the Justice System*. London: Palgrave Macmillan UK, pp. 17–30. https://doi.org/10.1007/978-1-349-08305-3_2.
Cohen, C., 2018. Fifteen: A decade after Lynndie: Non-ideal victims of non-ideal offenders—doubly anomalised, doubly invisibilised. In M. Duggan (Ed.), *Revisiting the 'Ideal Victim': Developments in Critical Victimology*. Bristol: Bristol University Press, pp. 279–296. https://doi.org/10.51952/9781447339151.ch015.
Daşlı, G., 2024. Victim agency, relational autonomy and transitional justice: Experience of Saturday Mothers. *International Journal of Transitional Justice*, ijae021. https://doi.org/10.1093/ijtj/ijae021.
Daşlı, G., Alıcı, N. and Flader, U., 2017. *Kadınların Barış Mücadelesinde Dünya Deneyimleri Sırbistan, Kosova, Sri Lanka, Suriye*. Demos Research Association.
de Alwis, M., 1997. Motherhood as a space of protest: Women's political participation in contemporary Sri Lanka. In *Appropriating Gender*, 1st ed. Routledge, p. 18.
de Alwis, M., 2009. Interrogating the political: Feminist peace activism in Sri Lanka. *Feminist Review*, 91, pp. 81–93. https://doi.org/10.1057/fr.2008.52.
De Clippel, E., 2022. *An Evolution from Maternal Activism to Political Motherhood: An Illustration of the Saturday Mothers of Istanbul*. Ghent University.

Dewhirst, P. and Kapur, A., 2015. *The disappeared and invisible: Revealing the enduring impact of enforced disappearance on women*. International Center for Transitional Justice. Briefing. Available at: https://www.ictj.org/sites/default/files/ICTJ-Briefing-Gender-Disappearances-2015.pdf (Accessed: 11 January 2025).

Frontline Defenders, 2021. *Authorities Should Seek Acquittal of All in the Saturday Mothers/People Trial*. Available at: https://www.frontlinedefenders.org/en/statement-report/authorities-should-seek-acquittal-all-saturday-motherspeople-trial (Accessed: 20 June 2024).

Gazete Duvar, 2022. *Cumartesi Anneleri: Hasan Ocak dosyasında cezasızlığa son verilsin*. Available at: https://www.gazeteduvar.com.tr/cumartesi-anneleri-hasan-ocak-dosyasinda-cezasizliga-son-verilsin-haber-1557222 (Accessed: 19 June 2024).

Gazete Duvar, 2024. *Teoman: Cumartesi Anneleri'nin teklifini reddetmeyi bir an bile düşünmedim*. Available at: https://www.gazeteduvar.com.tr/teoman-cumartesi-annelerinin-teklifini-reddetmeyi-bir-an-bile-dusunmedim-haber-1693503 (Accessed: 3 July 2024).

Göker, Z.G., 2013. Presence in silence: Feminist and democratic implications of the Saturday vigils in Turkey. In J. Beinin and F. Vairel (Eds.), *Social Movements, Mobilization, and Contestation in the Middle East and North Africa*, 2nd ed. Redwood City: Stanford University Press, pp. 149–166. https://doi.org/10.1515/9780804788038–010.

Göral, Ö.S., 2019. *Any Hopes for Truth? A Comparative Analysis of Enforced Disappearances and the Missing in the Middle East, North Africa and the Caucasus*. Istanbul: Truth Justice Memory Center.

Göral, Ö.S., 2021. Memory as experience in times of perpetual violence: The challenge of Saturday Mothers vis-à-vis cultural aphasia. *Kurdish Studies*, 9, pp. 77–95. https://doi.org/10.33182/ks.v9i1.569.

Günaysu, A., 2014a. *"Cumartesi" Nasıl Başladı, Neden Ara Verildi?* Available at: https://bianet.org/bianet/yasam/159385-cumartesi-nasil-basladi-neden-ara-verildi (Accessed: 23 August 2021).

Günaysu, A., 2014b. *Savaşa, milliyetçiliğe, ırkçılığa karşı: Arkadaşıma dokunma!* Available at: https://bianet.org/bianet/insan-haklari/160975-savasa-milliyetcilige-irkciliga-karsi-arkadasima-dokunma (Accessed: 23 August 2021).

Hearty, K., 2018. Victims of human rights abuses in transitional justice: Hierarchies, perpetrators and the struggle for peace. *International Journal of Human Rights*, 22, pp. 888–909. https://doi.org/10.1080/13642987.2018.1485656.

Helms, E., 2013. *Innocence and Victimhood: Gender, Nation, and Women's Activism in Postwar Bosnia-Herzegovina*. Madison, WI: The University of Wisconsin Press.

Interview no:7, Interview by Author, 2019.

Interview no:10, Interview by Author, 2019.

Interview no:11, Interview by Author, 2019.

Interview no:15, Interview by Author, 2020.

Interview no:18, Interview by Author, 2020.

Interview no:19, Interview by Author, 2020.

Interview no:21, Interview by Author, 2020.

Interview no:23, Interview by Author, 2020.

İnsan Hakları Derneği, 2018. *Cumartesi Anneleri 700. Hafta: Unutmuyoruz, Affetmiyoruz, Vazgeçmiyoruz*. Available at: https://www.ihd.org.tr/cumartesi-anneleri-700-hafta-unutmuyoruz-affetmiyoruz-vazgecmiyoruz/ (Accessed: 15 February 2025).

Karakuş, F., 1996. *Neden Kadinlar*. Available at: http://www.pazartesidergisi.com/pdf/16.pdf (Accessed: 18 February 2022).

Karakuş, F., 2022. *27 Mayıs 1995: Cumartesi İnsanları/Anneleri Galatasaray'da! Çatlak Zemin*. Available at: https://catlakzemin.com/27-mayis-1995-cumartesi-insanlari-anneleri-galatasarayda/ (Accessed: 4 March 24).

Karakuş, F., 2023. *27 Mayıs 1995: Cumartesi İnsanları/Anneleri Galatasaray'da! Çatlak Zemin*. https://catlakzemin.com/27-mayis-1995-cumartesi-insanlari-anneleri-galatasarayda/ (Accessed: 12 March 24).
Karaman, E.R., 2016. Remember, S/he was here once: Mothers call for justice and Peace in Turkey. *Journal of Middle East Women's Studies*, 12, pp. 382–410. https://doi.org/10.1215/15525864–3637576.
Karaman, E.R., 2023. Silencing historical traumas versus constructing resistance narratives: The Saturday Mothers and Peace Mothers in Turkey. In F.M. Göçek and A. Alemdaroğlu (Eds.), *Kurds in Turkey: Politics, Violence, and Resistance*. Vanderbilt University Press.
Kaya, O., Acar, Y.G., 2023. From collective action to collective resistance: Working with the Saturday Mothers. In E. Şen, E. Sandal Önal, M. Sefa Uysal, and Y.G. Acar (Eds.), *The Political Psychology of Kurds in Turkey*. Palgrave Studies in Political Psychology. Cham: Springer International Publishing, pp. 129–143. https://doi.org/10.1007/978-3-031-33291-3_7.
Kocabıçak, E., 2003. *Locating Thirdspace in the Specifities of Urban: A Case Study on Saturday Mothers, in Istiklal Street Istanbul*. Master's thesis, Middle East Technical University.
Koçali, F., 1996. *Kadinlarin Galatasary'i*. Available at: http://www.pazartesidergisi.com/pdf/16.pdf (Accessed: 11 February 2022).
Kovras, I., 2017. The daughters of Antigone in Latin America. In *Grassroots Activism and the Evolution of Transitional Justice*. Cambridge University Press, pp. 61–83. https://doi.org/10.1017/9781316711262.003.
Laqueur, T., 2002. The places of the dead in modernity. In C. Jones and D. Wahrman (Eds.), *The Age of Cultural Revolutions: Britain and France, 1750–1820*. Berkeley, CA: University of California Press, pp. 17–32.
Mater, N., 2014. *Erkekler Yüksek Politikayı Tercih Ediyor" previously published in Pazartesi, July 1996*. Republished in Filiz Koçali "Galatasaray'ın Kadınları". 25 October. https://bianet.org/biamag/yasam/159418-galatasaray-in-kadinlari.
Ni Aolain, F., Haynes, D.F. and Cahn, N., 2011. *On the Frontlines Gender, War, and the Post-Conflict Process*. Oxford University Press. https://doi.org/10.1093/acprof:oso/9780195396645.001.0001.
O'Rourke, C., 2012. Dealing with the past in a post-conflict society: Does the participation of women matter? Insights from Northern Ireland. *William Mary Journal of Race, Gender, and Social Justice*, 19, pp. 34–68.
Orhan, G., 2008. *From Motherhood to Activism: A History of Women in Transformation*. Master's thesis. Boğaziçi University, Istanbul.
Orozco Mendoza, E.F., 2016. Maternal activism. In *The Wiley Blackwell Encyclopedia of Gender and Sexuality Studies*. https://doi.org/10.1002/9781118663219.wbegss725.
Öztürk, Ç., 2014. *Rosa Arjantin'den Cumartesi'yi Selamlıyor*. https://bianet.org/yazi/rosa-arjantin-den-cumartesi-yi-selamliyor-159393 (Accessed: 7 August 2024).
Pişkin, T., 2018. Cumartesi Anneleri/İnsanları'nın Devletin "Gücüyle" 700 Haftalık İmtihanı. *Bianet*. https://bianet.org/yazi/cumartesi-anneleri-insanlari-nin-devletin-gucuyle-700-haftalik-imtihani-200259 (Accessed: 4 December 2024).
Saeed, H., 2016. Victims and victimhood: Individuals of inaction or active agents of change? Reflections on fieldwork in Afghanistan. *International Journal of Transitional Justice*, 10, pp. 168–178. https://doi.org/10.1093/ijtj/ijv032.
Saturday Mothers, 2021. Cumartesi Anneleri Berlin'de. *Dersim Kültür Derneği*, Available at: http://dersimkulturdernegi.com/cumartesi-anneleri-berlinde/ (Accessed: 23 February 2025).
Saturday Mothers, 2023. TARİHÇE. *Cumartesi Anneleri*. Available at: https://cumartesianneleri.org.tr/2023/08/02/tarihce/ (Accessed: 15 June 2024).

Schwöbel-Patel, C., 2018. The 'Ideal' victim of international criminal law. *European Journal of International Law*, 29, pp. 703–724. https://doi.org/10.1093/ejil/chy056
Sezer Şanlı, A., 2018. Yasın Protestoya Dönüşümünü İncelemek: Cumartesi Anneleri Hareketi Örneği. *Uluslararası İnsan Çalışmaları Dergisi*, 1, pp. 1–17. https://doi.org/10.35235/uicd.458095
Sezer Şanlı, A., 2020. Gündelik Hayatı Dönüştüren Eylem Olarak Protesto ve Protesto Aktörü Olarak Kadınlar: Cumartesi Anneleri Üzerine Bir Değerlendirme. *Fe Dergi: Feminist Eleştiri*, 12, pp. 44–58. https://doi.org/10.46655/federgi.745795
Şimga, H., Göker, Z.G., 2021. Women's perceptions on peace and justice: The case of the Kurdish issue in Turkey. *Women's Studies International Forum*, 87, p. 102499. https://doi.org/10.1016/j.wsif.2021.102499
T24, 2010. *Cumartesi Anneleri 300. kez Galatasaray Meydanı'nda*. Available at: https://t24.com.tr/haber/cumartesi-anneleri-300-kez-galatasaray-meydaninda,118756 (Accessed: 22 February 2025).
Tanrıkulu, N., 2014. Galatasaray Hafıza, İtaatsizlik ve Küreselleşmenin Mekanı. *Bianet*. Available at: https://bianet.org/yazi/galatasaray-hafiza-itaatsizlik-ve-kuresellesmenin-mekani-160801 (Accessed: 4 December 2024).
Toker Kılınç, N., Akbaş Demirel, C., Kõrükmez, L. and Biter, N., 2021. *Türkiye'de İnsan Hakları Mücadelesinin Değişim Hatları: İnsan Hakları Derneği Örneğinde Uluslararası Mekanizmalar, Yerelleşme ve Dayanışma*. Türkiye İnsan Hakları Vakfı.
Tosun, B., 2024. Cumartesi Anneleri'nin 29 Yılı. *Kıraathane Istanbul Edebiyat Evi*. Available at: https://www.youtube.com/watch?v=2EGZary2E2Q (Accessed: 16 September 2024).
Whetstone, C., 2020. *Nurturing Democracy in Armed Conflicts through Political Motherhood: A Comparative Study of Women's Political Participation in Argentina and Sri Lanka*. PhD thesis. University of Cincinnati.
Wright, S., 2016. "Ah . . . the power of mothers": Bereaved mothers as victim-heroes in media enacted crusades for justice. *Crime, Media, and Culture*, 12, pp. 327–343. https://doi.org/10.1177/1741659015623597
Zulver, J.M., 2022. *High-Risk Feminism in Colombia: Women's Mobilization in Violent Contexts*. 1st ed. [Online]. United States: Rutgers University Press.

Chapter 5

# The Construction and Complexities of Victimhood in the Kurdish Conflict

## 5.1 Introduction

In this chapter, I move to wider issues surrounding the complexities and nuances of victimhood in Turkey's Kurdish conflict. I examine how victimhood, a complex status shaped by political, psychological, and social factors, is constructed within the Kurdish conflict. First, I discuss how victims define themselves, what factors shape these definitions, and what various perceptions of victimhood tell us about the political agency of the victims. Second, I explore in detail two key elements of victimisation within the Kurdish conflict: ethnicity and gender. In this chapter, I identify that victimhood is a nuanced and complex experience that cannot be easily captured by the term 'victim'. Victimisation occurs in a multi-layered fashion and results in intergenerational consequences deepened by the intersection of ethnicity and gender. There is little literature on how conflict-affected Kurdish people perceive the components and implications of victimhood and victimisation is crucial to enhance victim-centred and agency-oriented transitional justice approaches and design and implement mechanisms accordingly.

## 5.2 Different Uses of the Term 'Victim' in Turkey

There are two different Turkish words used to translate the term for victim: *kurban* and *mağdur*. While both can refer to someone who has suffered harm, they carry distinct cultural, social, and political connotations. *Kurban* has strong religious undertones, with its literal translation meaning "the sacrificed".[1] This word evokes imagery of innocence and passivity, often amplifying the emotional and tragic aspects of victimhood. Over time, however, *kurban* has become less common in political, activist, and academic

1 This is in line with the original meaning of the English word 'victim', which derives from the Latin *victima*, meaning the animal or person killed and offered as a sacrifice to the gods or a supernatural power.

DOI: 10.4324/9781003432579-5

discourse, gradually being replaced by *mağdur.* However, its use has not entirely disappeared.

Mainstream media and certain academic publications still employ *kurban,* particularly referring to individuals in acts of violence committed by armed groups. In these contexts, *kurban* serves a specific narrative function. Framing the victims as *kurbans* accentuates the sense of terror and horror surrounding the violent act, by drawing a picture of an evil armed group that sacrifices innocent people. Media outlets that align with the state's perspective often avoid terms like *armed conflict*, opting instead for *terrorism*, and choose *kurban* to emphasize the brutality of such acts. This selective language use highlights how political affiliation can influence which term is chosen, as different groups use specific words to frame victimhood in ways that align with their agendas.

The distinction between *kurban* and *mağdur* extends beyond mere semantics, reflecting deeper cultural and political dynamics. While *kurban* underscores passivity and evokes imagery of innocence and sacrifice—often amplifying the emotional and tragic dimension of victimhood—*mağdur* portrays the individual as someone who has suffered injustice but still retains a sense of agency, especially in legal or social frameworks. This difference also influences how victimhood is perceived: *kurban* can dehumanize or reduce individuals to symbols of loss, stripping them of personal identity, whereas *mağdur* acknowledges—at least to some extent—their ongoing struggle for justice. *Mağdur* is also the legal term for those subjected to violations and it is more commonly used in peace and conflict terminology, as it fits within human rights narratives and legal frameworks.

However, *mağdur* is not without its complications. As explored at length in Chapter 5, the term has also taken on subtle negative connotations. Expressions like *mağdur edebiyatı* ("victim literature") are used dismissively to describe situations where someone is seen as exploiting their suffering to gain sympathy. In such cases, public discourse tends to praise resilience and strength over vulnerability, viewing overt displays of victimhood as disempowering or manipulative.

It is common for researchers and activists around the world to feel uncomfortable using the term *victim*, assuming it might have passive and apolitical connotations that strip people of agency and undermine the myriad complex experiences surrounding victimhood (Brett and Druliolle, 2018; de Waardt and Weber, 2019; Saeed, 2016). In feminist scholarship and practice, *survivor* is preferred as a more feminist term (Krystalli, 2020). The term *victim* is considered to hide some essential aspects of women's victimisation, including survival and resistance (Rudling, 2019). The term *survivor* is often associated with individuals whose victimisation experiences no longer dominate their lives, who have overcome passivity and regained agency. Which term is preferred over others changes from one country to another, from one person to another, and even within the same country. Some people might find the word *victim* inappropriate and pacifying, while others consider it to be empowering (Saeed, 2016). For example, in South Africa, those involved in the Khulumani process[2] usually referred to themselves during the Truth and Reconciliation Commission as victims, because "at that moment they still felt like victims of the past" (Hamber, 2009, p. 41). Similarly, in Colombia, women who identify as victims believe that the victim label provides a space for politics and enables certain claims to be made (Krystalli, 2020).

Consistent with global trends, feminist activists and researchers in Turkey prefer the term *survivor*, especially when addressing gender-based violence. For instance, the Association for Struggle Against Sexual Violence (*Cinsel Şiddetle Mücadele Derneği,* 2016) states that it is vital to change language that weakens and victimises the survivor:

> Instead of commonly used words like '*kurban* (sacrificed)', '*mağdur* (victim)' which weakens an individual who experienced sexual violence and gives the sense of despair, we find it important to use the word '*hayatta kalan*', that we adopted from survivor in English.

What this suggests, as does my research more generally, is that the term *survivor* exists primarily in relation to gendered violence but is very rarely used for state violence or the Kurdish conflict.

## 5.3 Victimhood as a Complex Political Identity

To understand what constitutes victimhood as a complex political identity, I discuss how Kurds, who have experienced or witnessed state violence, perceive and conceptualise victimhood. Specifically, I focus on the connotations of the term victim which helps us understand how victims identify and make sense of their victimhood. In Chapter 3, I outlined the debates around how victims and victimhood are seen in the field of transitional justice. This section links those debates to the Kurdish conflict and looks at how the victimhood scene reflects the literature. As discussed in Chapter 3, the meanings attached to the victim status in a particular society are shaped by a set of criteria, actors, practices, and social norms. Consequently, the conceptualisation of victimhood varies across different contexts, periods, and societies (Brett and Druliolle, 2018).

My interviews show that the term *victim* has wide-ranging connotations. I asked my interlocutors whether it is appropriate to use the term victim. Their reactions varied from a direct objection to hesitation. Almost without exception, they consider the term victim to be insufficient to capture the

2 Khulumani Support Group was founded in 1995 to assist those testifying before South Africa's Truth and Reconciliation Commission (TRC).

complex experiences and layers of victimhood. It is perceived as a limiting word that excludes other dimensions people's identities, most notably their power to resist and act. The agency of the victims is at the core of this discussion. Challenging the ascribed identities is a form of exercising political agency (Bouris, 2007), and for this reason, studying how victims relate to victim identity and how they resist and challenge that identity is crucial to acknowledging victims' political agency.

The common view is another term is needed to define and capture the complexity and gravity of the situation (Interview no:2, 2019). An Istanbul-based Kurdish researcher with expertise in forced displacement asserted that the term *victim* should not be used to identify the person, but the act could be named as victimisation (Interview no:4, 2019). But then she elaborated: "I say those who were victimised. Actually, I don't even say they were victimised. I say those whose rights were violated. Because victimisation is a heavily charged term, and I don't want them to be squeezed in this identity" (Interview no:4, 2019). The accounts of different interlocutors show that victim is seen as a restricting category, almost as a fixed category in which people are placed, a locked identity with no room for other roles.

However, even those who express discomfort with the word use it in their everyday language. For instance, an activist-leader whose family spent decades for justice for a disappeared believes that using the word victim is inappropriate. She thinks the Turkish language has a limited vocabulary to define certain things:

> Yes, I was victimised, but this was something that resulted in death. Loss, not being able to find the lost one, is very tragic, not even being able to find the bones. This is beyond victimisation . . . But yes, these families were victimised. They were exposed to violence, to trauma and yes, its Turkish equivalent is being victims. But we don't use it often. Honestly, we don't use the phrase being victimised very much. Because it remains light.
>
> (Interview no:23, 2020)

I asked her what a better word would be to reflect the gravity of what happened, and she provided no alternative. She reiterated that in Turkish, the term victim is used for lighter situations, such as getting fired from a job or being kicked out of a house. She expressed an inability to find the equivalent for such an intense situation as death. It shows that despite the perceived shortcomings of the word, no alternative term has been agreed upon.

An Istanbul-based Kurdish researcher drew a picture of gradually evolving complexities of victimhood encompassing various emotions (Interview no:5, 2019). He explained that until the 1990s, there was denial and shame around Kurdish identity. The rise of the Kurdish freedom movement in the 1990s allowed Kurds to embrace their identity more confidently. Before this recognition, they could not even say that they were victims. In his view, the empowerment of Kurds took place simultaneously with their politicisation, which involved embracing and owning their Kurdish identity. This new relationship with their ethnic identity enabled them to acknowledge their victimisation particularly because of that identity. He believes that this recognition led significant numbers of Kurds to resist their oppressors. He pointed out the shift in how people identify in various stages of the conflict. For example, during the clashes of 2015–2016, the feeling around victimhood was different. Following the self-governance declarations, Kurds did not identify as victims while fighting, believing that violent resistance could lead to victory. But when the clashes ended and they felt defeated, they started using the victim discourse, as it was the only thing they were left with. They would express sentiments such as:

> 'You took my son, my children, destroyed my house, but my daughter-in-law gave birth to two more children. You took one from me; now I have two.' They don't use the language of victimhood. But when the clashes are over, then they do. They start to say: 'My house was destroyed, I was tortured, we were maltreated.' Perhaps they were experiencing victimisation even more [while the clashes continued], but what they say is 'you cannot defeat us.' But then what happens when the hope fades? 'You destroyed my house, tortured my child, took my husband away.' What is left is this victim discourse.
>
> (Interview no:5, 2019)

This quote addresses the commonly attributed weakness, defeat, and disempowerment of the victim position. In the following quote the sentiments of shame and being defeated are associated with victimhood and they are contrasted with power, pride, self-confidence, and resistance:

> 'We experienced everything from this state. Our village was destroyed, we were forcibly disappeared, tortured. What else can we experience from this state?' The wall of fear was passed. With the self-governance declaration, that self-confidence reached its peak, and then we just fell from the peak.
>
> (Interview no:5, 2019)

As explained in Chapter 2, most of my interlocutors were practitioners, lawyers, and activists who were chosen for their expertise in the field and experience of working with the victims. Some, if not all, of my Kurdish expert interlocutors are likely to have faced direct violence. Even if they have not suffered from direct harm, their everyday life is constantly affected by the conflict, either because they reside in Diyarbakır or engage in political activities. Some of them were forcibly displaced, some have disappeared or killed family members, and some have relatives fighting as a guerilla. In the interviews,

I referred to victims either as a general category or referring to those who fall into their area of expertise such as forced displacement, torture, enforced disappearances. It means that, while talking about their understanding of the term *victim*, most of my interlocutors refer to others, not themselves. However, because some of them experienced victimisation themselves, it is only natural to assume that their accounts also reflect their personal feelings and understandings of what it means to identify as a victim. In the following subsections, I outline the different ways victim and victimhood are perceived in the Kurdish conflict.

## 5.4 Failing to Capture a Complex Identity

My interlocutors share the dominant understanding that labelling someone as a "victim" fails to capture the entirety of their political struggle, resistance, and mobilisation. (Interview no:2, 2019; Interview no:14, 2020; Interview no:17, 2020). Therefore, the full picture of their complex political identity is missed, their political agency is overlooked, they are portrayed as passive individuals and placed in an inferior position compared to perpetrators. As discussed in detail in Chapter 3, victims exercise political agency through challenging the roles and identities that the oppressor assigns. My interlocutors think of the individuals affected by the Kurdish conflict, especially those leading an active political struggle, as powerful political subjects. This is why they are concerned that describing them as victims assigns them passivity (Interview no:3, 2019) and takes away their capacity to act against the conditions victimising them; in other words, they have not transformed their victimhood status by resisting the oppressor.

Most interlocutors portrayed the concept of victim as the opposite of taking a stance and resisting oppression and violation. This is evident in my interview with a Diyarbakır-based journalist. Although he agrees that victim is the appropriate legal term, he does not think those who resist ongoing violations would identify as victims: "I am a rebel, I am a fighter, I am carrying out a popular struggle. Therefore, I am not a victim, I am in a position of being subjected to violence, violation, my rights denied" (Interview no:14, 2020). The following quote of a lawyer working with the families of the disappeared confirms this position:

> Especially for those who chose to stand up against state violence as part of a political struggle, those who see the search for justice as a continuation of the struggle, that their Kurdish identity was offended for years and now they want to be vocal about it, that passive essence [of the term victim] may be disturbing.
>
> (Interview no:3, 2019)

According to a Diyarbakır-based practitioner, using the term victim alone overlooks the potential and strength demonstrated by these individuals in their struggle (Interview no:17, 2020). She advocates for a term that encompasses both the mobilisation and resistance to provide a more complete understanding. This view is shared by a Diyarbakır-based lawyer who emphasises that even though *victim* is the correct legal term, it does not reflect the realities of the complexities of victims' situations (Interview no:15, 2020). If someone is harmed because of their active engagement in a political act, either by being vocal about politics or resisting oppression actively, the term victim can only refer to a legal category. He gives the example of relatives of the disappeared, highlights that they are part of a political struggle, and stresses the need for a definition to reflect that struggle (Interview no:15, 2020).

As someone who has been involved with the families of the victims as a lawyer and a human rights advocate for almost a decade, his focus on the families taking a political stance is noteworthy. He does not deny the victim category but points out the necessity of addressing political mobilisation. It shows that although the word victim does not have to have a negative connotation, this is only one part of a complex reality. The families are not only reacting to what happened to them, but they also advocate for broader political goals such as the resolution of the conflict and peacebuilding. Bozkurt and Kaya's (2014) work on women whose husbands forcibly disappeared also underlines this. Those women do not see themselves merely as individuals subjected to violence, but also as political subjects with views on political issues on the macro level.

Most of the time, security forces forcibly disappear or extrajudicially kill individuals specifically because of their political identity or political activities. Being highly aware of this, families of the disappeared make sure to acknowledge and honour political stances of their loved ones. A Diyarbakir-based lawyer involved in the families' justice struggle emphasised the significance of families receiving official recognition that their loved one was disappeared as part of a systematic state policy (Interview no:19, 2020). Acknowledging the reason behind the loss meant honouring the disappeared person's life and struggle. She also explained that in the court, they would make it clear that these people had not committed any crimes, and they were selected purposefully because they led a political struggle or said things aloud about the Kurdish issue. The families found it empowering when it was stated clearly that their loved ones were taken away because of their political ideas, beliefs, or a struggle. In a way, this shapes the families' struggle to date. This is confirmed by the following quote:

> All relatives of victims, when they are talking publicly, their first sentence, of course, is 'may our lost ones to be found, may they have at least a grave, may we pray for them, may we unite with them, may we make their memories live'. . . The second one is the demand that the state, the authorities of that time, this commander, that village guard, this policeman be tried. But what they constantly stress and what they fight for is the following: the bloodshed should end, the conflict should end, and the peace should

> be reached. The Kurds should be returned their rights. In fact, in its political sense, they carry out a real peace struggle. This is how I see it. Indeed, they always speak as political subjects and state that the resolution of this problem is still possible. 'Yes, our relatives lost their lives, yes, we suffered from quite a deep pain, we are experiencing things that are impossible to describe and hard to repair, but indeed there is a solution.
>
> (Interview no:15, 2020)

The victim position is associated with surrender, defeat, or disempowerment. One of my interlocutors contended the rejection of the term could be a defence mechanism to focus on its resistance aspect as opposed to suffering: "Yes, we suffered a lot, but we are still standing. We did not perish" (Interview no:4, 2019). Similarly, a Diyarbakır-based practitioner working with torture survivors juxtaposes victim identity with resistance, highlighting them as contrasting concepts. His following quote shows that, like others, he interprets the victim position as indicating a stance of surrendering rather than resisting:

> Under torture, one is, in fact, not a victim; they demonstrate their pride by standing upright. They may convey the message, 'Yes, you might be torturing my body, but you will never be able to touch my soul or my mind,' from deep within. This is why we refer to them as 'the one who was tortured', we don't say 'torture victim'.
>
> (Interview no: 20, 2020)

The concept of "standing upright" in the face of oppression resonates with concepts in other cultures, such as the Arabic word *sumud,* which means steadfastness, perseverance, and determination. *Sumud* has been used in terms of Palestinian resilience, i.e. in how Palestinians resist oppression (Shalhoub-Kevorkian, 2015; Sobout, 2017). Shalhoub-Kevorkian's work reveals that for many Palestinians, steadfastness, resistance, and survival are coping mechanisms to deal with the presence of the oppressor, but at the same time survival is equated with resistance.

I asked one of my interlocutors to clarify if he sees the victim (*mağdur*) and proud (*mağrur*) as opposing each other and whether the victim discourse undermines pride. His response demonstrates the attributed inferiority to the victim identity:

> It is precisely that. The reason why the victim is used is this: 'Look, this person was victimised.' As the tolerant society, and the kind person I am, let's save the victim from victimhood. Assuming responsibility for myself, in fact, I look down on that person. This means, they are in a bad place, oppressed, and damaged. It gives me the feeling: 'I am not going to allow them to be oppressed anymore, I take them under my wings. I am their saviour.'
>
> (Interview no:20, 2020)

Associating the victim position with lack of pride and dignity is not unique to the Kurdish case. For instance, the South African TRC, where many people, especially men, hesitate to testify because they did not want to be seen as victims who needed support and sympathy (Govier, 2015). De Waardt, who examines the politics of victimhood in post-conflict Peru, highlights a similar view in his interlocutors: "However, in his view, naming oneself as a victim implies a loss of dignity and an acceptance of defeat rather than an identity to be proud of" (de Waardt, 2016, p. 433). Her research illustrates a "dialectic interplay between external and internal definitions of the concept" (de Waardt, 2016, p. 449). Despite the negative connotations of the concept, victims use it as an external definition to make their experiences known to the public and assert their rightful claims. This is similar to the Kurdish conflict, where "victim" is the only term available for legal claims (see next section).

Similarly, interlocutors frequently argue that identifying as a victim implies an expectation from the victimiser, thereby placing the victim in a subordinate position. The term victim is used to describe someone beneath you, someone you may feel pity for, but it also establishes a hierarchy. If someone is labelled a victim, they might be seen as needing protection, requiring rescue. This act of rescue can only be carried out by someone in a higher position, typically the oppressor. An Istanbul-based Kurdish lawyer, who considers himself a victim, explained: "If you say you are a victim, it means that you victimised me, you are the reason. You need to recover or redress it. It entails a demand" (Interview no:9, 2019). He elaborated, "Asserting 'I am the victim, and you are the victimiser, take responsibility for that,' means you trust the state, submit to the state, and ask the state to do something" (Interview no:9, 2019).

In contrast to those who view this as a positive aspect of the term victim by addressing the party at fault (see next section), embracing victimhood is perceived as placing the victim in a vulnerable position, expecting assistance from the state (as the oppressor), who wields power. In parallel to the previous quotes, anticipating action from the state is considered degrading and submissive:

> She doesn't want to put herself in a weaker position against the state. This is the psychology of the resisting person. Because this also encompasses the psychology of being defeated. And she does not want to be in that situation.
>
> (Interview no:9, 2019)

## 5.5 Why is the Word Victim Still Used?

### *Victimhood as a Legal Category*

The rigidity and dominance of the legal terminology is the primary reason the term victim has so much presence in daily life, even if its implications do not match how victims identify. Law defines harm and rights based on the concept of victimhood, and one needs to be referred to as a victim to bring conflict-related human rights violations to court (Interview no:10, 2019). Therefore, judiciary, especially the court cases, is the primary area where victim is commonly used. A lawyer and human rights advocate working on enforced disappearances noted that the existence of a victimisation means that there is someone responsible for that violation: "Perhaps 'the one that suffered harm by the violation' is the correct definition. But when you change the terminology then you have some issues in the legal world about what you want to say" (Interview no:3, 2019).

A Diyarbakır-based lawyer working with the families of the disappeared explained that the families were more interested in the legal implications of being a victim. Since the legal terminology defines them as victims, they do not feel uncomfortable using it (Interview no:19, 2020). She commented that she had never discussed the appropriateness of the word with anyone, nor do the families hesitate to use it. Another Diyarbakır-based lawyer noted that "being harmed directly from the crime makes that person a victim" (Interview no:22, 2020). He contended that there is nothing problematic about using the word victim; the families use it during the trials, and he never came across anyone who was bothered by it. A lawyer, who is also a relative of a disappeared, felt similarly and perceives the victim as a neutral word that he did not question the meaning of. He thinks of it with its literal meaning (almost identical to its legal meaning), which is the person who was harmed due to a crime. He commented: "by no means do I see it as a word of humiliation, neither an elevating nor a degrading meaning. I haven't thought about it before, honestly. We are victims at the end" (Interview no:24, 2020).

Another lawyer directly affected by the conflict had no issue using it while filing a lawsuit, but he found it problematic when he reflected on the term during the interview. Up until the point I asked him his thoughts about the term victim, he had used it to refer to both himself and others. However, when he heard the question, the first thing he said was that it was not appropriate to use the term victim. When I asked what the right word would be instead, he acknowledged that victim was legally correct.

> There is victimisation, but it is not sufficient. I need to think about it. I guess it remains light. The word victim is insufficient against the sheerness of the victimisations that are experienced. How they use it changes from one person to another, one incident to another. A family who lost their child and who are political would not say 'we are victims.' They would say, 'you slaughtered our child'.
>
> (Interview no:9, 2019)

The fact that the legal terminology dictates the use of the term victim does not mean that there is conflict-specific legislation that defines victimhood.

Unlike some conflict or post-conflict countries with legislation that defines and determine the victim status, Turkey's institutional structure around conflict-related victimhood is limited. In those countries, an institutional system of varying degrees requires people to officially register as victims to attain victim status and be entitled to benefits. The benefits might include counselling and social support, a pension scheme for some in Northern Ireland (most recently for those permanently injured), vocational training, education opportunities, and financial compensation, as is the case in Colombia (Cronin-Furman and Krystalli, 2020).

For instance, in Northern Ireland, the Commission for Victims and Survivors (CVSNI) was created in 2008 as a public body "to improve the lives of all victims and survivors of the conflict in Northern Ireland" (CVSNI, 2022). The CVSNI was established by the Victims and Survivors (Northern Ireland) Order 2006, which also determined a definition of victims and survivors. Article 3 states that victims and survivors are individuals who have been physically or psychologically injured as a consequence of a conflict-related incident, who are regular caregivers of those injured, or who have been bereaved as the result of a conflict-related incident.[3] Colombia is a more recent example, where the state bureaucracy of victimhood goes earlier than the 2016 peace agreement. Even before the peace process began in 2012, the 2011 Law on Victims and Land Restitution established the Victims' Unit, a governmental body dedicated to those recognised as victims of the armed conflict by the state (Cronin-Furman and Krystalli, 2020). There is a comprehensive institutional transitional justice framework that registers and defines victims, enabling them to participate in transitional justice processes (de Waardt and Weber, 2019; Nussio et al., 2015).

An important reason for the lack of institutional framework for conflict-affected populations is that the official state narrative has always referred to the Kurdish issue as a terrorism issue and refused to recognise it as an armed conflict. Accordingly, Turkish governments have framed the PKK as a terrorist group and defined the state's armed forces' operations in the Kurdish region as counter-terrorism operations rather than armed conflict. Nejbir explains that "in doing so Turkey priorities its own counterterrorism and national security legal regime rather than international humanitarian law" (Nejbir, 2021, p. 41). Even during the peace process in 2014, the legislative framework that authorised the government to take the necessary steps to move forward was titled the Law to End Terror and Strengthen Social Integration.

Similarly, one of the few laws designed to address conflict-related victimhood is named Law on the Compensation of Damages That Occurred due

3 It should be noted that having a definition of victimhood comes with its own problems. For example, in Northern Ireland, the question of the definition of victimhood and who it includes or excludes has been part of a political contestation (Breen-Smyth, 2009).

to Terror and the Fight against Terror (2004). The law aimed at compensating individuals who experienced material damage because of the "terrorist attacks" or "fights against terrorism activities". As Biner asserts:

> Compensation was to be granted for losses resulting from physical damage to movable and immovable assets as well as losses that resulted because a person was denied access to his property during that period. Loss of life and injuries were also included in the compensation categories, but non-pecuniary damages were not.
>
> (Biner, 2013, p. 73)

Even though this law implied a victimhood category, the word victim is not present in the text of the law. For example, Article 1 states the purpose of the law as "to determine the basis and procedures of compensating the loss of the persons who experienced material damage resulting from terrorist acts or fight against terrorism activities" (Law on the Compensation of Damages That Occurred due to Terror and the Fight against Terror, 2004). The rest of the law refers to the victims as "the persons who experienced damage" without using the actual word victim. Although the real purpose of the law is to pay compensation to the displaced, the beneficiaries included other victims, and the government purposely presented the law as a mechanism for all victims of terrorism (Kurban, 2012). The law avoided formally recognising the victims of displacement, failed to acknowledge the state's displacement policy, and failed to establish a justice mechanism. The state did not use the law as an opportunity to extend an apology or acknowledge its responsibility for conflict-related losses and damages (Biner, 2013). Therefore, for the beneficiaries of the law, the compensation money was not considered as a reparation for their victim status, but rather as blood money or as a form of state charity (Biner, 2013; Kurban, 2012). The existence of the law does not undermine the absence of a comprehensive institutional context where one needs to register as the victim of the conflict to have access to some rights and benefits. The example of the Compensation Law demonstrates that the dominance of legal terminology around victimhood derives from the widespread use of the term victim in legal language, but not the conflict-specific laws. Therefore, once a comprehensive institutional framework has been established to deal with the victims of the conflict in future, the implications of the term victim are likely to shift.

### *Victimhood as an Indicator of Responsibility*

Addressing the responsible actor behind the violation is another key reason for using the word victim. My interlocutors believe that using the word victim directs attention to the perpetrator bearing responsibility for the violation and the victimhood. According to this view, using the word victim is critical to denote that someone is responsible for the human rights violation and that there is someone to hold accountable.[4] Thus, if you avoid using victim, you blur the fact that there are people who committed the crime and who need to be held accountable.

For instance, an Istanbul-based lawyer working on enforced disappearances commented that despite the victimhood identity's passive connotations, the word victim points to the state's responsibility (Interview no:10, 2019). An Istanbul-based Kurdish researcher also thinks the word victim is acceptable if it is used in a context that mentions not only the victimised, but also the victimiser (Interview no:4, 2019). In their opinion, if the focus is on the people and institutions who caused the victimisation, there is no problem with using it. Similarly, a researcher-practitioner working on the Kurdish issue argued that any hesitation in using the word victim ran the risk of undermining the injustice that the person suffered: "There is a loss, and there is a harm. When you don't tell that part fully, I feel that there is not a full demand for justice and peace" (Interview no:1, 2019). Likewise, the son of a man extrajudicially killed in the 1990s considers himself a victim without hesitation (Interview no:18, 2020). He emphasised that he is a victim, precisely because his father was murdered. He believes in the necessity of clearly stating that one is a victim because of state violence. The following quote accentuates that claiming victim status is necessary to highlight state violence:

> Yes, I mean, it is not something like some arguments happened over a piece of land in the village, some people were killed, and the police came but could not protect us. It is not the victimisation caused by that . . . We are talking about the victimisation created by the state's failure to carry out its task.
>
> (Interview no:18, 2020)

## 5.6 Multi-Layered Victimisation in the Kurdish Conflict

To better understand the construction of victimhood, we should examine more closely how victimisation has occurred within the context of the Kurdish conflict. I do this primarily by analysing my interlocutors' responses in relation to victimhood. Regarding the groups most affected by the conflict, most of my interlocutors consider the intersection of multiple categories, including ethnicity, gender, language, sexual identity, and class. They understand that the experience of human rights violations becomes more layered and deepened over time and display intergenerational consequences.

4 Krystalli writes about a similar understanding of Colombian woman. She notes that the word victim demonstrates that there is a person who suffered from the harm done by a victimiser and underscores the need for a process to address and repair the harm. For more details see Krystalli (2020).

Multi-layered and intergenerational victimisation perpetuates social inequalities, ultimately leaving a huge portion of Kurds on the margins of society without equal access to resources. For example, in instances of forced displacement, many families live in impoverished conditions in the new urban centres to which they relocate. The absence of the usual income resources means that children are compelled to engage in labour and receive either minimal or no education. This has a profound impact on future generations, manifesting in a range of outcomes, including poor physical and mental health and a lack of socioeconomic opportunities. A researcher working with forcibly displaced families in Istanbul concluded that, as a result, it is predominantly Kurds who occupy the lowest-paid jobs in major urban centres. The following quote encapsulates the multifaceted nature of intergenerational victimisation:

> When people first arrived here [Istanbul], mothers and fathers remained entirely outside the economy. They were taking care of their farm back in their village. What could they do here? Nothing. The cheapest accommodation would be basements which caused many health issues. The kids had to drop out of school, they had to work for the family's survival. Where would they work? In textile, restaurants, cleaning jobs. A whole generation had to stay out of education. This is a violation of [the right to] access to education.
>
> (Interview no:2, 2019)

A Diyarbakır-based journalist noted that through such intergenerational impacts of the conflict, the state manages to victimise the whole Kurdish society:

> The size, root and depth of the harm turn into something else, very much so. It goes beyond individual victims. You go through each household, each individual. His father has been in a revolutionary group, you imprison his child. You punish him. You punish him with his family. You punish them altogether, the whole society.
>
> (Interview no:14, 2020)

Long-lasting intergenerational effects of conflict have been well established in other contexts as well.[5] For example, Hamber and Lundy point to the transgenerational needs of the victims of historical institutional abuses (Hamber and Lundy, 2020). They indicate that the victims point to the long-term

5 See for example Devakumar, D., Birch, M., Osrin, D. et al., 2014. The intergenerational effects of war on the health of children. *BMC Medicine*, 12, 57. https://doi.org/10.1186/1741-7015-12-57

impact of the loss of opportunities and express the need for transitional justice measures to address transgenerational needs. Thus, women and children face state violence both directly, as in the cases of sexual violence, forced displacement, enforced disappearances, and indirectly, as in living with the consequences that carry over generations.[6]

In the following two sections, I elaborate on this multi-layered understanding, focusing on ethnicity and gender as the two key aspects highlighted in my interviews. Their intersection is at the heart of multi-layered victimisation. Furthermore, these aspects of victimisation also shed light on the mobilisation of organised victims' groups and help us understand the prominence of women and younger generations in the victim groups.

## *Ethnicity*

The impact of the Kurdish ethnic identity on experiences of victimisation was a central theme in my exploration, particularly in relation to the state's assimilationist policies (see Chapter 2). Due to the existential impact of state violence on Kurds, victimisation has become an indispensable aspect of the Kurdish identity (Üngör and Işık, 2021). When I inquired in the interviews about the primary victims of the ongoing armed conflict, the most common response was the Kurdish people. Most of them stressed the widespread effect of the conflict on the entire Kurdish population, irrespective of political affiliations, largely stemming from entrenched ethnicity-based discrimination. The complex ethnopolitical nature of the Kurdish conflict (Yeğen, 1999) means that even Kurds residing in relatively less war-affected parts of the Kurdish region are not immune to various forms of victimisation. Ethnic discrimination of Kurds is in line with the wider patterns of ethnic exclusion in nation-states of the twentieth century, and it is not limited to politically active Kurds (Tezcür and Gurses, 2017). Even a supporter of the ruling party would be impacted because their social and economic context is inevitably shaped by the conflict (Gurses, 2012).

The war pervades the fabric of everyday lives of the inhabitants in the Kurdish region, manifesting through state violence and oppression. The multifaceted nature of the conflict is palpable in various parts of the Kurdish region, ranging from a heavy military presence to the securitisation of everyday life and the destruction of the environment and cultural heritage. Therefore, the denial of their identity not only prompted Kurds to mobilise as a collectively victimised group but also, coupled with elevated levels of poverty and underdevelopment in the Kurdish region, discrimination has been perceived through both material and cultural assimilation lenses (Mohammed

6 Intergenerational impact of the conflict can also be observed in the formation of victim movements. See Chapter 6 for the intergenerational aspect of the Saturday Mothers movement.

and Romano, 2023). A journalist who witnessed different periods of state violence in the region explained to me the following:

> This entire geography suffers from the Kurdish conflict. Security dams block every single river in the region. This is a matter of depriving this geography of water, drying it out, causing desertification, and changing its climate. This naturally means that everyone living in Kurdistan is impacted.
> (Interview no:14, 2020)

Indeed, due to the protracted armed conflict and the state's discriminatory economic policies that have overlooked the pressing local needs, the Kurdish region has suffered significant levels of poverty, underdevelopment, and economic deprivation (Yadirgi, 2022). Animal husbandry and agriculture, the main sources of livelihood, have been damaged severely by the Turkish state's colonial extraction of resources, which has reduced the Kurdish region's capacity to be self-sufficient in feeding its population (Pimbert, 2021).

An Istanbul-based researcher who holds extensive experience working with the families of the disappeared asserts that claiming that the whole society were equally affected would be inaccurate, as such a blanket statement obscures the nuanced reality of the situation (Interview no:10, 2019). In a broader context, she contends that historically, it is the Kurdish citizens of Turkey who have been systematically victimised as a collective group by the Turkish Republic. Indeed, the war's impact on the rest of the society in Turkey is mostly based on the indirect outcomes of living in a country where the war is a significant factor shaping the political, economic, and social context.

In her work that discusses the victimhood definitions in Northern Ireland, Marie Breen-Smyth (2009) argues that the *we are all victims* discourse renders invisible the different ways people are affected by armed conflict. Revisiting the same topic in a more recent work, she comments that extending the victimhood concept to an entire identity group equalises the actual sufferers of violence with the other members of the group who are ascribed the victim identity only because of their potential suffering (Breen-Smyth, 2018). Similarly, although more broadly on victimhood, Buruma (1999, p. 5) points out that equalising distinct types of victimhood tends to erase the distinctions between the diverse ways different victims suffered. He claims that "in fact, it is ahistorical, because the actual experiences of historical victims get blended in a kind of soup of pain." In the case of the Kurdish conflict, claiming that the whole of society or the entire Kurdish population is victimised, might undermine the pain suffered by certain individuals because of the intersection of ethnicity, gender, class, and political identity.

### Gender

Gendered experiences of armed conflict emerged as another predominant theme when I inquired about the most conflict-affected groups. In particular, the interlocutors based in the Kurdish region, almost without exception, indicated that women and children are the primary victims, and delved into the complex layers of their victimisation. A Diyarbakır-based interlocutor shed lights on the multi-layered victimisation experienced specifically by women who are relatives of the disappeared, stating:

> She lost her child, husband, her whole income, and has been impoverished. She has no place to go, no home, no accommodation. They are all destroyed, and she has been through it all. She was tortured, she was imprisoned, the lawsuits about her are still going on.
>
> (Interview no:14, 2020)

This observation aligns with what feminist scholarship reveals about the gendered repercussions of war; while all gender identities experience the effects of conflict, women often experience distinct and disproportionate challenges compared to men (Ní Aoláin et al., 2011; Weber, 2021). Feminist theorists argue that war is not gender-neutral and that it amplifies existing gender inequalities (Enloe, 2000). Women frequently experience heightened vulnerability to sexual and gender-based violence, displacement, and the erosion of social and economic rights during and after conflict (Pankhurst, 2008). Due to gender norms, they often encounter more challenges in accessing property, land, and the labour market, as well as in receiving social services like healthcare and education (Weber, 2021). Ní Aoláin et al. (2017) contend that:

> During conflict, women directly experience various impacts, many related to sexual violence, including unwanted pregnancies, sexually transmitted diseases, and community stigma. Given the strictures of community and socially determined family roles, the impact of economic devastation, forced displacement, health deterioration, and loss of education fall in highly gender-stratified ways on women and girls.

Language plays a key role in the way in which women are disproportionately impacted by the conflict. An interlocutor suggested that women are disadvantaged in social life compared to men, because they did not speak Turkish or go to school and thus did not have the opportunity to be in public and engage with Turkish (Interview no:14, 2020). Women's mobility and social interactions are often regulated by men, thereby restricting their ability to engage with others, which diminishes their likelihood to acquire proficiency in Turkish (Üstündağ, 2023). Women's limited access to education and employment also serve to shield them from the influence of the Turkish language in their daily lives. By viewing the Kurdish language as illegal and illegitimate, the state policy has increasingly put Kurdish women in a vulnerable position in relation to gendered ethnic violence (Erel and Acik, 2020). Kurdish is invalid on the state level, yet many Kurdish women do not fully understand what is said to them in Turkish, which puts them in a muted social position (Bozkurt and Kaya, 2014). However, this also gave them the chance to preserve and transmit the language to next generations, and "many Kurds believe that Kurdish survived the Turkish state's linguicide thanks to women" (Üstündağ, 2023, p. 35).

The state's attempts to eradicate the Kurdish language, consequently aiming to eliminate the Kurdish identity, have also resulted in Kurdish-speaking children experiencing violence and social stigma (Coşkun et al., 2013). Parents isolate the children from the Kurdish culture, he argues, trying to prevent them from being humiliated and discriminated against by not letting them learn Kurdish. Not teaching the language is a widespread practice undertaken by parents to protect their children. He argues that this results in the children's alienation from their identity, "because these kids start living on a denial of themselves. They experience more health problems, they smoke more, and they experience internal unrest more. This is reflected on the family, and it becomes a vicious cycle" (Interview no:18, 2020).

DISA's 2012 report on the mother tongue and education of Kurdish children revealed that forcibly teaching Turkish in schools results in political, economic, and social challenges (Derince, 2012). Kurdish children encounter significant communication barriers with educators because of the exclusion of Kurdish language in educational settings. The types of violence that children suffer because Kurdish is not used in education includes stigmatisation, discrimination, low self-esteem, the sense of failure, dropping out of school, and ultimately reproducing socioeconomic inequalities. On some occasions, Kurdish children end up associating their culture with inferior values and feeling detached from their identities. The parents lose the chance to get involved with their children's education due to the gap between Kurdish as the language of the household and Turkish as the one in the public and institutional sphere.

Enforced disappearances and forced displacement are among the most severe human rights violations in which the gender dimension is evident. Enforced disappearances are gendered crimes, and 97 per cent of the cases are male victims (Erel and Acik, 2020). In many cases, this left single mothers with the burden of sustaining the family as well as searching for justice. Göksel argues that within "the intersecting processes of war and forced migration", multi-layered outcomes of forced displacement are experienced most severely by women, who, in most cases, lost their husbands, sons, or brothers either through extrajudicial killings or enforced disappearances, or because they joined the guerrilla movement (Göksel, 2018, p. 7). It is also part of the reason why women are also the most active in the search for peace, justice, and truth, as is the case with Saturday Mothers (Göksel, 2018).

I had the privilege of hearing Halime Bayram speak powerfully about this intersection at an international conference on transitional justice held in Istanbul in February 2025. Bayram, an activist in the Kurdish women's movement and a member of the Saturday Mothers (*Dayiken Şemiye)* in Diyarbakır, shared her deeply personal story. Her brother, Mehmet Şirin Bayram, was forcibly disappeared in Diyarbakır in 1996, an event that profoundly shaped her family's life. In her moving speech, Bayram offered a detailed account of how enforced disappearances alter the lives of the women left behind. Drawing on her mother's lived experience, she highlighted the unique challenges faced by Kurdish women, particularly the role language plays in their pursuit of justice. Her mother, who spoke only Kurdish and not Turkish, faced significant barriers when trying to seek answers about her son's disappearance. Since legal authorities only recognise Turkish in official procedures, her mother's inability to communicate in the imposed language severely hampered her fight for justice.

Bayram recounted how her mother, driven by fear and resilience, made immense efforts to learn Turkish. She began speaking to her children in Turkish at home, despite it not being her mother tongue, out of a haunting fear—that if another child were to be abducted, she would at least have the linguistic tools to seek justice. This example illustrates how assimilationist language policies intersect with conflict-related human rights violations, creating multi-layered hardships and victimisation for Kurdish families. At the same conference, Besna Tosun, a Saturday Mothers activist and relative of the disappeared, expanded on this theme, explaining how the inability to submit legal applications in Kurdish has prevented countless families from pursuing justice for their disappeared loved ones. In some cases, it was not until decades later—when the children of the disappeared had grown up—that legal action was finally initiated, sometimes 20 years after the initial disappearance. These testimonies starkly reveal how state-imposed language barriers compound the harm suffered because of enforced disappearances, turning the pursuit of justice into yet another site of struggle for Kurdish people.

In addition to the hardships women face due to the act of disappearance, including moving to a new place and providing for the family while mourning for the loved one, longer-term challenges while searching for truth and justice are also present (Davidovic, 2018). When a man is forcibly disappeared, his wife has "the burden of decision making regarding new familial and residential arrangements, as well as the burden of dealing with social and economic hardship" (Gökalp, 2010, p. 564). The embedded patriarchal relations in society means the social and economic affairs of the family are usually arranged by men, which leaves the women in an even more difficult position after the loss of the husband. Bozkurt and Kaya emphasise the increased burden on the wives of the disappeared as follows:

> Because they are Kurdish, they are women, they can't use Kurdish in the public sphere, can't get an education also due to the conditions of war in the geography they live in, because they lack any leverage for negotiation due

> to the same reasons, and have to settle for any job they find, these women end up in the most disadvantaged position of the labour market as well.
>
> (Bozkurt and Kaya, 2014, p. 42)

Forced displacement, even without the death of a husband, creates a heavy burden on women. In one of the interviews, a Diyarbakır-based lawyer explains:

> Yes, men experience economic difficulties, but women have to deal with the kids and face psychological problems such as anger and violence of men. Men deal with the difficulties outside the house but then come back home and bother the women. Women have to get along with it or at least survive it. I think women are very much victims here, without any doubts . . . Plus, every family has lost at least one or two kids either because they joined the organisation [PKK] or were disappeared. In this respect, as well, women are very much the victims.
>
> (Interview no:19, 2020)

Displacement disrupts the social and economic lives of the family dramatically. For example, many families grow their products in their villages, and they lose their livelihood when they move to bigger cities. This contrasts with life in the village which many women recall positively (Çağlayan et al., 2011). Even though the economic conditions in the village may be limited, their lives are based on self-sufficiency and supported through the local solidarity networks of neighbours and relatives. Forced displacement not only creates the loss of income opportunities, but it also disrupts the linguistic, cultural, temporal and spatial dimensions of social life.

However, women in some cases acquired new power in their households and communities in these processes. Female-headed households formed as an outcome of the conflict enabled some women to challenge the traditional gender roles in the family and community and undertake new roles to generate income, which ultimately empowered them (Gökalp, 2010). This experience chimes with international research which also finds that conflict can play a role in challenging and redefining existing power relations and gendered hierarchies and thus enhance women's agency, create new spaces for empowerment and leadership (Ni Aoláin et al., 2017; Björkdahl and Selimovic, 2015; O'Rourke, 2012; Weber, 2018).

Gendered experiences of conflict-related human rights violations are also seen in social reactions of communities in the aftermath of the violation. A Diyarbakir-based interlocutor working with torture survivors argued social dynamics are often in men's favour. His observation is that men support one another and heal faster, whereas women stay with what they went through:

> For instance, when a man survives torture, it is said that he was subjected to torture for the revolution, for the country. However, when it happens to

> a woman, people would say 'What was she doing there as a woman? No wonder why this happened to her'.
>
> (Interview no:20, 2020)

Men are perceived as heroic, and they might acquire a more respected social status after going through state violence, which helps them deal with the violations. For women, heroic notions of surviving and resistance do not play out in the same way. Traditional gender roles associate women with familial duties in private space rather than the more visible roles men are assigned in public space. The same interlocutor argues that it becomes even worse when it comes to Kurdish queer activists, because they cannot benefit from community support. He notes:

> Of course, there is a hegemonic class and the oppressed within the Kurds as well. Women and LGBTI are affected more because they cannot get the social support as men would do. 'He resists, and he advocates for rights although he is gay. We barely accepted him being gay, and now how come he is involved in this?'
>
> (Interview no:20, 2020)

## 5.7 Moving Beyond the Binary Understandings of Victimhood

My findings show that there is a common binary view that identifying as a victim and leading a political struggle are mutually exclusive. Most of my interviews entail an understanding of victimhood which is that recognition of victims' vulnerabilities automatically means stripping them of their agency. Perceiving victim status as lacking political subjectivity is seen in other contexts. Krystalli explains that dominant narratives around victimhood in Colombia portray victimhood as lacking the necessary conditions for political subjectivity and agency; as something that needs to be left behind, to be transcended and transformed into something positive, something powerful such as political subjects who enjoy full citizenship (Krystalli, 2020). Similarly, in Turkey, the assumed binary opposition between political agency and vulnerability of victim identity informs the assumption that victimhood follows a linear process where victims empower and overcome their vulnerability (if this is at all possible or indeed necessary), then become political actors, and finally go beyond victimhood. Highlighting only one aspect of victimhood reproduces the binary framework.

Butler argues that the binary opposition established between agency and vulnerability draws on a masculinist ideal and it is therefore a feminist task to undo it (Butler, 2014):

> political resistance relies fundamentally on the mobilization of vulnerability, which means that vulnerability can be a way of being exposed and

> agentic at the same time. Such collective forms of resistance are structured very differently than the idea of a political subject that establishes its agency by vanquishing its vulnerability—this is the masculinist ideal we surely ought to continue to oppose.
>
> (Butler, 2014, p. 24)

To fulfil the feminist task of undoing the binary we need to understand "the way vulnerability enters into agency" (Butler, 2014, p. 25). Butler unpacks the critique, which argues that marking groups as vulnerable may fix those groups in "a political position of powerlessness and lack of agency" (Butler, 2014, p. 25). However, "vulnerability is neither fully passive nor fully active, but operating in a middle region, a constituent feature of a human animal both affected and acting" (Butler, 2014, p. 26). Studying the organised victims and the Saturday Mothers specifically, who have mobilised their vulnerability and made themselves even more vulnerable by exposing their bodily presence on a highly visible public square, attests how vulnerability can embed and generate agency.

Through criticising vulnerability studies, Cole also refers to the masculinist ideology which seeks to achieve invulnerability and "disavows weakness and dependence in any form" (Cole, 2016, p. 263). In parallel to the connotations of victimhood in Turkey described earlier, vulnerability is universally associated with several "negative conditions, disabling qualities and diminished capacities" including helplessness, weakness, fragility, and dependency (Cole, 2016, p. 264). It is often perceived "as a condition best avoided, but otherwise a problem to solve through various forms of securitization" (Cole, 2016, p. 264). This is, in her view, a subtle way of seeing victimhood almost as a pathological condition.

One of my findings described earlier was how using the term victim points at the victimiser. Notably, Cole acknowledges that "victimization refers to being acted upon" (Cole, 2016, p. 271). Some of my interlocutors share this understanding that calling people *mağdur* (victim) acts as an indicator and reminder that someone *onları mağdur etti* (victimised them). She contends that trying to reveal a hidden agency in victimhood treats inaction, passivity, and weakness as shameful. To put it in her words: "Victims do not lack agency in all circumstances—they can resist, rebel and retaliate—but they are not the primary actors in the context of their victimization" (Cole, 2016, p. 271).

The dominant narratives around victimhood in Turkey may promote the masculinist ideology of achieving invulnerability in the way Cole understands it (Cole, 2016). The desire to transcend vulnerability into empowered political agency means that feeling weak, dependent, and detached can be associated with negative meanings. I argue that the prevalent political terminology that overemphasises victims' empowerment and resistance risks ignoring some other integral parts of the victimisation experience, including suffering, trauma, pain, grief, shame, and the longer-term psychosocial effects. Difficult emotions that may emerge could be seen as a sign of political weakness, whereas grief and loss in the face of colonial repression generate complex non-linear processes.

In fact, victims do not have to fully transcend the difficult emotions to exercise political agency or consistently get involved in transformative collective mobilisation. Drawing on her ethnographic study with displaced and bereaved Kurdish mothers in Diyarbakır, Yildirim captures and conveys this beautifully:

> in this colonial setting of necropolitical destruction and displacement, feeling spaced-out is an assertion of political critique . . . These noncathartic states need not be organized, collective, or even resistant in any standard sense to be considered as a form of outrage at colonial oppression and as expressions of dissent.
>
> (Yıldırım, 2021)

Rather than viewing victimhood and empowerment mutually exclusive, I advocate for a more nuanced and multidimensional understanding of victimhood that accommodates vulnerability, silent suffering, and weakness as much as agentic powers, enabling, and resistance. A lawyer I interviewed supports this: "Being a victim does not necessarily mean giving up or being defeated. I keep on fighting even though I am a victim. We are all victims in fact, I don't think it is a wrong term" (Interview no:7, 2019).

Shifting away from a binary perspective towards a more nuanced interpretation of victimhood is needed to encompass different positionalities, capture various components, and to better reflect the complexities of how victims suffer, survive, mobilise, withdraw, lead, empower, and pursue collective goals, often simultaneously.

As discussed earlier, victims assert their own narrative and reclaim their autonomy by challenging the prescribed roles and identities enforced on them. Vulnerability is not a barrier to challenging the conditions and roles that victimised them. Vulnerability and agency can coexist; emotions such as pain, grief, anger, and despair can endure alongside agency, empowerment, resilience and resistance. Complex political victims are capable of navigating the conditions that lead to their victim status and especially through collective efforts, such as in the case of the Saturday Mothers movement.

## 5.8 Conclusion

This chapter has extensively analysed the construction and complexities of victimhood within the context of Turkey's Kurdish conflict, revealing that conflict-affected victimisation is a complex and multi-layered experience that has to be understood in a nuanced and non-binary manner. Drawing on the different conceptions of victimhood put forward by my interlocutors, I have demonstrated that the term victim does not fully capture the complexities of victimhood. It is considered a limiting word that excludes some critical dimensions of one's identity. The term victim is seen as disempowering because it undermines the political agency of victims, situating them in an inferior position relative to the oppressor. Although those victimised by state violence during the conflict can be potent political actors, as is shown in this book and many others, the victim label is seen as contradictory to this position by assigning them passively. However, despite the absence of a legislative or institutional framework that regulates the category of victimhood in relation to the conflict, the general legal terminology requires the use of the word victim. There are also those who have a different view and suggest that the term victim addresses the responsibility of the oppressor, especially in a legal setting. Bridging the gap between the legal terminology and the reality of the struggle is a crucial task yet to be fulfilled.

The intersection of ethnicity and gender lie at the foundation of the complex layers that form victimhood. These interconnecting factors not only shape the experiences of conflict-affected individuals but also underscore the multifaceted nature of their vulnerabilities and challenges. For example, enforced disappearance and forced displacement led to a perpetual deprivation of socio-economic opportunities that impact subsequent generations. The repercussions of victimisation extend beyond direct and immediate consequences, contributing to the systematic marginalisation and exclusion of Kurdish people.

Brett and Druliolle draw attention to a potential tension "between being defined as a victim within transitional justice and peacebuilding mechanisms, on the one hand, and instances of self-identification as a victim on the other" (Brett and Druliolle, 2018, p. 5). For this reason, we should understand the dynamics of how those most affected by the conflict make sense of, and relate to, the victim identity. Capturing the implications of victim status and connotations of victimhood may help design peacebuilding and transitional justice mechanisms in line with the demands and experiences of those who have been most affected by the conflict. Once the conflict has ended and a reconciliation process has started, this will be even more relevant for creating long-term, sustainable peace.

In the next chapter, I analyse the Saturday Mothers movement's contribution to transitional justice pillars to see how organised victims' movements can advance the goals of transitional justice where there is no official willingness to embrace transitional justice mechanisms.

## Reference List

Biner, Z.Ö., 2013. The logic of reconciliation: Between the right to compensation and the right to justice in Turkey. *Humanity: An International Journal of Human Rights, Humanitarianism, and Development*, 4, pp. 73–91. https://doi.org/10.1353/hum.2013.0002

Björkdahl, A., Selimovic, J.M., 2015. Gendering agency in transitional justice. *Security Dialogue*, 46, pp. 165–182. https://doi.org/10.1177/0967010614552547
Bouris, E., 2007. *Complex Political Victims*. 1st ed. Boulder, CO: Lynne Rienner Publishers.
Breen-Smyth, M., 2009. Hierarchies of pain and responsibility: Victims and war by other means in Northern Ireland. *Tripodos*, 25, pp. 27–40.
Breen-Smyth, M., 2018. Suffering, victims and survivors in the Northern Ireland conflict: Definitions, policies, and politics. In P. Terhoeven (Ed.), *Victimhood and Acknowledgement*. De Gruyter, pp. 39–58. https://doi.org/10.1515/9783110581508-003
Brett, R. and Druliolle, V., 2018. The politics of victimhood in post-conflict societies. *The Politics of Victimhood in Post-conflict Societies*. https://doi.org/10.1007/978-3-319-70202-5
Buruma, I., 1999. The joys and perils of victimhood. *New York Review of Books*.
Butler, J., 2014. Rethinking vulnerability and resistance. In *Plenary Conference XV Symposium of the International Association of Women Philosophers (IAPh)*, University of Alcalá, Madrid, 24 June, pp. 1–19.
Çağlayan, H., Özar, Ş. and Doğan Tepe, A., 2011. *Ne Değişti? Kürt Kadınların Zorunlu Göç Deneyimi*. Ayizi Kitap.
Cole, A., 2016. All of us are vulnerable, but some are more vulnerable than others: The Political ambiguity of vulnerability studies, an ambivalent critique. *Critical Horizons*, 17, pp. 260–277. https://doi.org/10.1080/14409917.2016.1153896
Commission for Victims and Survivors, 2022. *About Us*. Available at: https://www.cvsni.org/about-us/ (Accessed: 11 September 2021).
Coşkun, V., Derince, Ş. and Uçarlar, N., 2013. *Scar of Tongue: Consequences of the Ban on the Use of Mother Tongue in Education and Experiences of Kurdish Students in Turkey*. Diyarbakir, Turkey: DISA Publications. https://doi.org/10.1007/s10993-012-9251-x
Cronin-Furman, K., Krystalli, R., 2020. The things they carry: Victims' documentation of forced disappearance in Colombia and Sri Lanka. *European Journal of International Relations*, 29–30. https://doi.org/10.1177/1354066120946479
Davidovic, M., 2018. Mother-activism before the European Court of Human Rights: Gender sensitivity towards Kurdish mothers and wives in enforced disappearance cases. *Silent Conflict in the East of Turkey between the Turkish Government and Kurdistan Workers'*, 133–153.
de Waardt, M., 2016. Naming and shaming victims: The semantics of victimhood. *International Journal of Transitional Justice*, 10, pp. 432–450. https://doi.org/10.1093/ijtj/ijw011
de Waardt, M., Weber, S., 2019. Beyond victims' mere presence: An empirical analysis of victim participation in transitional justice in Colombia. *Journal of Human Rights Practice*, 11. https://doi.org/10.1093/jhuman/huz002
Derince, M.Ş., 2012. Anadili Temelli Çokdilli ve Çokdiyalektli DİNAMİK Eğitim: Kürt öğrencilerin eğitiminde kullanılabilecek Modeller. *Diyarbakır Siyasal ve Sosyal Araştırmalar Enstitüsü (DİSA)*, önce Anadili Analiz Raporları. DiSA.
Enloe, C.H., 2000. *Maneuvers: The International Politics of Militarizing Women's Lives*. Berkeley, CA: University of California Press.
Erel, U., Acik, N., 2020. Enacting intersectional multilayered citizenship: Kurdish women's politics. *Gender, Place & Culture*, 27, pp. 479–501. https://doi.org/10.1080/0966369X.2019.1596883
Govier, T., 2015. *Victims and Victimhood*. Peterborough, ON: Broadview Press.
Gökalp, D., 2010. A gendered analysis of violence, justice and citizenship: Kurdish women facing war and displacement in Turkey. *Women's Studies International Forum*, 33, pp. 561–569. https://doi.org/10.1016/j.wsif.2010.09.005
Göksel, N., 2018. Losing the one, caring for the all: The activism of the peace mothers in Turkey. *Social Sciences*, 7, p. 174. https://doi.org/10.3390/socsci7100174

Gurses, M., 2012. Environmental consequences of civil war: Evidence from the Kurdish conflict in Turkey. *Civil Wars*, 14, pp. 254–271. https://doi.org/10.1080/13698249.2012.679495
Hamber, B., 2009. *Transforming Societies after Political Violence. Truth, Reconciliation, and Mental Health*. Springer. https://doi.org/10.1007/978-0-387-89427-0
Hamber, B., Lundy, P., 2020. Lessons from transitional justice? Toward a new framing of a victim-centered approach in the case of historical institutional abuse. *Victims & Offenders*, 00, pp. 1–27. https://doi.org/10.1080/15564886.2020.1743803
Interview no:1, Interview by Author, 2019.
Interview no:2, Interview by Author, 2019.
Interview no:3, Interview by Author, 2019.
Interview no:4, Interview by Author, 2019.
Interview no:5, Interview by Author, 2019.
Interview no:7, Interview by Author, 2019.
Interview no:9, Interview by Author, 2019.
Interview no:10, Interview by Author, 2019.
Interview no:14, Interview by Author, 2020.
Interview no:15, Interview by Author, 2020.
Interview no:17, Interview by Author, 2020.
Interview no:18, Interview by Author, 2020.
Interview no:19, Interview by Author, 2020.
Interview no:20, Interview by Author, 2020.
Interview no:22, Interview by Author, 2020.
Interview no:23, Interview by Author, 2020.
Interview no:24, Interview by Author, 2020.
Bozkurt, H. and Kaya, Ö., 2014. *Holding Up the Photograph*. Truth Justice Memory Center. Available at: https://hakikatadalethafiza.org/sites/default/files/2023-01/holding-up-the-photograph.pdf (Accessed: 7 April 2024).
Krystalli, R., 2020. Women, peace, and victimhood. *Global Observatory*, pp. 11–13.
Kurban, D., 2012. Reparations and displacement in Turkey. Lessons learned from the compensation law. In *Case Studies on Transitional Justice and Displacement*. ICTJ, pp. 1–13.
Law on the Compensation of Damages That Occurred due to Terror and the Fight against Terror Law no: 5233. Available at: https://www.brookings.edu/wp-content/uploads/2016/07/Turkey_Law5233_2004.pdf (Accessed: 5 March 2025).
Mohammed, S.J. and Romano, D., 2023. The Kurdish conflict in Turkey: The central role of identity recognition (or lack thereof). *Ethnopolitics*, 0, pp. 1–18. https://doi.org/10.1080/17449057.2023.2275229
Nejbir, D.A., 2021. *Turkey's Destruction of Kurdish Graveyards*. Geneva: Mesapotamia Observatory of Justice. Available at: https://mojust.org/turkeys-destruction-of-kurdish-graves-2/ (Accessed: 11 January 2022).
Ní Aoláin, F., Cahn, N. and Haynes, D.F., 2017. *The Oxford Handbook of Gender and Conflict*. Oxford University Press. https://doi.org/10.1093/oxfordhb/9780199300983.001.0001
Ní Aoláin, F., Haynes, D.F. and Cahn, N.R., 2011. *On the Frontlines: Gender, War, and the Post-Conflict Process*. New York: Oxford University Press. https://doi.org/10.1093/acprof:oso/9780195396645.001.0001
Nussio, E., Rettberg, A. and Ugarriza, J.E., 2015. Victims, nonvictims and their opinions on transitional justice: Findings from the Colombian case. *International Journal of Transitional Justice*, 9, pp. 336–354. https://doi.org/10.1093/ijtj/ijv006
O'Rourke, C., 2012. Dealing with the past in a post-conflict society: Does the participation of women matter? Insights from Northern Ireland. *William & Mary Journal of Race, Gender, and Social Justice*, 19, pp. 34–68.

Pankhurst, D. (Ed.), 2008. *Gendered Peace*. Routledge. https://doi.org/10.4324/9780203939130

Pimbert, M.P., 2021. Regenerating Kurdish ecologies through food sovereignty, agroecology, and economies of care. In *Ecological Solidarity in the Kurdish Freedom Movement. Thought, Practice, Challenges, and Opportunities*. Lexington Books.

Rudling, A., 2019. "I'm Not that Chained-Up Little Person": Four paragons of victimhood in transitional justice discourse. *Human Rights Quarterly*, 41, pp. 421–440.

Saeed, H., 2016. Victims and victimhood: Individuals of inaction or active agents of change? Reflections on fieldwork in Afghanistan. *International Journal of Transitional Justice*, 10, pp. 168–178. https://doi.org/10.1093/ijtj/ijv032

Shalhoub-Kevorkian, N., 2015. Death and dying in my Jerusalem: The power of liminality. In B. Hamber and E. Gallagher (Eds.), *Psychosocial Perspectives on Peacebuilding*. Cham: Springer. https://doi.org/10.1007/978-3-319-09937-8_8

Sobout, A., 2017. *Reshaping Transition: Urbicide and Grassroots Perspectives of Justice in Nahr el Bared Refugee Camp in Lebanon*. PhD thesis. Ulster University.

Tezcür, G. and Gurses, M., 2017. Ethnic exclusion and mobilization: The Kurdish conflict in Turkey. *Comparative Politics*, 49, pp. 213–230. https://doi.org/10.5129/001041517820201378

Üngör, U.Ü. and Işık, A., 2021. Mass violence and Kurds: Introduction to the special issue. *Kurdish Studies*, 9, pp. 1–9. https://doi.org/10.33182/ks.v9i1.634

Üstündağ, N., 2023. *The Mother, the Politician, and the Guerrilla: Women's Political Imagination in the Kurdish Movement*, 1st ed. Fordham University Press. https://doi.org/10.2307/jj.6380563

Weber, S., 2018. From victims and mothers to citizens: Gender-just transformative reparations and the need for public and private transitions. *International Journal of Transitional Justice*, 12. https://doi.org/10.1093/ijtj/ijx030

Weber, S., 2021. Gender and transitional justice. In H.O. Yusuf and H. Van Der Merwe (Eds.), *Transitional Justice: Theories, Mechanisms and Debates*. Routledge. pp. 206–228. https://doi.org/10.4324/9781315760568–10

Yadirgi, V., 2022. The Kurdish question in contemporary Turkey: a political economy perspective. In H.O. Yusuf and H. Van Der Merwe (Eds.), *The Routledge Handbook on Contemporary Turkey*. Routledge. pp. 282–296.

Yeğen, M., 1999. The Kurdish question in Turkish state discourse. *Journal of Contemporary History*, 34, pp. 555–568.

Yıldırım, U., 2021. Spaced-out states decolonizing trauma in a war-torn Middle Eastern City. *Current Anthropology*, 62, pp. 717–740. https://doi.org/10.1086/718206

Chapter 6

# Saturday Mothers' Contributions to the Pillars of Transitional Justice

## 6.1 Introduction

Through a persistent struggle that has been expanding towards a broader network since 1995, the Saturday Mothers movement has worked to stop enforced disappearances and bring the perpetrators to justice. I discussed in Chapter 4 the factors contributing to the Saturday Mothers' evolving into a long-lasting social movement. That chapter also showed that the Saturday Mothers movement has been studied extensively within the social movements and feminist literature. However, the movement's achievements have not been analysed from a transitional justice lens. A close examination of their pivotal role helps us grasp the challenges of dealing with the past in Turkey and expands our understanding of grassroots organisations' potential in achieving their goals in non-transitional, oppressive settings which is helpful for other contexts across the world.

In the next sections, I discuss Saturday Mothers' achievements through the four pillars of transitional justice: truth, justice, reparations, and guarantees of non-recurrence (UN, 2010). However, since reparations, in a narrow sense, refers to providing direct benefits to victims (de Greiff, 2006) and the state has not provided any reparations in response to the Saturday Mother movement's efforts, I exclude them from my discussion. Instead, I discuss memorialisation as a separate pillar. In the 2016 report, Memorialisation and Reparations, Ereshnee Naidu refers to memorialisation as a new pillar "as it serves many purposes including truth-telling, civic engagement, community rebuilding, recognition, and can fulfil a range of transitional justice goals during all phases of conflict" (Thiagarajah, 2016). Although I do not examine the Saturday Mothers movement's efforts through a separate pillar of reparations, my analysis recognises the interconnectedness of transitional justice pillars and that it entails different components of symbolic reparations. For example, memorialisation and commemorations are recognised as a form of symbolic reparations (Ay, 2019; de Greiff, 2006; Greeley et al., 2020). Moreover, exhumations have been part of reparation policies and have become a vital theme of reparations for civil society in Peru (Azevedo, 2016; Delacroix,

DOI: 10.4324/9781003432579-6

2022). Acknowledgement, recognition, and perpetrators' confessions may also be seen as part of reparations (Hamber and Wilson, 2002).

First, I explore the truth pillar through two lenses: the Saturday Mothers movement's demand for a truth commission and the creation of a space for truth-recovery. Then, I move on to elaborate on the justice pillar. I begin with the efforts to achieve justice and then explain the prosecutions in 2000. I also discuss how the families reacted to those prosecutions and how they were affected by the process. In the next section, I discuss how they contributed to guarantees of non-recurrence. The two primary ways in which they have done so are the preventive role they played and the sustainable movement they created. Finally, I examine how Saturday Mothers have built memorialisation processes. I argue that not only did they add the issue of enforced disappearances into collective memory, but they also marked Galatasaray Square as a memory site.

## 6.2 Truth

> On that day, on that square, we ask for the fates of our relatives. This is our most natural right. We don't do any harm to anyone. We only say who is guilty. Because we say who is guilty, unfortunately, we have faced a lot of problems [with the authorities] in some periods.
>
> (Interview no:21, 2020)

An activist leader from the Saturday Mothers explained with this quote how truth-seeking is a challenging yet indispensable part of the Saturday Mothers' struggle. Since the very beginning, they have demanded truth and engaged simultaneously in truth-seeking and truth-recovery activities. Whenever they shared their experiences, they were met with denial and rejection. As a result, their greatest motivation became ensuring that "what they had endured was known and heard by everyone" (Arcan, interviewed by İnsan Hakları Okulu, 2022). The ongoing denial of the truth of enforced disappearances, impunity of perpetrators, and the lack of justice make truth and official recognition of enforced disappearance an urgent need and demand for families.

It is not merely a need to know what happened as families often know many details of the act including the names of those who took their relative from home. Some families keep in mind the perpetrators' names to be able to list them when justice is finally delivered in a courtroom (Göral et al., 2013). In some cases, the person who abducted their loved one is their relative or neighbour whom they continued to see for a long time after the incident. A lawyer working on enforced disappeared cases indicated the following:

> The relatives of the disappeared can name one by one who came and took [the person] from home, brought, etc. Despite that, these people are not

> being investigated, brought to justice, or punished. If by accident they are brought to court, as it has happened in the Temizöz case, they are being acquitted at the end of years-long prosecutions.
>
> (Interview no:3, 2019)

Receiving an official acknowledgment, therefore, means that what families have known for a long time will become public knowledge. This could end the denial that makes the holder of that knowledge visible (Interview no:2, 2019). At the same time, it denotes recognising the significance, value, and dignity of victims and their families. What becomes public and official knowledge can also be treated with more care and seriousness. It is the necessary first step of what should lead to a comprehensive and broader official set-up to deliver justice and providing reparations. However, as Kodikara establishes in her work on Sri Lanka, "in ethnonationalist, deeply divided contexts such as Sri Lanka, truth is not just a second-best option to justice but is an equally radically destabilizing and unsettling commodity" (Kodikara, 2023, p. 172). Dempster's argument explains why an official truth-recovery mechanism has a wide range of implications for families of enforced disappearance:

> Internationally, acknowledgement that a 'disappeared' loved one has been killed is more than a specific transitional mechanism, rather it is a form of recognition that is manifest in various aspects of the response to a 'disappearance' and can have practical, financial, legal, emotional, and psychological benefits for those whose loved one has been 'disappeared'.
>
> (Dempster, 2019, p. 196)

Truth commissions are one of the primary mechanisms offered in the international transitional justice toolkit. They seldom reveal previously unknown facts, but they still make fundamental contributions to the recognition of victims and their experiences (de Greiff, 2012). In line with this, relatives of the disappeared and human rights defenders have routinely expressed the demand for a truth commission for enforced disappearances (Evrensel, 2011). For example, in a Saturday sit-in in 2011, Serpil Başkaya, the daughter of the disappeared Hüseyin Başkaya, read the weekly statement emphasising the demand for a truth commission in which human rights organisations, legal experts, and intellectuals will work together (Evrensel, 2011). In a press statement released in 2015, the İHD Commission Against Enforced Disappearances Under Custody stressed "the need for a truth commission to investigate the reasons behind the crimes against humanity in Turkey, first and foremost enforced disappearances, and to find the perpetrators" (İHD, 2015). During the International Week for the Fight against Forced Disappearances in 2023, İHD Diyarbakır demanded "the founding of a Dealing with the Past and Truth Commission for similar sufferings not to be repeated again in these lands, for truth to be revealed, and for societal peace to be built" (İHD Diyarbakır, 2023). Instead of outlining a specific framework for how a truth commission should operate, these statements emphasize the broader necessity of such a commission as a crucial mechanism to investigate cases of enforced disappearances, uncover the truth behind various instances of state violence, promote non-recurrence, and foster societal peace and reconciliation.

Besides advocating for truth-recovery mechanisms, Saturday Mothers themselves contributed to truth-recovery and attempted to construct a new truth regime against the state's untruths (Sezer Şanlı, 2018). Most notably, Saturday sit-ins have operated

> as an informal truth commission wherein the families of the disappeared share their testimonies, publicly ask for the fate of their loved ones to be revealed, and demand those who are responsible for these disappearances to be identified and put on trial.
>
> (Can, 2014, p. 161)

The specific format of using a public square to tell the story of a disappeared person every week at the same hour is itself a truth-telling activity. Through testimony sharing, they render visible the stories of the disappeared who could otherwise have remained anonymous. The process of testimony sharing requires preparatory work done by the İHD Commission Against Enforced Disappearances Under Custody. After deciding who will be commemorated that week, they start working on the details of that person's disappearance story (Can, 2014). They contact the lawyers to receive updates on the case's legal status and invite witnesses to share their testimonies during the sit-in. If the disappeared person's family are not among the regular attendees, the commission invites them to attend that week.

During sit-ins, families and organisers share details about the disappeared person's personality, political views, and the context of their disappearance (Can, 2014). They also disclose information about the alleged perpetrators and recount any interactions they had with security officers in their search for answers. This public sharing goes beyond documenting the disappearance itself; it highlights the family's pursuit of truth and justice and the barriers they have faced in achieving accountability. The format of the gatherings creates a powerful platform for families to express their experiences of loss and their ongoing struggle for justice publicly, shedding light on the persistence of impunity.

As an outcome of the Saturday Mothers' determined truth-seeking activities, a parliamentary sub-commission was established in 2011 "to investigate the death of Cemil Kırbayır, who was taken into custody on 13 September 1980" (TBMM, 2011). The sub-commission was set up only a few days after the landmark meeting between the Saturday Mothers and then-Prime Minister Erdoğan (Bianet, 2011). Berfo Kırbayır (Mother Berfo or *Berfo Ana*, as she is widely known), the most symbolic face of the Saturday Mothers Movement, was among the attendees (Tahincioğlu, 2024). The sub-commission collected documents and held hearings to listen to the testimonies of witnesses, police, and intelligence members who had interrogated Kırbayır. It produced a 350-page report which established that the torture in custody caused Kırbayır's death and the public servants interrogating him disappeared his body (TBMM, 2011). It was the first time that an official state body acknowledged the disappearances in custody. The sub-commission's investigation also revealed that there was no lawsuit filed regarding the case. Mikail Kırbayır, Cemil Kırbayır's brother made a speech in a sit-in and highlighted the importance of the parliamentary investigation:

> They said he ran away. We said he was murdered. The state lied to the family for three decades. But the parliamentary sub-commission made a meticulous investigation only to find that he did not run away, he was killed by state officials, and his body was somehow disappeared.
>
> (Kırbayır, cited in Can, 2014, p. 189)

The sub-commission only dealt with one case out of many disappearances, its report has not led to a criminal investigation to hold the perpetrators accountable, and its work has not led to a broader official attempt or concrete measures for truth-recovery. However, considering the previous lack of official cooperation in any form of accountability, it was a remarkable effort to officially acknowledge disappearances. In a context where official denial and impunity regarding enforced disappearances continued, it was the Saturday Mothers movement's effort that made this important truth-recovery step possible.

## 6.3 Justice

### *Justice-Seeking Efforts*

Justice has been the main demand of the Saturday Mothers movement. They have campaigned to ensure the prosecution of perpetrators and the end of the decades-long impunity. An interlocutor expressed the justice demands of the families as follows:

> The demand for justice includes firstly getting back the disappeared person either alive or dead. They want the bones if that is the case [if it is possible]. This is their first demand before everything else. I mean they want a stone, a headstone. Then they want whoever did this to be tried.
>
> (Interview no:20, 2020)

An activist leader explained how ensuring justice will lead to other steps towards dealing with the past:

> One of our most essential demands is that the perpetrators to be found and put on trial. This will bring along what I just mentioned, the delivery

> of justice, the state's dealing with the past, and the preparation of a new constitution. All of these will create a chain reaction, I mean, they will pave the way for one another.
>
> (Interview no:23, 2020)

Families of the disappeared alongside the İHD members and lawyers have sought justice in numerous ways. During the 1990s and the early 2000s, the families wrote countless petitions to the local and national judicial authorities. Yet local authorities ignored them, provided no answers, and delivered no judicial action. That period was marked by total impunity because none of the perpetrators had been tried or convicted (Göral, 2019a). For families, seeking justice is not just about achieving an outcome; it is also about demonstrating unwavering persistence throughout the process. Continuously striving for justice even without concrete responses shows commitment to the cause and a refusal to let the issue fade. They might not believe that justice will be fully delivered, and they may know the results will be unsatisfactory. But every step towards accountability is still particularly important. My interlocutor whose family member was disappeared makes this point truly clear:

> If you ask me, personally, I don't really think they [perpetrators] can be prosecuted. Yet, in future, if we can have even the tiniest contribution to the end of impunity . . . when someone else is disappeared, any security officer shall at least know they will be prosecuted and punished. Yes, we won't experience this, perhaps we won't witness it, but at least the ones after us should see and experience it. At least, the state shall never dare to do anything like that again.
>
> (Interview no:23, 2020)

When there was no response from local or national judicial authorities, the families went to the European Court of Human Rights (ECtHR), a key platform for families to ask for justice. As a tool for legal mobilisation and social transformation, filing lawsuits before the ECtHR became essential for holding the Turkish state accountable in the eyes of a wider audience (Uçarlar, 2015). The hearings before the ECtHR provided the applicants with the opportunity to be heard publicly in a legal forum for the first time (Çali, 2010). The ECtHR ruled that Turkey had violated the right to life and was responsible for torture and maltreatment. Hundreds of judgements issued by the ECtHR contributed to documenting state-sponsored human rights violations (Kurban, 2014) and challenging the official policies of denial and silence (Budak, 2015; Çali, 2010; Jongerden, 2017; Uçarlar, 2015). The cases from Turkey played a significant role in shaping the reasoning of the ECtHR regarding enforced disappearances (Göral, 2019a).

### *Prosecutions in the 2000s*

As mentioned earlier, Saturday Mothers resumed the sit-ins after a 10-year break following the Ergenekon trials in 2009. The start of the trials marked a turning point in terms of shaking up the culture of impunity (Budak, 2015). They raised expectations for dealing with the past for the families, lawyers, and activists, who sought justice for the 1990s' human rights violations (Alpkaya et al., 2017). Several high-ranking military officers were tried on charges of plotting a coup d'état. Many of them were also involved in the 1990s crimes in the Kurdish region, including enforced disappearances (Göral, 2019a). The trials brought the 1990s crimes to the forefront of public debate. Those cases were a crucial legal component in the justice struggle and the fight against impunity (Göral, 2019a). It was the first time that the most senior military officers responsible for conflict-related human rights violations were put on trial.

The trials served as a catalyst for mobilising around demands for justice. Human rights actors, including the Saturday Mothers, became even more vocal about seeking accountability for the crimes committed in the Kurdish region. Saturday Mothers claimed that the trials should include the Gendarmerie Intelligence Organisation (JİTEM, *Jandarma İstihbarat ve Terörle Mücadele Grup Komutanlığı*) to recover the truth behind the enforced disappearances and unsolved murders (Karaman, 2016). Mothers started to list the perpetrators who were also involved in the Ergenekon case. In one of the Saturday sit-ins, Jiyan Tosun, the daughter of Fehmi Tosun, who had disappeared on 10 October 1995, summarised the reason for the resumption:

> We want the case files of the enforced disappearances to be included into the Ergenekon investigations. We want all extra-judicial secret structures like the Special Warfare Forces, Gendarmerie Intelligence and Anti-Terror Unit, Ergenekon to be fully investigated with all their crimes in the Ergenekon case.
> (Bianet, 2009a)

As mentioned earlier, justice-related demands got more concrete during this period and focused heavily on the inclusion of the enforced disappearance cases into the Ergenekon investigations and the prosecutions of the perpetrators. At the same sit-in, Tosun continued to list the individuals whom Saturday Mothers demanded to see put on trial:

> Imprisoned JİTEM commanders for what they did on behalf of the state, for the people they disappeared, for mass graves, and death wells;[1] the

1 Some of the disappeared were known to be buried in wells in the Kurdish region, which are referred to as death wells by human rights organisations.

generals and military officers who are pointed as the responsible ones for enforced disappearances in ECtHR rulings; state of emergency governors and chief police officers who are pointed at as the responsible ones for enforced disappearances in JİTEM members' confessions.

(Bianet, 2009a)

The evidence collected during the Ergenekon trials created hopes and expectations for families that the truth would be finally revealed, and justice would be achieved. This cautious optimism led many people to file complaints to prosecutors with the help of the local bar associations (Sevi̇mli̇ et al., 2021). These complaints paved the way for several JİTEM-related court cases in the subsequent years. While the trials were ongoing, Saturday Mothers also voiced their demands for exhumations and the opening of mass graves and wells in some sit-ins (Bianet, 2009b). Based on testimonies given in court, the prosecutors ordered the excavation of some of those wells and the uncovering mass graves in the Kurdish region (Karaman, 2016). These orders resulted in the discovery of the remains of several disappeared individuals (Bozkurt and Kaya, 2014).

It was the first time the perpetrators of severe crimes were in the court as defendants and brought face-to-face with the families of the disappeared. This was an important initial step for families, who had identified perpetrators and high-ranking military officials for many years. In most cases, they knew the names and identities of those who abducted their lost ones, tortured them, or those who ordered their disappearances. In some cases, families continued to live in the same village or neighbourhood as the perpetrators and had to face them for several years.

Families of the disappeared closely followed the trials, attended hearings, voiced their demands through sit-ins, and played a crucial role in expanding calls for justice to a wider audience, thereby attracting even more attention (Göral, 2021; Kaya, 2012). Once the crime of enforced disappearance became subject to judicial proceedings, it became harder to ignore or deny. The issue gained broader public attention, and demands for justice for enforced disappearances in the 1990s grew in visibility. After 2008, sit-ins began to draw the support of artists, intellectuals, human rights initiatives, and political parties. Galatasaray Square, through Saturday sit-ins, became a focal point for voicing demands related to Turkey's human rights record, with the Saturday Mothers' gatherings serving as a platform where diverse groups could channel their calls for justice. Despite the trials' limited outcomes, the civil society actors involved viewed them as an ongoing effort to pressure the state to acknowledge responsibility and address impunity.

Soon after the start of the trials, it became evident that they would be superficial and cosmetic, with little prospect for success. First, the trials were removed from their original city where the crimes had taken place and the families were based. Trials were moved to remote cities for security reasons, presenting a barrier for families and lawyers to be present at the hearings. Moreover, it became harder to get testimonies from the witnesses who lived in the area where the disappearances took place (Sevi̇mli̇ et al., 2021). Second, during the hearings, lawyers and families constantly pointed at proof and evidence that the court should collect. In most cases, the lawyers' demands to broaden the prosecution around this new evidence were rejected (Sevi̇mli̇ et al., 2021). Some of the defendants also made confessions and gave details about disappearances. However, the prosecutions did not go deep enough to consider the evidence and confessions to reveal the truth. Third, most defendants, despite being charged with gross human rights violations, were not arrested. After several years, they started to be acquitted one by one. Despite explicit confessions, witness statements, and other evidence presented, the perpetrators were absolved from guilt. Dinçer (2020) points out that the judicial proceedings initiated between 2008 and 2014, known as "confrontation trials," largely ended in impunity. Many defendants were acquitted, or charges were dismissed due to statutes of limitations, turning the justice system into an instrument of impunity.

The cases brought against the perpetrators of human rights violations during ongoing conflicts might prepare the groundwork for the transition that will take place at a later stage (Sarkin, 2016). Even if those cases end up serving impunity, they are still important in bringing the issue to the attention of the public and in some cases attracting the international community's attention. In Turkey as well, these trials, despite the disappointing outcomes, were considered a breaking point in the Turkey Republic's history (Budak, 2015). They were an unprecedented attempt to judge ex-commanders, military chefs, as well as the coup plotters. Since silence and denial have been such important tools for the Turkish state's approach to human rights violations, these prosecutions opened up a space, at least for a while, to address past crimes.

### *Trials' Impact on Families*

My interlocutors highlighted that the trials initially had a healing and empowering impact on families. They gave rise to a cautious sense of relief and provided the families with the opportunity to face the perpetrators. The trials became sites of encounters between the families and perpetrators, the families of the disappeared and the families of the perpetrators, the lawyers, and the court panel (Göral, 2019b). One of the lawyers who represented the families shared the observation that for families, being in a courtroom where the perpetrators sat in the defendant's seat, "facing an army of lawyers making compelling arguments in support of the families" was undoubtedly a significant relief (Interview no:16, 2020). Even the existence of such a platform was refreshing and groundbreaking.

Considering how enforced disappearance was used to spread fear among the families, neighbours, and the wider society and how, out of fear, some families could not even go to the police or judiciary, it was remarkable to see the creators of the fear in a different position. The people who used to hold such massive authority in their hometowns now had to listen to the accusations and be present at the trials. Another lawyer emphasised that she observed the families' empowerment during the hearings:

> I monitored all those trials. It was the first time I observed it [the positive impact] that clearly. You know the families have lived so closely with [the perpetrators] for so many years, they know their loves ones were taken by them. But at the end, it is a small place, they have constantly lived together, and perhaps they couldn't raise voices on many issues. But it was really good for them to claim their rights and speak very clearly and confidently in the court. We had observed clearly that they gained self-esteem. Yes, the outcomes were bad, but the fact that the perpetrators remained arrested and that they stood trial had an incredibly positive impact on the families.
>
> (Interview no:19)

The trials also provided the families with public acknowledgement of their suffering, something they had worked hard to achieve for years. Although they knew perfectly who was responsible for the loss of their loved ones, having a formal process made it impossible for anyone to deny what happened to their loved ones (Göral et al., 2013). The key issue, therefore, was not so much about revealing the unknown truth but was more about making it public knowledge and getting the respect and dignity they deserved. It meant that they proved to the wider society that they were not lying, and there was truth to what they had been claiming for years. Although they were initiated for other purposes and ultimately became instrumentalised, the truth that families had shared for years was finally brought to light, covered by various media outlets, and acknowledged by society at large. An interlocutor emphasised the importance of this truth-recovery aspect for families:

> They said that what mattered to them was to see the defendants being tried, and they would follow the cases no matter how long they took. They knew that the trials were not going to bring justice, but it was important that the entire world would know what happened to them was not a lie. The whole society now knows that their loved ones were killed by this, and that person and they hold the truth, not a lie.
>
> (Interview no:3)

How the trials served for truth-recovery and brought some relief and sense of dignity to families is evident in a striking example one of my interlocutors provides. There was a mother of a forcibly disappeared man who, out of fear, had to tell the authorities that the reason for her son's death was a heart attack. She was afraid that if she told the truth, something similar could happen to herself or her other children. In a way, she could not claim her son's death without fear. But because she was supported by many lawyers during the trials, she felt safe and empowered to tell the truth, and the official records were changed to correct the reason of death (Interview no:16, 2020).

Another aspect that contributed to families' empowerment and healing was the recognition of the political nature of the crime and the political identity of the disappeared. An interlocutor explained that for families, the official acknowledgement of the fact that their loved one was disappeared as part of a systematic state policy was crucial (Interview no:19, 2020). Instead of portraying the disappeared people as innocent victims who were randomly chosen, it was important to acknowledge that was a reason behind the loss. It meant honouring the disappeared person's life and struggle. She clarified the relationship between revealing the political, social, and historical aspect of disappearances and the families' wellbeing as follows:

> I mean, sometimes, the lawyers would say things like "those disappeared people had committed no crime, they were not sinful, they were innocent." We would oppose it. Of course, they had committed no crime, but they were selected purposefully. I mean, perhaps they led a political struggle in a political party, or they said things aloud about the Kurdish issue. These people were taken away because they had a political identity. We [as lawyers] thought this part needed to be highlighted and we tried to highlight it. The families generally share this view too. And the fact that it was addressed was good for them. I mean, yes, surely, they were not guilty, but the families feel better when it is stated that they had political ideas, beliefs, or struggle.
>
> (Interview no:19, 2020)

Families and lawyers saw the trials as important platforms to make their struggle and demands heard while at the same time doubting the unlikeliness of a full reckoning with the past (Interview no:22, 2020). One reason for not being completely convinced was the broader developments related to the Kurdish issue. For instance, while the trials were underway, the oppression of Kurdish politicians intensified. In a climate where violence and oppression continued to be heavily present, families understood that full justice could not be achieved.

There was, however, hope that this process might at least pave the way for future mechanisms. It was this hope that made them attend the hearings consistently (Interview no:15). For the first time, many families began to think this could be the starting the point of a wider process of justice, recognition, and accountability for past crimes. As one interlocutor established: "We were thinking that the groundwork could be done, some things could be revealed, and those investigations could be expanded" (Interview no:22,

2020). Regardless of whether they were hopeful or pessimistic, families made every effort to attend as many hearings as possible, often traveling long distances on limited budgets. Though families and lawyers alike remained cautious, distrusting the state to deliver justice, they were determined to be present, following the proceedings until the end and refusing to abandon their demand for justice. A lawyer monitoring the trials emphasised the families' persistence:

> Most cases were relocated for security reasons, yet families continued to attend. Sometimes, multiple family members would go, while other times they would alternate, attending every other hearing. Regardless, they remained steadfast, following the proceedings until the very end.
>
> (Interview no:3, 2019)

In the end, however, there was disappointment. The following quote illustrates how, despite their initial caution, families were ultimately disappointed by the trials' failure to deliver justice:

> The families endured, and continue to endure, the disappointment a thousand times more. But there is also this: because this problem goes back more than a hundred years, those who witnessed the intense periods of the 80s and 90s are politically aware people who know more or less what they can and cannot expect from the state. They recognised that a genuine reckoning with the past could only be possible through a mechanism of societal peace.
>
> (Interview no:15, 2020)

Some believe that the existence of an official mechanism may have done more harm than good, as it closed the door on a genuine accountability process. Now, the state could claim that these individuals came clean as a result of a series of legal procedures. Some argue that the families felt as if they had been used to legitimise the whitewashing of the perpetrators (Interview no:20). My interlocutor, who followed the trials as a relative of the disappeared reflected that if the trials had been handled differently, they could have made a groundbreaking impact and a restorative effect. If, for example, these people were given "back-to-back life sentences then it would shake things off and certainly everything would be much more different today". He noted that he would take this as an official apology (Interview no:21, 2020). At the Saturday gathering on 14 September 2019, activist leader Maside Ocak reflected on the Kızıltepe JİTEM trial, emphasising the entrenched impunity and the significant obstacles faced in the pursuit of justice:

> The truth was covered with a thick veil by the court. Truth and justice were obliterated by the statute of limitations. This case, which was brought to the judiciary with immense difficulty, became yet another example of the

> tradition of impunity . . . Then answer this: if we cannot seek justice in the courts for our children, who were taken into custody by state security forces, tortured to death in official state buildings, and buried in wells, where should we seek it?
>
> (Gazete Duvar, 2019)

Even though the perpetrators remained unpunished and therefore impunity prevailed, these trials are among the most concrete justice mechanisms regarding state violence. They were instrumentalised, distanced from their true purpose, and used by state actors as tools in internal power struggles. They enabled some actions to reveal those behind crimes such as village burnings and raids and, most importantly, exhumations and identifications of bodies of several disappeared (Yoleri, 2023).

## 6.4 Guarantees of Non-Recurrence

The Guarantees of Non-Recurrence Pillar of transitional justice comprises measures aimed at ensuring the human rights violations do not repeat (Shala, 2024). These measures most often have taken the form of institutional reforms (Kinder, 2021). However, civil society interventions at the societal level can also serve as a key preventive mechanism, contributing to Guarantees of Non-Recurrence (de Greiff, 2015). The Saturday Mothers movement considers their most important achievement as preventing more disappearances from happening, confirming the role of social movements and civil society more broadly in helping achieve this pillar.

This book stated earlier that one of key demands of the Saturday Mothers movement has been to make sure that those enforced disappearances will never happen again (see Chapter 4). Indeed, since the Saturday sit-ins first started in 1995, the remains of approximately 70 of the disappeared were found over 15 years (Pişkin, 2018). This has been highlighted multiple times in my interviews, and prominent activist leaders have expressed pride in it during their public interviews. For example, Maside Ocak—Hasan Ocak's sister and a member of the İHD commission—emphasised the same point in a media interview in 2013:

> There were 495 people disappeared between 1995–1996, but the number between 1996 and 1999 was only nine. We haven't found yet where our disappeared are, their perpetrators haven't been tried yet, but we stopped new disappearances.
>
> (Ocak, cited in Arslan, 2013)

İHD states that no enforced disappearances took place since 2004 (İHD, 2015). However, 2004 is also the year that the state of emergency rule ended. It is not quite possible to know whether it is solely the Saturday Mothers movement that stopped further disappearances. Yet, it can be argued that they created a certain deterrent effect on security forces. Police knew if they tortured or killed someone in custody, their families had a place to go. Physically, that place is Galatasaray Square, but symbolically it is the Saturday Mothers. They knew that there was a group of people who would follow up on the case, bring it to the forefront of public opinion, and carry it to a public space. An interlocutor argued that because the movement insisted on telling the truth, they managed to create fear in the authorities of being exposed in the square and they started to hesitate:

> There are some people who could survive after custody. We know that they heard sentences like 'We would now kill you too, but then your mother would go sit among those Saturday Mothers'. We know it all. I mean, seriously, this demonstration, this longest-lasting, most humane demonstration of Turkey prevented many deaths. Because we shouted there to enlighten many incidents without fearing from anyone, people started to take some of their steps more correctly.
>
> (Interview no:21)

Similarly, Maside Ocak stressed the same point in an interview marking the 1000th sit-in in May 2024: Her repeated emphasis of the movement's success of creating a barrier in stopping further disappearances illustrates the importance of what continues to be a main drive for continued collective action:

> This was a crucial sentiment for us. When we had to pause our activities in 1999, that year saw only ten cases of individuals disappearing in custody. During that time, many who joined us at Galatasaray expressed, 'They were going to disappear me in custody, but thank the existence of the Saturday Mothers.' When we first gathered in Galatasaray, we had three primary demands, one of which was an end to disappearances in custody. By the time we paused at our 200th week, we had witnessed that our movement had established a barrier against enforced disappearances—a policy embedded in the state apparatus of this country. Through our efforts, we were able to prevent disappearances and protect individuals' right to life.
>
> (Elvan, 2024)

In week 600 of the gatherings in Diyarbakır in August 2020, İHD Diyarbakır referred to the struggle of the Saturday Mothers movement as the longest-lasting civil disobedience protest of the country (İHD Diyarbakır, 2020). Indeed, the preventive role played by the movement is the outcome of building a sustainable social movement. One of the most important achievements of the Saturday Mothers is that they created the most sustainable and visible movements in Turkey despite continuous police violence and criminalisation efforts. Nobody had expected that the weekly vigils against enforced disappearances started as a movement of relatives of the disappeared would turn into the longest-running civil disobedience movement in Turkey (Karaman, 2016; Sezer Şanlı, 2018). Saturday Mothers transformed their suffering and long-term mourning into collective resistance (Aydın, 2018; Sezer Şanlı, 2018). The Saturday Mothers emerged not only as the most organised group among those who experienced state violence, but also as one of the most prominent and widely publicised protest movements in Istanbul (Baydar and Ivegen, 2006, p. 691). An activist leader indicated that the mere existence of this movement for such a long time is a success:

> Those who came there [the sit-ins] joined this movement to find out the fate of their loved ones and for no other people to experience this suffering. And if we can still sustain this for approximately twenty-five years, in my opinion, this should be perceived as a movement that has achieved and continues to achieve its goal.
>
> (Interview no:21)

One of the primary reasons for Saturday Mothers' persistence is the desire for non-recurrence of the crime of enforced disappearance. One of the relatives explained to me: "To create a healthy society that is healed from traumas, these events definitely should not repeat. The biggest reason of our persistence is this: that these losses should not happen again" (Interview no:23). The pain of the act of disappearance is so much that it is impossible for the families to let it go. She expands as follows:

> Being a relative of the disappeared, if you ask me, is one of the most painful things in the world. Especially if you cannot find your disappeared relative, if you cannot even reach their corpse, dead body, that pain is indescribable. And you carry this pain with you for a lifetime.
>
> (Interview no:23)

She highlights that persistence and stubbornness stem from having directly experienced an immense pain and wanting to prevent other people from enduring the same. This quote shows that the pain caused by the act of the disappearance is a driving force for families to continue to mobilise.

Among the reasons for the perseverance of the mobilisation over decades is the families' deep sense of responsibility towards their loved ones. By continuing their collective action to hold state authorities accountable, they respect, honour, and carry forward the struggle for which their relatives were disappeared. Being highly aware of the unlikeliness of achieving justice goals in the short term, they remain committed to a long-term vision of realising their goals:

> They are conscious of the reason their relatives were disappeared. They are part of the struggle carried out by their relatives, they know they are

> part of it, and this is what they are continuing. This is also why they sustain this movement. I mean this is the fundamental motivation of doing this every week. Otherwise, they are not in the expectation that justice will be delivered immediately, truth will be recovered, reconciliation will happen in near future.
>
> (Interview no:16)

In relation to this long-term vision, the continuity of the protests across generations is a key aspect of what made the Saturday Mothers movement sustainable. The age range of participants vary between 5–85, highlighting the intergenerational aspect of the movement (Kaya et al., 2024). The new generations such as grandchildren, nephews, and nieces take part in gatherings. Every new generation inherits the struggle, which makes the children of the disappeared the most pivotal actors in the search for truth and justice (Göral et al., 2013). Activist leader Sebla Arcan, a member of the İHD Commission, noted this intergenerational and empowering nature of the movement in an interview:

> Children born after we began our sit-ins are now our lawyers. Today, we sit in the square with the fourth generation. While mental health science suggests that trauma is passed down through generations, the Saturday Mothers have instead transmitted resistance and resilience. They created an unprecedented struggle. Without a doubt, this struggle has empowered all of us who are part of it. The reason we have been able to sustain this struggle for 1,000 weeks is this: we demand justice—not only for the disappeared but for all.
>
> (Elvan, 2024)

Arcan highlighted this point in a conversation, saying, "We passed on the struggle, not the trauma, from generation to generation" (Arcan, personal communication, 28 December 2024). For some participants, the stories they grew up hearing have become their own, even though they may not be old enough to remember the act of disappearance (Göral et al., 2013). This phenomenon is observed in other cities as well, as highlighted by an activist from Diyarbakır. Family members born two generations after the disappearance now attend the gatherings. The activist finds it notable that individuals who never met the disappeared person and are not directly affected as a child or sibling have committed to this struggle and actively engage with the enduring effects of the traumatic event (Interview no:20, 2020).

Some families attend as the entire family, and in some families, it is one or two people who are actively involved. Usually, if parents are included in the movement, the younger generations have close ties too, even though they might not be attending every gathering. A recent study revealed that "Participants who grew up witnessing the involvement of their parents or grandparents mentioned an internalised sense of responsibility to perpetuate the movement's legacy" (Kaya et al., 2024, p. 11). In fact, "I grew up among Saturday Mothers" is a common expression of the children of the disappeared. Some of these young people later become active members with leading and organising roles. Maside Ocak, a second-generation participant in the movement, emphasised the role of "inheriting and carrying on the parent's legacy" in an interview marking the 1000th week in 2024:

> The fourth generation has now grown up. I have learned so much from this struggle. For 1,000 weeks, we have been defending the right to life. For 40 years, we have carried the weight of seeing how families' wounds bleed again each week to prevent them from being forgotten. I am honoured to be part of this difficult struggle and to stand as a barrier against people disappearing in custody. I inherited this honourable struggle from my father—not just from him, but from I am the custodian of all the relatives of the disappeared who left us without ever finding justice.
>
> (Güngör, 2024)

One of my interlocutors explained how she and her family members attend the gatherings sometimes in rotation. Her mother started to attend the Saturday Mothers sit-ins in 1995, shortly after the first sit-in took place. She joined her mother in the 2000s and from then on, she became an active participant of the Saturday Mothers movement. Both her parents would participate every week unless they had health issues. If she or her mother cannot join for health reasons, the other attends that week, and this ensures the participation of at least one member of the family.

Research on success and effectiveness of social movements and collective action confirms that perseverance of activism is itself success (Bosco, 2006). Researching the Plaza da Mayo mothers, Bosco confirms that

> Collective action can also be a goal itself. For the Madres, becoming activists and remaining together as activists through the construction of emotional networks has been inseparable from their more explicit goals regarding the struggle for human rights in Argentina.
>
> (Bosco, 2006, p. 361)

Similarly, for Saturday Mothers, maintaining their community of families and activists in the face of police violence and forced breaks to activism is an impressive outcome of this long-term collective action.

## 6.5 Memorialisation Processes

Saturday Mothers have kept reminding the public that enforced disappearances took place and have not let this topic disappear from society's memory. Thanks to their protests, "Istanbul's most important spaces became haunted by the figure of the disappeared" (Göral, 2021, p. 83). They have marked Galatasaray Square as a site of memory (*lieux de mémoire*), a place "where memory crystalises and secretes itself" (Nora, 1989, p. 7), of the grassroots mobilisation for truth and justice after enforced disappearances.

> there is no spontaneous memory, that we must deliberately create archives, maintain anniversaries, organize celebrations, pronounce eulogies, and notarize bills because such activities no longer occur naturally. The defence, by certain minorities, of a privileged memory that has retreated to jealously protected enclaves in this sense intensely illuminates the truth of *lieux de memoire* that without commemorative vigilance, history would soon sweep them away.
>
> (Nora, 1989, p. 12)

Through commemorative vigilance and repeated use of symbols Saturday Mothers have rendered visible the issue of enforced disappearances to a wide audience and anchored the memory of the disappeared and ongoing struggle for democracy and justice into collective memory (Kurban, 2020; Sezer Şanlı, 2018; Göker, 2021). Göral (2021) argues that through their memory-making acts, the Saturday Mothers have confronted cultural aphasia (Chapter 2), a state marked by the absence of appropriate words and concepts to articulate specific realities. By recounting and reiterating the stories of disappearances, identifying the perpetrators, and sharing concrete experiences from the aftermath, they create a performance of resilience, persistently challenging and disrupting the voids and refusals inherent in cultural aphasia (Göral, 2021).

Public testimonies are at the heart of the sit-ins, with the Saturday Mothers holding photographs of the disappeared in silence to reinforce their message. "Commemorative symbols such as plaques, murals, monuments, museums and conflict-related sites have the capacity to carry meaning" and they constitute the sites of memory "because of their ability to embody the past and stimulate remembering in fixed locales" (McDowell and Braniff 2014, p. 14). Nimet Tanrıkulu, an activist in the movement, highlights this meaning-carrying feature of Galatasaray Square even in the physical absence of Saturday Mothers:

> Galatasaray is, above all, a place of memory today. Even if it's not 12:00 on a Saturday or the Saturday Mothers/Saturday People are not present, the door of that high school continues to speak to passers-by about the disappeared and the past 20 years of the country's struggle against enforced disappearances.
>
> (Tanrıkulu, 2014)

The Saturday Mothers' memory practices have been essential not only in recalling instances of enforced disappearances but also in denouncing the persistent absence of justice and accountability. Galatasaray Square, as a site of memory, has become the symbol of the struggle for justice and resistance against impunity and silence for enforced disappearances. This resistance stands firm against the state's long-standing attempts to deny and silence calls for truth and justice. A relative of a disappeared journalist described this struggle as "keeping a society's memory alive," shedding light on the interconnected struggles of commemorating the disappeared while exposing systemic injustice, unaccountability, and impunity:

> I mean, the fact that they [Saturday People] come there every week and support and that everyone holds a photograph . . . this is also refreshing the memory and keeping the community's memory alive. In other words, if Galatasaray Square and the Saturday Mothers' struggle did not exist, nobody would know after 1995 who the relatives of the disappeared are, whether people found their lost ones' bodies, and if there is impunity or not. Nobody would know. Everyone would forget about it. They would forget about the disappeared as well. But the Saturday Mothers are keeping a society's memory alive.
>
> (Interview no:23, 2020)

A parallel memory-making and meaning-creating work is seen with the relatives of the disappeared in Diyarbakir. Abdullah Zeytun, a lawyer and the former director of İHD Diyarbakır, explains how Koşuyolu Park is one of the memory-carrying spaces where the mobilisation for justice and truth is expressed in a public place (Zeytun, interviewed by Erbay, 2018). He underlines that the ban aims at withdrawing the struggle of relatives of the disappeared from the social space and making it forgotten:

> However, the relatives of the disappeared and human rights advocate do not define the limits of the struggle for truth and justice only by "place". They will make all the spaces that are related to social memory a part of their struggle.
>
> (Zeytun, interviewed by Erbay, 2018)

As Zeytun's quote illustrates, even the ban on Galatasaray Square and Koşuyolu Park underscores the significance of these spaces as sites of memory. When Galatasaray Square was banned in 2018, police barricades blocked all streets leading to the square on Saturdays, making it inaccessible to the public (Yoleri, interviewed by Truth Justice Memory Centre, 2020). Ironically, this restriction reinforced the square's symbolic role as a site of memory, with the absence of the Saturday Mothers marked by a heavy police presence that altered the atmosphere of the entire neighbourhood. Galatasaray Square, iconic for the Saturday sit-ins, was not only restricted but also surrounded, representing an attempt to erase memory, undermine commemoration efforts, and cut off the mothers' interactions with passersby and the public. This very visibility of the ban enhanced the square's symbolic importance, as the police barricades became a continuous reminder of the movement's struggle, extending beyond the usual one-hour Saturday gatherings.

Another vital aspect of the Saturday Mothers' contribution to memorialisation lies in the personal significance of the gatherings for the families involved. By following the same format on a weekly basis, the families embrace and honour the memories of their loved ones, gathering ritualistically with the memories of lost fathers, sons, daughters, and siblings. They come to the square not only to seek answers about their loved ones' fates but also to commemorate them and preserve their memories. A relative of a disappeared lawyer described Galatasaray Square as "the place where we meet our disappeared" (Interview no:21, 2020). By gathering there every Saturday, they pay respect to the lives and legacies of the disappeared, fulfilling a profound sense of duty. Zübeyde Tepe, the mother of Ferhat Tepe who was disappeared in 1993, points to the symbolic significance of the square for families:

> That place, Galatasaray Square, has become a symbol for our children and for us, and now it even appears in our dreams. When we go there, we feel as if they never died. When I hold Ferhat's photo in my hand there, I feel as if he is right beside me.
>
> (Güngör, 2024)

Gülseren Yoleri, a lawyer and the İHD İstanbul director, highlights the value of the Galatasaray Square for the families as a site of memory and comments that its spiritual importance will never get lost despite the bans to access the square:

> Galatasaray is a space of memory ingrained in minds and hearts. Relatives of the disappeared also describe it as 'a place of reunion' with the disappeared. Every Saturday at 12:00 noon, the disappeared, their relatives, and those who lost their loves while searching for them, come together in the square. This is a powerful emotion; therefore, its value is immense. This is why, in the spiritual sense, the loss of the square is impossible.
>
> (Yoleri, interviewed by Truth Justice Memory Centre, 2020)

The Saturday Mothers movement serves as a memory work that heals the trauma of the relatives of the disappeared (Sezer Şanlı, 2018). The act of gathering becomes an empowering form of collective commemoration. Existing research on community mobilisation in public spaces confirms this. Those affected by state violence can benefit from public displays of justice-seeking and engagement with the political space by gaining a sense of solidarity and empowerment (Hamber, 2015). Those who were harmed, who engage in collective self-advocacy to focus on their own needs, constitute important political resources and become more productive, healthier, and happier (Breen-Smyth, 2018). A relative of a disappeared explained that through the Saturday Mothers' organised mobilisation participants transcend their individual suffering and transform it into something collective:

> Actually, I always fought for my dad. But after I joined them [Saturday Mothers] I started to fight for everyone. In fact, I started to forget the issue of my dad a little bit, I started to forget the thing about my dad's murder. Because, it is actually remarkably interesting, you give up on chasing the problems about yourself. Because the pride of doing a collective work is something quite different.
>
> (Interview no:21, 2020)

In a personal discussion, Sebla Arcan emphasised that the Saturday Mothers' press statements and criminal complaints also function as a form of archival work. These efforts ensure that the facts surrounding the disappearances are meticulously documented and will remain accessible when structural change occurs and a meaningful reckoning with the state's past crimes becomes possible (Arcan, personal communication, 28 December 2024). Their dedication to producing these records serves a forward-looking purpose—not only intervening in the present societal and political landscape but also demonstrating a commitment to preserving these accounts. In doing so, they are creating a valuable archive for a future in which there is official recognition and the political will to pursue accountability and justice for the crime of enforced disappearances.

Another tool for commemorating the disappeared has been the International Week for the Fight against Forced Disappearances, commemorated every year since 1995 by İHD. On the first anniversary of 17 May 1995, the day Hasan Ocak's body were founded, the Ocak family and political organisations supporting the struggle against the disappearances organised an international assembly in Istanbul. The assembly took place on 17–31 May 1996 in Istanbul with the support of trade unions, political parties, and organisations. The Saturday sit-in on 17 May opened the assembly in which relatives of the disappeared, human rights advocates, intellectuals, and union members participated from Turkey as well as Chile, Colombia, Philippines, Sri Lanka, Palestine, and France, among others (ETHA, 2019). Two key resolutions that were passed during the assembly were to establish the International Committee Against Disappearances and to dedicate a week to disappearances each year. Each year during those two weeks, several commemoration practices take place.

## 6.6 Conclusion

Those who mobilise around an experience of victimisation can play a vital role in advancing the transitional justice process by pressuring governments that perpetuate impunity and supporting those committed to driving the process forward (Weis, 2015, p. 71). This chapter provided a comprehensive understanding of the Saturday Mothers movement's role in advancing the goals of transitional justice in Turkey. Their key demands have been reflecting the transitional justice pillars of truth, justice, guarantees of non-recurrence, and memorialisation. Not only did they focus on these key goals in their speeches and activities, but they also made concrete gains such as contributing to ending disappearances.

Such achievements were made in the context of an ongoing armed conflict without an official transitional justice agenda, and in the absence of genuine state willingness to acknowledge its responsibility in past crimes. As will be explored in the next chapter, there were periods when the state was seemingly willing to cooperate to deliver truth, justice, and accountability. Several judicial developments and the establishment of a parliamentary sub-commission to reveal the whereabouts of Cemil Kirbayir (explained earlier in this chapter) took place in that period when the political climate was more favourable to achieve certain gains in an official level. In parallel to other transitional justice initiatives that will be explored in Chapter 7, these official advancements have not achieved the overall goals of truth or justice. Yet, the Saturday Mothers movement laid a solid foundation for a broader transitional justice path to be followed. They created a public space through which the notions of truth, justice, memorialisation, and non-recurrence have gained visibility and support from a variety of actors. Most importantly, they raised awareness on one of the most severe and systematic human rights abuses in the history of the Turkish Republic: enforced disappearances. Together with other grassroots actors including activist groups, civil society organisations, and practitioners, they moved forward the transitional justice trajectory of Turkey. In the next chapter, I undertake a detailed analysis of transitional justice imaginaries of other grassroots actors, exploring the prospects and implications for transitional justice in the current context.

## Reference List

Alpkaya, G., Ataktürk Sevimli, E., Ballıktaş Bingöllü, B., Çiftçioğlu, K., Gebeş, Melis. and Yavan, D., 2017. *Dava İzleme: Duruşma Salonunda Devlet ve Yurttaş Raporu.* Truth Justice Memory Center. Available at: https://hakikatadalethafiza.org/sites/default/files/2022-12/dava_izleme_raporu.pdf (Accessed: 8 March 2025).

Arslan, R., 2013. *Cumartesi Anneleri: Bir mezar taşı kaç hafta, kaç anne eder?* Available at: https://www.bbc.com/turkce/haberler/2013/10/131020_cumartesi_anneleri_rengin (Accessed: 26 February 2025).

Ay, E., 2019. *Remembering without Confronting. Memorialization as a Reparation without Coming to Terms with the Past: Case study: Ulucanlar Prison Museum.* Master's thesis. The European Master's Programme in Human Rights and Democratisation.

Aydın, D., 2018. Kürdistan'da Direnişe Dönüşen Yas: Cumartesi Anneleri, Barış Anneleri ve MEYA-DER. *Jineoloji Dergisi*, pp. 1–24.

Azevedo, V.R., 2016. Restoring the dignity of the war's disappeared? Exhumations of mass graves, restorative justice and compassion policies in Peru. *Human Remains and Violence*, 2, pp. 39–55.

Baydar, G. and Ivegen, B., 2006. Territories, identities, and thresholds: The Saturday Mothers phenomenon in İstanbul. *Signs,* 31, pp. 689–715. https://doi.org/10.1086/498986

Bianet, 2009a. *Cumartesi Anneleri: Fehmi Tosun Nerede?*. Available at: https://bianet.org/haber/cumartesi-anneleri-fehmi-tosun-nerede-112849 (Accessed: 26 February 2025).

Bianet, 2009b. *Cumartesi Anneleri: Devlet Kuyuları Açsın, Karanlığı Yensin.* Available at: https://bianet.org/haber/cumartesi-anneleri-devlet-kuyulari-acsin-karanligi-yensin-112572 (Accessed: 25 February 2025).

Bianet, 2011. Kırbayır'ın İşkencede Öldürüldüğü Meclis Raporuyla Kanıtlandı. *Bianet.* Available at: https://bianet.org/haber/kirbayir-in-iskencede-olduruldugu-meclis-raporuyla-kanitlandi-130236 (Accessed: 26 February 2025).

Bosco, F.J., 2006. The Madres de Plaza de Mayo and three decades of human rights' activism: Embeddedness, emotions, and social movements. *Annals of the Association of American Geographers*, 96, pp. 342–365. https://doi.org/10.1111/j.1467-8306.2006.00481.x

Bozkurt, H. and Kaya, Ö., 2014. *Holding Up the Photograph.* Truth Justice Memory Center. Available at: https://hakikatadalethafiza.org/sites/default/files/2023-01/holding-up-the-photograph.pdf (Accessed: 7 April 2024).

Breen-Smyth, M., 2018. Suffering, victims and survivors in the Northern Ireland conflict: Definitions, policies, and politics. In P. Terhoeven (Ed.), *Victimhood and Acknowledgement.* De Gruyter, pp. 39–58. https://doi.org/10.1515/9783110581508–003

Budak, Y., 2015. Dealing with the past: Transitional justice, ongoing conflict and the Kurdish issue in Turkey. *International Journal of Transitional Justice*, 9(2), pp. 219–238. https://doi.org/10.1093/ijtj/ijv002

Çali, B., 2010. The logics of supranational human rights litigation, official acknowledgment, and human rights reform: The Southeast Turkey cases before the European Court of Human Rights, 1996–2006. *Law & Society Inquiry*, 35, pp. 311–337. https://doi.org/10.1111/j.1747–4469.2010.01187.x

Can, B., 2014. *Making: The Cases of Torture and Enforced Disappearances in Post-1980 Turkey.* PhD thesis, University of Pennsylvania.

de Greiff, P., 2006. Introduction: Repairing the past: Compensation for victims of human rights violations. In *The Handbook of Reparations.* https://doi.org/10.1093/0199291926.001.0001

de Greiff, P., 2012. Theorizing transitional justice. *International Journal of Transitional Justice*, 51, pp. 31–77.

de Greiff, P., 2015. *Statement by Pablo de Greiff, Special Rapporteur on the Promotion of Truth, Justice, Reparation and Guarantees of Non-recurrence at the Human Rights Council Thirtieth Session.* Available at: https://www.ohchr.org/en/statements/2015/09/statement-pablo-de-greiff-special-rapporteur-promotion-truth-justice-reparation (Accessed: 30 January 2023).

Delacroix, D., 2022. Controlling victims: Forced exhumations in the Peruvian Andes. *Peacebuilding*, pp. 1–15. https://doi.org/10.1080/21647259.2022.2098453

Dempster, L., 2019. *Transitional Justice and the "Disappeared" of Northern Ireland: Silence, Memory, and the Construction of the Past.* Routledge.

Dinçer, H., 2020. 90'lardan Bugüne Türkiye'de Cezasızlık Politikalarının Bilançosu: Savaşın Gölgesinde Adalete Bağırmak. *Toplum ve Bilim*, 152, pp. 40–72.

Elvan, G., 2024. *Ocak ve Sebla Arcan anlattı: Cumartesi Anneleri'nin 1000 haftalık eylemi.* Video interview with Ocak, M. and Arcan, S. Available at: https://www.youtube.com/watch?v=DLSV4dJLn9w (Accessed: 22 September 2024).

ETHA, 2019. *En uzun sokluklu mücadele: Kayıplar mücadelesi*. Available at: http://www.etha15.com/haberdetay/en-uzun-sokluklu-mucadele-kayiplar-mucadelesi-104139 (Accessed: 20 September 2021).

Evrensel, 2011. *Kayıplar için bir hakikat komisyonu kurulsun*. Available at: https://www.evrensel.net/haber/96/kayiplar-icin-bir-hakikat-komisyonu-kurulsun (Accessed: 11 January 2020).

Gazete Duvar, 2019. Cumartesi Anneleri: Diyarbakır'daki annelerin acılarını en iyi biz biliriz, *Gazete Duvar*, 14 September. Available at: https://www.gazeteduvar.com.tr/gundem/2019/09/14/cumartesi-anneleri-diyarbakirdaki-annelerin-acilarini-en-iyi-biz-biliriz (Accessed: 12 March 2025).

Göker, Z.G., 2021. Galatasaray Meydanı'nda Vücut Bulan Vicdan ve Adalet: Cumartesi Anneleri/İnsanları. *beyond.istanbul*. Available at: https://medium.com/beyond-istanbul/galatasaray-meydan%C4%B1nda-v%C3%BCcut-bulan-vicdan-ve-adalet-cumartesi-anneleri-i%CC%87nsanlar%C4%B1-73d2ff6bcdf8 (Accessed: 15 June 2024).

Göral, Ö.S., 2019a. *Any Hopes for Truth? A Comparative Analysis of Enforced Disappearances and the Missing in the Middle East, North Africa and the Caucasus*. Truth Justice Memory Center.

Göral, Ö.S., 2019b. İmkansız bir talep olarak adaleti beklemek: Kaybedilenler ve yakınları. In Z.Ö. Biner and Ö. Biner (Eds.), *Beklerken. Zamanın Bilgisi ve Öznenin Dönüşümü*, İletişim, 2019, pp. 45–87.

Göral, Ö.S., 2021. 'Memory as experience in times of perpetual violence: The challenge of Saturday Mothers vis-à-vis cultural aphasia'. *Kurdish Studies*, 9, pp. 77–95. https://doi.org/10.33182/ks.v9i1.569

Göral, Ö.S., Işık, A. and Kaya, Ö., 2013. *The Unspoken Truth: Enforced Disappearances*. Truth Justice Memory Center.

Greeley, R.A., Orwicz, M.R., Falconi, J.L., Reyes, A.M., Rosenberg, F.J. and Laplante, L.J., 2020. Repairing symbolic reparations: Assessing the effectiveness of memorialization in the inter-American system of human rights. *International Journal of Transitional Justice*, 14, pp. 165–192. https://doi.org/10.1093/ijtj/ijaa002

Güngör, D., 2024. 1000 haftadır mücadeleleri sürüyor: Çocuklarımız nerede? *BirGün*.

Hamber, B., 2015. Dealing with painful memories and violent pasts: Towards a framework for contextual understanding. *Transformation of War-Related Identities*. https://doi.org/10.1215/15525864-3637576

Hamber, B. and Wilson, R.A., 2002. Symbolic closure through memory, reparation and revenge in post-conflict societies. *Journal of Human Rights*, 1, pp. 35–53. https://doi.org/10.1080/14754830110111553

İnsan Hakları Derneği, 2015. *Kayıplar Bulunsun, Failler Yargılansın!* Available at: https://www.ihd.org.tr/kayiplar-bulunsun-failler-yargilansin-2/ (Accessed: 17 November 2020).

İnsanHakları Derneği Diyarbakır, 2020. *Ülkenin en uzun sivil itaatsizlik eylemini gerçekleştiren kayıp yakınları ile insan hakları savunucularının yegane talepleri* [. . .]. Available at: https://twitter.com/amedihd/status/1291437130066137091 (Accessed: 22 August 2021) .

İnsanHakları Derneği Diyarbakır, 2023. Available at: https://www.gazeteduvar.com.tr/ihd-diyarbakir-yuzlesme-ve-hakikatleri-arastirma-komisyonu-kurulsun-haber-1618942

Interview no:2, Interview by Author, 2019.

Interview no:3, Interview by Author, 2019.

Interview no:13, Interview by Author, 2019.

Interview no:15, Interview by Author, 2020.

Interview no:16, Interview by Author, 2020.

Interview no:19, Interview by Author, 2020.

Interview no:20, Interview by Author, 2020.

Interview no:21, Interview by Author, 2020.

Interview no:22, Interview by Author, 2020.
Interview no:23, Interview by Author, 2020.
Jongerden, J., 2017. Looking beyond the state: Transitional justice and the Kurdish issue in Turkey. *Ethnic and Racial Studies*, pp. 1–18. https://doi.org/10.1080/01419870.2017.1330486
Karaman, E.R., 2016. Remember, S/he was here once: Mothers call for justice and Peace in Turkey. *Journal of Middle East Women's Studies*, 12 (£), pp. 382–410.
Kaya, Ö., 2012. *The Saturday Mothers of Cizre in Their 100th Week*. Available at: https://hakikatadalethafiza.org/en/1003/ (Accessed: 20 October 2022).
Kaya, Ö., Acar, Y.G., Agar, C.C. and Neville, F., 2024. Resistance from generation to generation: The Saturday Mothers in Istanbul. *Journal of Community & Applied Social Psychology*, 34, p. e2843. https://doi.org/10.1002/casp.2843
Kinder, E., 2021. Non-recurrence, reconciliation, and transitional justice: Situating accountability in Northern Ireland's oral history archive. *International Journal of Human Rights*, 25, pp. 509–528. https://doi.org/10.1080/13642987.2020.1746649
Kodikara, C., 2023. The office on missing persons in Sri Lanka: Why truth is a radical proposition. *International Journal of Transitional Justice*, 17, pp. 15–31. https://doi.org/10.1093/ijtj/ijac025
Kurban, D., 2014. *Europe as an Agent of Change*. The Role of the European Court of Human Rights and the EU in Turkey's Kurdish Policies, SWP Research Paper. Stiftung Wissenschaft und Politik (SWP).
Kurban, D., 2020. *Limits of Supranational Justice: The European Court of Human Rights and Turkey's Kurdish Conflict*. Cambridge: Cambridge University Press. https://doi.org/10.1017/9781108776585
McDowell, S. and Braniff, M., 2014. *Commemoration as Conflict: Space, Memory and Identity in Peace Processes*. Basingstoke: Palgrave Macmillan.
Nora, P., 1989. Between memory and history: Les Lieux de Memoire. *Representations*, 26, pp. 7–24.
Personal communication with Sebla Arcan, 28 December 2024.
Pişkin, T., 2018. *Cumartesi Anneleri/İnsanları'nın Devletin "Gücüyle" 700 Haftalık İmtihanı*. Available at: https://bianet.org/yazi/cumartesi-anneleri-insanlari-nin-devletin-gucuyle-700-haftalik-imtihani-200259 (Accessed: 12 April 2024).
Sarkin, J., 2016. Refocusing transitional justice to focus not only on the past, but also to concentrate on ongoing conflicts and enduring human rights crises. *Journal of International Humanitarian Legal Studies*, 7, pp. 294–329. https://doi.org/10.1163/18781527–00702002
Sebla Arcan ile "Niçin Kayıplar Mücadelesi?" 2022. *İnsan Hakları Okulu*. Available at: https://www.insanhaklariokulu.org/sebla-arcan-ile-nicin-kayiplar-mucadelesi-youtube-kanalimizda/
Sevimli, E.A., Kiliç, E., Zeren, G., Gebeş, M. and Zıngıl, Ö., 2021. *1990'lı Yıllardaki Ağır İnsan Hakları İhlallerinde Cezasızlık Sorunu: Kovuşturma Süreci*. Available at: https://hakikatadalethafiza.org/sites/default/files/2022-12/cezasizlik_kovusturmasureci.pdf (Accessed: 18 March 2025).
Sezer Şanlı, A., 2018. Yasın Protestoya Dönüşümünü İncelemek: Cumartesi Anneleri Hareketi Örneği. *Uluslararası İnsan Çalışmaları Dergisi*, 1, pp. 1–17. https://doi.org/10.35235/uicd.458095
Shala, N., 2024. *Guarantees of Non-Repetition in International Human Rights Law and Transitional Justice: Building Peace after Conflict*. 1st ed. London: Routledge. https://doi.org/10.4324/9781003458104
Tahincioğlu, G. (host), 2024. Cumartesi Anneleri 1000 Hafta. Guest: Mikail Kirbayir. *Spotify*. Available at: https://open.spotify.com/episode/3NQILYLGmVs63JlG5iGIte?si=8e5997a72db44252 (Accessed: 26 February 2025).

Tanrıkulu, N., 2014. *Galatasaray hafıza, itaatsizlik ve küreselleşmenin mekanı*. Available at: https://m.bianet.org/bianet/insan-haklari/200259-cumartesi-anneleri-insanlari-nin-devletin-gucuyle-700-haftalik-imtihani (Accessed: 22 April 2021).
Thiagarajah, L.G., 2016. *Memorialisation and Reparations: A Report of Four Dialogues*. Available at: https://ices.lk/wp-content/uploads/2017/02/Memorialisation-and-Reparations-Report-of-Dialogues-Book-6th-Proof.pdf (Accessed: 26 August 2021).
TruthJustice Memory Center, 2020. *Galatasaray Square: A Recognized Memory Space*. Available at: https://hakikatadalethafiza.org/en/news/galatasaray-square-recognized-memory-space (Accessed: 26 February 2025).
Türkiye Büyük Millet Meclisi, 2011. *Cemil Kirbayir Raporu*. Available at: http://www.tbmm.gov.tr/komisyon/insanhaklari/docs/2011/cemil_kirbayir_raporu.pdf (Accessed: 10 January 2021).
Uçarlar, N., 2015. *Nothing in Its Right Place. Demands of Justice and Coming to Terms with the Past in the Post-Conflict Period*. DİSA Publications.
United Nations, 2010. *Guidance Note of the Secretary General United Nations Approach to Transitional Justice*. New York: United Nations Secretary General.
Weis, V.V., 2015. The relevance of victim's organizations in transitional justice processes. The case of "Abuelas De Plaza De Mayo" in Argentina. *SSRN Electronic Journal*. https://doi.org/10.2139/ssrn.2688361
Yoleri, G., 2023. *100 yıldan eski bir devlet pratiği: Gözaltında kayıplar*. Available at: https://www.gazeteduvar.com.tr/100-yildan-eski-bir-devlet-pratigi-gozaltinda-kayiplar-haber-1640031 (Accessed: 31 December 2024).
Zeytun, A., 2018. *Koşuyolu Parkı'na 'kayıp yakınları' bariyeri*. Interviewed by Vecdi Erbay, 14 September. Available at: https://www.gazeteduvar.com.tr/gundem/2018/09/14/kosuyolu-parkina-kayip-yakinlari-bariyeri (Accessed: 14 June 2021).

Chapter 7

# Fragmented Transitions

## Civil Society, State Responses, and Transitional Justice in Turkey's Kurdish Conflict

### 7.1 Introduction

Turkey's Kurdish conflict provides a unique lens through which to explore how civil society drives transitional justice efforts, even in the absence of a formal transition. Although no official processes are in place, a multitude of grassroots initiatives make Turkey an insightful case study of "transitional justice in non-transitions" (Hansen, 2017). This chapter examines how civil society actors have employed the tools of transitional justice to address the Kurdish conflict despite the lack of a peace process and in the face of growing authoritarianism. It also reveals the interplay between bottom-up advocacy and top-down responses.

Focusing on two pivotal developments in the past two decades, the Truth and Justice Commission for the Diyarbakır Prison and the Apology for the Dersim Massacre, the chapter highlights how both measures, although originating from different ends of the spectrum (one led by civil society and the other initiated by the prime minister), were ultimately propelled by sustained activism and advocacy efforts from lawyers, human rights advocates, and activists (including the Saturday Mothers) most affected by the conflict. These efforts prompted both public discourse and official engagement.

By examining these two processes, the chapter sheds light on Turkey's fragmented transitional justice landscape, identifying what has been achieved and what remains absent. In doing so, it deepens our understanding of the dynamic relationship between grassroots mobilisation and state-level actions in confronting the country's troubled past.

### 7.2 The Truth and Justice Commission for the Diyarbakır Prison

A truth commission as a truth-recovery mechanism has been the civil society's most demanded transitional justice mechanism in Turkey (Baser, 2017). Various actors, including civil society professionals, victim and survivor groups, human rights defenders, and politicians, have frequently demanded the establishment of a truth commission, while journalists and commentators

DOI: 10.4324/9781003432579-7

widely wrote about the benefits of establishing one (Hamsici, 2013; Işık, 2011; (Serhat, 2021). Several NGOs organised events and invited foreign experts to discuss truth commissions from a comparative perspective (Truth Justice Memory Centre, 2011). Opposition parties also addressed the need for a truth commission to resolve the conflict, and even some members of the ruling party expressed their support for such a commission.

The prominence of the demand for a truth commission was also apparent in the 2015 *Newroz* celebrations in Diyarbakır, showing that truth-recovery is key to transitional justice imaginaries in Turkey (Daloglu, 2013).[1] The celebrations took place while the peace process was ongoing, and hopes were still high for continuing the process. The imprisoned PKK leader Abdullah Öcalan's message was read to over one million attendees (Evrensel, 2015). His message included the proposal for establishing a truth and reconciliation commission (AGOS, 2015). Öcalan has been the most influential political figure in the Kurdish movement (Gerber and Brincat, 2021). He was also the leading actor shaping the peace process and mapping out Kurdish aspirations. His Newroz message came only one month after the Dolmabahçe Declaration, which was released by a joint press statement by the parties to the peace process. It was the first time a mutually agreed road map was announced regarding resolving the Kurdish conflict (Çiçek and Coşkun, 2016). In his message, Öcalan referred to the Declaration and pointed at the truth commission as an initial step ahead. Although the state officials did not make calls for a truth commission explicit, it was clear that this message could not be sent without the government's knowledge and approval. Therefore, reading the message to large crowds meant that all sides of the peace talks had agreed on a truth commission to be established as an essential step ahead. The peace process collapsed a couple of months after the declaration; thus, the agreed steps have never materialised. However, it is remarkable how many actors have raised the demands for a truth commission.

My interviews demonstrate that a state-led, truth-seeking process would represent an official willingness to acknowledge the past state violence, ensure the public recognition of the state violence, and pave the way to end the impunity (Interview no:3; Interview no:14; Interview no:22). The Truth and Justice Commission for Diyarbakır Prison emerged in the absence of an official mechanism and served as a concrete example of how transitional justice can be pursued, even to some extent in an ongoing conflict. Having worked between 2007 and 2012, this unofficial, civil society-led truth commission

1 Newroz is a traditional Kurdish celebration of the spring. It has acquired a political significance and has been associated with the resistance of the Kurdish people. After a week of celebrations in different cities, the final and largest celebration is organised in Diyarbakır on 21 March each year, where political representatives and activists from the Kurdish political movement attend and give speeches.

demonstrated a proactive approach to achieving justice and truth without relying on the state.

On the 27th anniversary of the military coup of September 12, 1980, the 78'ers Initiative,[2] together with a group of activists, academics, lawyers, human rights defenders, and psychologists, established the Truth and Justice Commission for Diyarbakır Prison (the 'Commission') (Önderoğlu, 2010; Türker, 2008). The Commission was the first instance of a specific tool for TJ in Turkey, aiming at 'facing the truth' as the initial step towards democratisation and conflict resolution (Truth and Justice Commission for Diyarbakır Prison, 2009). Commission members believed that if democratisation and resolution of the conflict were genuinely demanded, "facing the truth" should be the first step, and Diyarbakır Military Prison (DMP) held a unique and critical place in that truth (The Truth and Justice Commission for Diyarbakır Prison, 2009).

The DMP was infamous for severe human rights violations, including systematic sexualised torture and ill-treatment committed against thousands of Kurdish political prisoners in the aftermath of the 1980 military coup. Due to its role in radicalising large numbers of Kurds who later joined the PKK, the prison holds a key place in the Kurdish collective memory and resistance (Zeydanlıoğlu, 2009). Commission members expressed that what happened in the DMP contributed significantly to the ongoing conflict, explicitly highlighting that many ex-prisoners 'went up to the mountain'.[3] They also noted that in Kurds' collective memory, the prison held a painful place, whereas, in the rest of Turkey, what happened in prison and its consequences were not much known (Türker, 2008). Therefore, they articulated the commission's objectives as initiating a judicial process for human rights violations committed between 1980–1984 in prison, starting a process of revealing the truth and confronting the past, and transforming the prison into a museum that would function as a memory site (CNN Türk, 2010). The Commission's objectives, therefore, aligned and sought to pave the way for justice, truth, and memorialisation.

Especially in countries where there has been little or no meaningful accountability or transitional justice process, grassroots actors try to challenge the governments' "amnesiac tendencies" through engaging in truth projects (McAuliffe, 2019). In such contexts where official truth commissions are not feasible due to political constraints, civil-society-led, unofficial truth projects could constitute viable alternatives (Bickford, 2007). Although official truth commissions may be more likely to bring about country-wide dialogue processes about the past, grassroots unofficial truth projects have

2 78'er Initiative comprises a group of activists from the 78s generation, the term used to broadly refer to left-wing activists who experienced the 1980 military coup.

3 "Going up to the mountain" refers to taking up arms and joining the PKK forces located in the mountains.

their own strengths. They can be perceived by community as more legitimate interlocutors and therefore deliver truth-telling more efficiently. They may also challenge the official truth projects' tendency to instrumentalise victim experience and rely on international templates (McAuliffe, 2019).

The Truth and Justice Commission for the Diyarbakır Prison is an example of unofficial truth projects, such as *Brasil: Nunca Mais* (Brazil, Never Again), The Ardoyne Community Project from Northern Ireland, The Greensboro Truth and Community Reconciliation Project from the United States, and SERAJ from Uruguay, which share similar characteristics to official truth commissions, despite lacking some key features such as bureaucratic structure and state support (Bickford, 2007).

The Commission was established "to set an example of this structure (truth commissions), which has significant effects on healing the wounds of society and restoring its functionality" (The Truth and Justice Commission for the Diyarbakır Prison, 2011). The Commission members also confirmed in a 2009 manifesto that "they worked like a type of an unofficial truth commission for two years" (The Truth and Justice Commission for the Diyarbakır Prison, 2009). Not only did the members portray their work as such, but the Commission's goals and activities also mimicked those of official truth commissions. The following speech by the 78'er Initiative demonstrates that the activists were deliberate in their attempt to create a truth commission in Turkey similar to the international examples:

> The Truth and Justice Commission for the Diyarbakır Prison is a civil society movement, and it does not have any ties to any political parties. It is not at all a judicial body. They [truth commissions] have been established under different names worldwide in the countries where military coups took place. Its aim is not to take revenge but to ensure the law's goal is achieved and justice is delivered by revealing the truth. It will be one of the founding stones on the way toward peace by healing the trauma created in that period. Trauma makes people muted. Our commission aims at creating an atmosphere for the victims to become unmuted and re-establish their word.
>
> (Türker, 2008)

The Commission's activities between 2007–2011 were very much aligned with how official truth commissions work worldwide. Through in-depth interviews conducted both in Kurdish cities and western Turkey, it collected testimonies from nearly 500 ex-prisoners, mostly Kurds, all of whom survived and witnessed different forms of constant torture during their time in prison. Celalettin Can, a prominent activist from the 78'er Initiative and a former prisoner in the DMP, played an active role in identifying and having initial conversations with former prisoners he was in touch with (Can, 2022b).

The Commission was fully independent, both in its decision-making and financing. To provide a full and objective account of the human rights violations in the prison, they conducted interviews with members of different political groups, without prioritising any specific group (Can, 2022b). As opposed to relying on donor grants, the Commission's work was self-financed through the members' own resources, solidarity networks, the support of the local community (for example, by arranging accommodation for commission members), and local municipalities' support (such as by providing meeting venues for free) (Can, 2022b).

Drawing on 800 hours of torture survivor testimonies, 466 forensic medical forms, and 450 trauma test forms, the Commission put together a 7,000-page-long document (Andaolu Kültür, 2010; Truth and Justice Commission for Diyarbakir Prison, 2011). In 2012, the Commission released its Final Report, which was based on first-hand accounts of systematic torture. The report identified military officers alleged to be the perpetrators and detailed the physical and psychological impact of torture on the prisoners.[4] One of the most striking findings was that, even 30 years after their release from prison, 15% of the interviewees still experienced post-traumatic stress disorder, and 71% continued to suffer from torture-related health issues (Truth and Justice Commission for Diyarbakir Prison, 2011).

The Commission's findings from a sociological, psychological, and legal perspective were also shared with the public through the "Turkey is confronting its past" symposiums in Diyarbakir, Ankara, and Istanbul (Bianet, 2011). These symposiums were covered widely in the media and facilitated the dissemination of the commission's findings to society. The symposiums, therefore, were influential in responding to a problem identified by the commission: that society knew little about the human rights violations committed in the DMP. The symposiums provided a platform for torture survivors, who were eager to publicly share their experiences and the meaning of what happened to them (Gülsen, 2022). In addition to playing a critical role in making the survivors' experiences public knowledge, they also delivered a healing impact by openly recognising their experience with an audience of politicians, activists, journalists, and academics (Diken, 2010; Gülsen, 2022).

In the Istanbul symposium organised in 2011, Commission members shared recommendations including a Parliamentary Inquiry, broad social dissemination of findings, prosecution and removal of de facto immunity for perpetrators, artistic works, support for victims (i.e. physical and psychological

4 During and after my PhD research, I have tried to access this long document and get a hold of the original and detailed findings, thinking it would add more layers to future studies. Other researchers and practitioners who work on the topic have also failed to reach the document. The risks of revealing such a document to public in politically sensitive times brings with risks. I hope one day the socio-political circumstances allow for public access to this document so that the Commission's thoughtful and valuable findings can be learned from.

rehabilitation), compensation, a human rights and memory museum, and resolution of the Turkish-Kurdish issue on the basis of justice, equality, and democracy (Truth and Justice Commission for Diyarbakır Prison, 2011).

Following on the recommendations, in 2009 the Commission began to focus primarily on campaigning for transforming the prison into a human rights museum. By 2013, the campaign had gathered 100,000 signatures, which were presented to the government and the parties in the parliament (Meryem, 2018). While the Commission was still operating in 2010, then-prime minister Recep Tayyip Erdoğan made a speech in Diyarbakır addressing the torture committed in the DMP. He announced that the government wanted to dismantle the old prison's premises and construct a new one to delete the painful memory of the 1980 military coup (Karakaş, 2016). His speech was unprecedented in recognising the legacy of the DMP at the highest level. However, his approach to memory contradicted the grassroots actors' demands for building a memory site. The government's response to such demands at the time often included acknowledging past violations while rejecting memorialisation demands. More recently, in 2021, during a visit to Diyarbakir, Erdoğan said that the DMP would be turned into a cultural centre. While not clarifying what a cultural centre would entail, his speech was met with mixed reactions. Some welcomed the decision as a step toward dealing with the past, while some considered it an attempt to erase the memory (McKernan, 2021).

In late 2015, the Parliament acted on one of the other recommendations of the Commission and launched a parliamentary investigative commission under the Human Rights Inquiry Committee. "The sub-commission to investigate the Diyarbakir Prison Nr. 5 established after the 12 September military coup" was proposed by Orhan Miroğlu, an AKP parliamentarian, and a former prisoner in the DMP. The HDP and CHP supported his proposal, and the sub-commission started its work under Miroğlu as the head of the commission in early 2016. He stated that the victims' demands for memorialisation and dealing with the past were among the commission's objectives (Karabağlı, 2015).[5] The sub-commission members decided to investigate the period that started with the state of emergency rule in Diyarbakir on 24/4/1979 and ended on 31/12/1984.

It was the first time the DMP was subject to an official public investigation. The proposal text for the sub-commission included commitments to certain transitional justice goals, such as developing reparative justice mechanisms for victims and coming to terms with past trauma and suffering. It stated that drawing on torture victims' testimonies, the sub-commission's goal was to publish a comprehensive report to share its findings with the public, the

5 MHP, ultra nationalist political party was the only party that did not support and therefore did not give any members to this sub-commission.

parliament, and various public bodies (Karabağlı, 2015). It was remarkable that the parliamentarians from different political parties explicitly committed to such goals, even though they did not expressly refer to TJ transitional justice. The sub-commission was established a only a few months after the peace process collapsed, and thus discourse on dealing with the past was still popular. In their first meeting, Miroğlu indicated that to understand why the Kurdish conflict moved into a ground of terror and violence, there was a need for genuine confrontation with the DMP (Karabağlı, 2017). Connecting the issue with the "terrorism problem" provided a legitimate reason for such a commission to be supported. Moreover, the DMP was a product of the 1980 coup d'etat, and the political parties, including the AKP, had a firm position against military coups. That was another factor that provided the sub-commission with legitimacy.

Until September 2017, when it finished its work in an unsatisfactory manner, the sub-commission held hearings and listened to the testimonies of more than 30 torture survivors and a former prison officer, who had been previously sentenced for his involvement in torture. In that period the sub-commission was criticised for failing to work closely with civil society organisations working on the issue (Gülsen, 2022). Anadolu Agency, the state-sponsored media agency, assisted the sub-commission in media reviewing. When the government decided to call an early election in 2018, the work of parliamentary commissions was put on hold. The sub-commission's 50-page report was completed and shared with all commission members. However, the launch of the report was suspended, and it has never been shared with the public. Miroğlu stated that the report is still held in the archives of the Human Rights Inquiry Committee in the parliament, and it could be shared publicly if there is a favourable political climate (Rûpela Nû, 2021). The failure to disseminate the report resulted in a limited impact (Daşlı and Murphy, 2024).

In line with the recommendation for "prosecution and removal of de facto immunity for perpetrators", the Commission was committed to securing justice for victims. With the help of the data collected by the commission, 310 ex-prisoners filed a criminal complaint to the Diyarbakır Chief Public Prosecutor's Office in 2010. The Commission members made a press statement on behalf of the applicants, demanding that the human rights violations committed in the DMP should be treated as crimes against humanity, and the perpetrators should be punished accordingly. Following that day, a criminal process started investigating the 1980–1988 period in the DMP, and the number of applicants had risen to 1,000 by 2012 (Sabah, 2012). In what was an unprecedented attempt to hold the torture perpetrators accountable, the prosecutor started investigating the civil servants and military personnel who worked in the DMP at the time, but such efforts were ultimately futile. After the collapse of the peace process, the prosecutor was moved to a different city, and then the investigation was dismissed because of the statute of limitations (Can, 2022a). The Truth and Justice Commission for the Diyarbakır

Prison is highly important in demonstrating how civil society-led initiatives can contribute to truth, justice and memorialisation during an ongoing conflict and prompt change at the grassroots and official levels. The work of the Commission on truth, justice, and memory pillars enabled the official recognition of human rights violations in the DMP in an unprecedented manner. The campaign succeeded in sparking a vibrant public discourse and prompting official action, thus amplifying the potential of civil society-led truth projects to challenge state policies of denial and impunity. However, the initially expanded space gradually diminished, and despite the vocal civil society campaign, the demands remained unfulfilled.

The Commission's work is remarkable not only because it demonstrates civil society's eagerness to take the lead in dealing with the past in the absence of a peace process but also because it occurred during a period more conducive to such efforts, contrasting with the current authoritarian context. Celalettin Can confirms that they worked in a relatively relaxed environment reaching to a wide audience, including the government officials (Can, 2022b).

In transitional justice research, there is an ongoing debate about how to assess the impact and effectiveness of truth commissions (Bakiner, 2013; Ferrara, 2019; Hirsch et al., 2012) with an emphasis on the need for a long-term perspective to evaluate these commissions' institutional, social, and political changes (Brahm, 2007). While these discussions primarily focus on official truth commissions, the same need applies to unofficial mechanisms. However, assessing the long-term impact of unofficial transitional justice initiatives presents additional challenges.

Because the Commission took place in a context of non-transition and was not accompanied by complementary transitional justice measures, nor was its report made public, its effectiveness in fostering healing, justice, and recognition for survivors of human rights violations in the DMP remains uncertain. The lack of a published report complicates transparency and makes it difficult to follow up with participants or conduct a long-term study on its impact. Moreover, in contexts where a broader transitional justice framework is weak or non-existent, those who testify before an unofficial truth commission are less likely to receive long-term psychosocial support or compensation. This lack of sustained care makes it even more challenging to reconnect with participants and evaluate the commission's effects on issues that are deeply personal, sensitive, and potentially retraumatising.

## 7.3 Apology for the Dersim Massacre

The Truth and Justice Commission for the Diyarbakır Prison is emblematic of civil society-led transitional justice mechanisms without an official transitional justice process. Another transitional justice attempt from the same era was Erdoğan's Dersim Apology. This came from the top down. A massive military operation took place in 1937–1938 in the Dersim region, populated mostly by Kurdish-Alevi citizens. It resulted in the death of approximately 14,000 civilians and the forced displacement of 12,000 people (Dinç, 2021). The official discourse saw the massacre as the state's legitimate self-defence against an uprising (Ayata and Hakyemez, 2013). In 2009, for the first time, Erdoğan referred to the "Dersim Massacre" during his parliamentary speech, symbolising a paradigm shift in the official narrative (Ayata and Hakyemez, 2013). A public discussion followed the speech, focusing on what happened in 1938, and "the silence about Dersim cracked at the official level" (Ayata and Hakyemez, 2013, p. 137). From that moment, various scholars and cultural works engaged with what happened in Dersim. Civil society organisations carried out memorialisation activities and ran panels and festivals gathering a wider audience and media attention than in previous years (Dinç, 2021).

Erdoğan's partial apology for the 1938 Dersim Massacre came on 23 November 2011, when he referred to what happened in Dersim as the most tragic event in our history. Demonstrating his awareness about state apologies, he said: "I shall apologise, and I am apologising if there is a need for apology on behalf of the state and if there is a [state apology] literature as such" (BBC Turkce, 2011). It was the first time in Turkey's history that a head of state declared that he would apologise for a past atrocity (Ayata and Hakyemez, 2013; Bakiner, 2013; Dinç, 2021). Erdoğan wanted to be seen as the one who shifted the state discourse from denial to reconciliation by publicly addressing official taboos (Ayata and Hakyemez, 2013). Indeed, a few months before the apology, he had claimed that his government had ended the denialist politics (Dinç, 2021). Erdoğan's half-hearted, reluctant, and conditional apology was a calculated political move to further the state agenda (Dinç, 2021) and distinguish his government from the official state narrative.

Erdoğan's apology sparked social mobilisation. For example, İHD immediately released a statement referring to Erdoğan's apology as a historical moment and starting point to be followed by a set of other crucial steps: an official apology, compensation to be paid to the victims' families, and a broader process to deal with the past (İHD, 2011). The statement included a detailed proposal for a truth commission for Turkey to deal with the past. Moreover, public campaigns were launched to replace the name of the second busiest airport in Istanbul, named after Turkey's first female war pilot, Sabiha Gökçen. She took part in the carpet-bombing of Dersim (Bakiner, 2013).

Furthermore, the survivors of the massacre sent hundreds of petitions to the parliament's Petition Committee, demanding a written apology, the return of the seized property, a museum dedicated to the victims, the opening of archives, and an investigation commission. The Petition Committee considered the demands to some extent and established "the sub-commission for repairing the victimisations that emerged during and after Dersim Incidents" in 2012. It was set up under the Petition Committee, which raised serious concerns about its effectiveness and capacity to conduct efficient investigations (Truth Justice Memory Centre, 2013). This sub-commission could be seen as "the first truth-commission-like entity in Turkey's human rights history" (Bakiner, 2013, p. 702). It was mandated to provide policy recommendations, but not to provide any compensation. It collected testimonies from victims, survivors, and the families of the victims, as well as gathering documents from military archives and the prime minister's office (Evrensel, 2012). However, the collected data has not led to a thorough investigation process. In parallel to the sub-commission on the DMP, the sub-commission on the Dersim Massacre did not pave the way for a broader attempt or concrete measures to deal with the past. It failed to address the survivors' demands in the petition such as finding out the locations of the graves, compensation of material losses, and dedicating resources to make documentaries. The sub-commission remained an incomplete effort.

A satisfactory official apology should meet three categories: framing, content, and future commitments (Verdeja, 2010). The first category relates to how, where, and by whom the apology is extended. The framing seems appropriate in the case of Erdoğan's Dersim speech, as it came from the head of state and was widely disseminated by the media. This assured "that the acknowledgment given to victims is shown to the broader public as well, signalling to the entire population the state's admission of crimes and its commitment to a new relationship to its citizens" (Verdeja, 2010, p. 571). However, the second criterion, content, was not fulfilled because the apology did not provide a full account of what exactly happened, nor did it entail a detailed analysis of how and why the massacre occurred. Instead, Erdoğan referred to it with rather broad terms such as "one of the most tragic and painful events in our recent history" (BBC Türkçe, 2011). An apology should also include some reflection about the social and moral outcomes of the act and explicitly indicate the state's responsibility (Verdeja, 2010). Instead of taking full responsibility on behalf of the state, Erdoğan pointed to a different perpetrator. He referred to the CHP as the responsible party and argued that "it is not the AKP government who needs to apologise" (BBC Türkçe, 2011). In the rest of the speech, he pointed at the opposition leader Kemal Kılıçdaroğlu[6] as the one who must apologise. The intention was to undermine Kılıçdaroğlu's political power as his immediate political rival, and challenge Kemalist ideology.

The final criterion for a satisfactory apology "concerns implicit and explicit commitments to the future" (Verdeja, 2010, p. 571). Commitment refers to material reparation as well as symbolic recognition. For an apology

6 Kılıçdaroğlu's party, the Republican People Party (*Cumhuriyet Halk Partisi*), is known to be representing the founding ideology of the state, Kemalism, and it was in power during the Dersim Massacre. AKP, at least on the discursive level, built itself against Kemalism.

to be considered complete and satisfactory by a majority of the victims, it has to be part of a larger package that includes an official commitment to policy changes and legal and other measures to eliminate impunity and guarantees for accountability (Lundy and Rolston, 2016). By extending the apology, Erdoğan fulfilled the symbolic aspect to a certain extent. However, although followed by a sub-commission, the apology failed to commit to the other elements. It led neither to a fully-fledged truth commission or parliamentary commission nor was it complemented by other measures such as reparations (Bakiner, 2013; Dinç, 2021). It was also not followed by any measures of accountability. However, despite all the failures, Erdoğan's apology had a healing impact on the Dersim community (Dinç, 2021).

On 28 December 2011, only a month after Erdoğan's apology, another massacre was added to the lengthy list of atrocities. Turkish warplanes bombed 34 Kurdish civilians in the Roboski province of Şırnak. The continued state violence against Kurds made it difficult to believe that the state was ready to reckon with its past. Erdoğan's apology was not followed by a genuine effort to deal with the past that enabled the massacre. Therefore, the Kurds perceived the apology as a politically motivated manoeuvre aimed at increasing electoral support (Çelik, 2021). It was seen as an attempt by Erdoğan's government to signal a willingness to confront the past while simultaneously constructing a new truth regime by reshaping the official narrative (Ayata and Hakyemez, 2013).

## 7.4 Conclusion

Civil society organisations, victim and survivor groups, lawyers, and activists have spearheaded efforts to address past injustices and implement transitional justice in Turkey. Grassroots transitional justice initiatives have much potential for driving a transitional justice agenda even in the absence of state-led processes, as it also applies in other cases (Durdiyeva, 2023). These bottom-up initiatives, focused on accountability and recognition, pressured the government into reluctantly adopting a limited transitional justice discourse and taking some concrete steps towards recognition. However, these actions were arguably driven by pragmatic reasons, primarily aligning with the political agenda of the time.

Analysing the grassroots actors' achievements using a transitional justice lens, even if actors do not always use this terminology, shows that there is a wealth of experience that could prove useful when the political conditions are more favourable to implement a fully-fledged set of transitional justice mechanisms. It is important to recognise the significant differences between the past and present socio-political contexts, which the next section explores in greater detail. When the two cases analysed in this chapter occurred, the armed conflict was ongoing, and no comprehensive official transitional justice framework was in place. Nonetheless, the political climate was more receptive to initiatives that brought past atrocities and crimes into public debate. The government at the time sought to distance itself from previous regimes by condemning them and challenging their legacy of denial and silence, as part of its effort to consolidate power. In recent years, shifting government priorities have moved transitional justice further from the political agenda. This change has also influenced the transitional justice visions and activities of civil society. The next section sheds light on this change.

## Reference List

AGOS, 2015. *Öcalan's Newroz Message: I Call Upon the PKK to Hold Congress*. Available at: http://www.agos.com.tr/en/article/10963/ocalans-newroz-message-i-call-upon-the-pkk-to-hold-congress (Accessed: 17 October 2021).

Anadolu Kültür, 2010. *Sivil Toplumun Kürt Sorununun Çözümüne Etkin Katılımı İçin Kapasite Geliştirme*. Available at: https://hakikatadalethafiza.org/kaynak/sivil-toplumun-kurt-sorununun-cozumune-etkin-katilimi-icin-kapasite-gelistirme-projesi-stk-gorusmeleri-raporu/ (Accessed: 22 March 2022).

Ayata, B. and Hakyemez, S., 2013. The AKP's engagement with Turkey's past crimes: An analysis of PM Erdoğan's "Dersim apology". *Dialectical Anthropology*, 37, pp. 131–143. https://doi.org/10.1007/s10624-013-9304-3

Bakiner, O., 2013. Is Turkey coming to terms with its past? Politics of memory and majoritarian conservatism. *Nationalities Papers*, 41, pp. 691–708. https://doi.org/10.1080/00905992.2013.770732

Baser, B., 2017. Intricacies of engaging diasporas in conflict resolution and transitional justice: The Kurdish diaspora and the peace process in Turkey. *Civil Wars*, 19, pp. 470–494. https://doi.org/10.1080/13698249.2017.1396528

BBC Türkçe, 2011. *Basbakan Erdogan'dan Dersim ozru*. Available at: https://www.bbc.com/turkce/haberler/2011/11/111123_dersim (Accessed: 4 April 2021).

Bianet, 2011. *Yüzleşme Sırası İstanbul'da*. Available at: https://bianet.org/bianet/bilim/134378-yuzlesme-sirasi-istanbul-da (Accessed: 9 April 2022).

Bickford, L., 2007. Unofficial truth projects. *Human Rights Quarterly*, 29, pp. 994–1035. https://doi.org/10.1353/hrq.2007.0036

Brahm, E., 2007. Uncovering the truth: Examining truth commission success and impact. *International Studies Perspectives*, 8, pp. 16–35.

Can, C., 2022a. Bir daha asla!" diyebilmek için... Diyarbakır 5 No'lu Askeri Cezaeviyıkılmasın! İnsan Hakları Müzesi olsun! *Independent Türkçe*. Available at: https://www.indyturk.com/node/498971/t%C3%BCrki%CC%87yeden-sesler/bir-daha-asla-diyebilmek-i%C3%A7in%E2%80%A6-diyarbak%C4%B1r-5-nolu-askeri-cezaevi (Accessed: 7 May 2022).

Can, C., 2022b. Diyarbakır Askeri Cezaevi anlatılmaz, yaşanır. *Memorialize Turkey*. Available at: https://memorializeturkey.com/tr/celalettin-can (Accessed: 14 September 2024).

Çelik, A.B., 2021. Inclusive citizenship and societal reconciliation within Turkey's Kurdish issue. *Southeast European and Black Sea Studies*, 21, pp. 313–332. https://doi.org/10.1080/14683857.2021.1909284

Çiçek, C. and Coşkun, V., 2016. *The Peace Process from Dolmabahçe to Present-Day: Understanding Failure and Finding New Paths*. Istanbul: Peace Foundation. Available at: https://tr.boell.org/sites/default/files/ingilizce.pdf (Accessed: 17 December 2021).

CNN Türk, 2010. *Diyarbakır Cezaevi için toplu suç duyurusu*. Available at: https://www.cnnturk.com/2010/turkiye/10/11/diyarbakir.cezaevi.icin.toplu.suc.duyurusu/592627.0/index.html (Accessed: 10 December 2021).

Daloglu, T., 2013. *Turkish Reconciliation Commission Gains Key Parliamentary Support*. Available at: https://www.al-monitor.com/originals/2013/04/bdp-parliamentary-commissionnazmi-gur-turkey-erdogan.html (Accessed: 16 July 2021).
Daşlı, G. and Murphy, E., 2024. Moving beyond binary identities in transitional justice: Recognising the complexity of agency in agonistic spaces. *International Journal of Human Rights*, pp. 1–20. https://doi.org/10.1080/13642987.2024.2430288
Diken, Ş., 2010. Bir Hafıza Anıtı, Diyarbakır 5 Nolu'ya Dair! *Bianet*. Available at: https://m.bianet.org/bianet/insan-haklari/125174-bir-hafiza-aniti-diyarbakir-5-nolu-ya-dair (Accessed: 7 November 2021).
Dinç, P., 2021. Dersim 1937–1938: Shifts and continuities in the state discourse and reasoning under Kemalism and Erdoğanism. In *The Kurds in Erdogan's "New" Turkey*. Routledge.
Durdiyeva, S., 2023. Role of civil society in transitional justice: The case of Russia. In *Transitional Justice*. Oxon: Routledge. https://doi.org/10.4324/9781003293873
Evrensel, 2012. *Dersim belgeleri Meclis'te*. Available at: https://www.evrensel.net/haber/24874/dersim-belgeleri-mecliste (Accessed: 10 October 2021).
Evrensel, 2015. *Tarihi 2015 Diyarbakir Newroz'u*. Available at: https://www.evrensel.net/fotograf/128/tarihi-2015-diyarbakir-newrozu (Accessed: 13 March 2021).
Ferrara, A., 2019. Assessing the long-term impact and legacy of truth commissions. In J. Sarkin (Ed.), *The Global Impact and Legacy of Truth Commissions*, Series on Transitional Justice. Intersentia, pp. 75–98. https://doi.org/10.1017/9781780687957.003
Gerber, D. and Brincat, S., 2021. When Öcalan met Bookchin: The Kurdish freedom movement and the political theory of democratic confederalism. *Geopolitics*, 26(4), 973–997.
Gülsen, E., 2022. *Restorative Role of Public Memorials and Memorialization after the Periods of Violence and Oppression: The Case of Turkey*. PhD thesis. Middle East Technical University, Social Sciences Institute. Available at: https://open.metu.edu.tr/handle/11511/95247 (Accessed: 26 February 2025).
Hamsici, M., 2013. *Barışa Giden Yol'da 'hakikat ve uzlaşma'*. Available at: https://www.bbc.com/turkce/haberler/2013/01/130121_peace_process_11_southafrica (Accessed: 20 July 2021).
Hansen, T., 2017. The time and space of transitional justice. In C. Lawther, L. Moffett, and D. Jacobs (Eds.), *Research Handbook on Transitional Justice*. UK: Edward Elgar Publishing, pp. 34–51.
Hirsch, M.B.-J., MacKenzie, M. and Sesay, M., 2012. Measuring the impacts of truth and reconciliation commissions: Placing the global 'success' of TRCs in local perspective. *Cooperation and Conflict*, 47, pp. 386–403. https://doi.org/10.1177/0010836712454273
Interview no:3, Interview by Author, 2019.
Interview no:14, Interview by Author, 2020.
Interview no:22, Interview by Author, 2020.
Işık, S., 2011. *Hakikat Komisyonu Kurulurken*. Available at: https://m.bianet.org/bianet/siyaset/134431-hakikat-komisyonu-kurulurken (Accessed: 12 October 2021).
İnsan Hakları Derneği, 2011. *Dersim katliami icin ozur dilemek bir baslangictir*. Available at: https://www.ihd.org.tr/ba20111125a/ (Accessed: 17 March 2021).
Karabağlı, H., 2015. TBMM'de dönemin işkenceleriyle ünlü Diyarbakır 5 No'lu Cezaevi ile ilgili alt komisyon kuruldu. *T24*. Available at: https://t24.com.tr/haber/tbmmde-donemin-iskenceleriyle-unlu-diyarbakir-5-nolu-cezaevi-ile-ilgili-alt-komisyon-kuruldu,320748 (Accessed: 15 March 2022).
Karabağlı, H., 2017. TBMM Diyarbakır 5 No'lu Cezaevi Alt Komisyonu dağılıyor: Dışarıdan bir itibarsızlaştırma yaşadık. *T24*. Available at: https://t24.com.tr/haber/tbmm-diyarbakir-5-nolu-cezaevi-alt-komisyonu-dagiliyor-disaridan-bir-itibarsizlastirma-yasadik,442427 (Accessed: 22 May 2023).

Karakaş, B., 2016. Hani Diyarbakır Cezaevi müze olacaktı? *P24*. Available at: http://platform24.org/yazarlar/1922/hani-diyarbakir-cezaevi-muze-olacakti (Accessed: 8 December 2021).
Lundy, P. and Rolston, B., 2016. Redress for past harms? Official apologies in Northern Ireland. *International Journal of Human Rights*, 20, pp. 104–122. https://doi.org/10.1080/13642987.2015.1050235
McAuliffe, P., 2019. Surrogacy and resistance: Evolving Patterns in unofficial truth commissions and truth projects. In *The Global Impact and Legacy of Truth Commissions*. Intersentia, pp. 269–292. https://doi.org/10.1017/9781780687957.011
McKernan, B., 2021. 'Tell those stories': Kurds call for torture prison to be turned into place of healing. *The Guardian*. Available at: https://www.theguardian.com/world/2021/jul/18/tell-those-stories-kurds-call-for-torture-prison-to-be-turned-into-place-of-healing (Accessed: 12 April 2022).
Meryem, D., 2018. Türkiye'de Yüzleşme Müzeleri ve Yüzleşilemeyen Diyarbakır Cezaevi. *Sivil Sayfalar,* 24 May. Available at: https://memorializeturkey.com/en/memorial/diyarbakir-military-prison-project/ (Accessed: 9 November 2021).
Önderoğlu, E., 2010. Torturers will be called to account. *Bianet*. Available at: https://m.bianet.org/bianet/minorities/125076-torturers-will-be-called-to-account (Accessed: 18 August 2022).
Rûpela Nû, 2021. *Meclis'in hazırladığı Diyarbakır Cezaevi raporu 3 yıldır açıklanmadı*. Available at: http://www.rupelanu.org/meclisin-hazirladigi-diyarbakir-cezaevi-raporu-3-yildir-aciklanmadi-16125h.htm (Accessed: 3 January 2022).
SABAH, 2012. *12 Eylül'deki işkencelere soruşturma*. Available at: https://www.sabah.com.tr/gundem/2012/04/06/12-eyluldeki-iskencelere-sorusturma (Accessed: 12 November 2021).
Serhat, R., 2021. *Katledilen avukat Medet Serhat'ın oğlu Rumet Serhat yazdı: Üniversiteye hazırlanırken öldürülen babanızın otopsisini okumak*. Available at: https://t24.com.tr/haber/katledilen-avukat-medet-serhat-in-oglu-rumet-serhat-yazdi-universiteye-hazirlanirken-oldurulen-babanizin-otopsisini-okumak,994106 (Accessed: 26 February 2025).
Truth and Justice Commission for Diyarbakır Prison, 2009. Diyarbakır Cezaevi Okul Değil, İnsan Hakları Müzesi Olmalıdır. *Birikim*. Available at: https://birikimdergisi.com/guncel/773/diyarbakir-cezaevi-okul-degil-insan-haklari-muzesi-olmalidir (Accessed: 22 December 2021).
Truth and Justice Commission for Diyarbakir Prison, 2011. Türkiye Diyarbakır Askeri Cezaevi Gerçeği Ile Yüzleşiyor III. *SEMPOZYUM*. Available at: https://static.bianet.org/files/doc_files/000/000/370/original/111203-DC-Sempozyum_Sunum_%C3%96zetleri.pdf
TruthJustice Memory Center, 2013. *Alevi katliamlari için hakikat komisyonu*. Available at: https://hakikatadalethafiza.org/haberler/alevi-katliamlari-icin-hakikat-komisyonu (Accessed: 6 May 2025).
Türker, Y., 2008. *Diyarbakır Cezaevi*. Available at: https://acikradyo.com.tr/arsiv-icerigi/diyarbakir-cezaevi (Accessed: 2 December 2024).
Verdeja, E., 2010. Official apologies in the aftermath of political violence. *Methaphilosophy,* 41(4), 563–581.
Zeydanlıoğlu, W., 2009. Torture and Turkification in the Diyarbakır military prison. *Rights Citizenship Torture Perspectives Evil Law State*, 18, pp. 73–92.

Chapter 8

# Transitional Justice Imaginaries in Turkey

## 8.1 Introduction

This chapter focuses on grassroots actors' conceptualisations, visions, and aspirations of transitional justice in the given context of an ongoing conflict and an authoritarian regime. By analysing their transitional justice imaginaries in Turkey as a case of non-transition in a deeply conflicted society and by adopting a forward-looking approach (Hansen, 2011), the chapter sheds a light on the challenges, barriers, and limitations to transitional justice as well as prospects for it. Exploring grassroots actors' understanding of transition and transitional justice provides insights into the motivations and lack thereof for engaging with transitional justice at different times. It also allows us to link the grassroots actors' demands and priorities with transitional justice.

## 8.2 Transition as a Bottom-Up, Long-Term, Non-Linear Process

A nuanced understanding of transition is common among my interlocutors involved in justice-seeking efforts. They view transition as a long-term, non-linear process that unfolds gradually over time rather than being confined to a singular moment, transition highlights the ongoing relevance of justice initiatives both before and after a peace agreement. One interlocutor noted that transitional periods cannot be considered as uniform blocks, and they are often marked by disruptions and setbacks. Bearing in mind the complexity of such processes, transitional justice emerges as a practical tool for taking initiative for in the prolonged periods of transition:

> You cannot transition to peace just in one day. It starts, stops, and then resumes—perhaps it will take sixty years. Am I going to wait sixty years to implement transitional justice? That would be a passive position. What we call as transition is not necessarily done by others. You are a party to it, and it is a struggle you lead to crate that transition. I can always use transitional justice as part of my struggle to transition.
>
> (Interview no:3)

DOI: 10.4324/9781003432579-8

The idea of transition as a long-term process comes with the belief that those working towards transitional justice goals must take initiative rather than simply wait for the right moment (Sarkin, 2016, p. 309) proposes that the scope of transitional justice should extend beyond (and before) post-transition periods, advocating for proactive measures during ongoing conflicts. He emphasises that "Transitional justice can become a useful tool for deterrence if put in practice to help ensure human rights violations do not (re)occur" (Sarkin, 2016, p. 309).

This need for action resonates with my interlocutors, who similarly reject the idea of waiting for higher authorities, warring parties, or political elites to drive the transition. They stress that such passivity undermines the agency of grassroots actors. Instead, they advocate for a bottom-up approach. As one interlocutor observed, a slow but ongoing transition has been made possible by the Kurdish people's resistance. However, they called for a faster and more comprehensive transformation, stating: "We need a stronger willpower without waiting for the state. We need to make sure that the state feels the civil structure has the willpower to co-exist as equal citizens" (Interview no:8). This understanding brings the agency forward while placing the responsibility for leading transitional justice during ongoing conflicts on civil society and human rights advocates. This bottom-up, agency-driven approach reflects the view that the transition is a dynamic terrain for political struggle. It could be fought for and initiated on the grassroots level.

In Chapter 3, I discussed critiques by critical peace and transformative justice scholars of top-down, externally driven approaches to transitional justice (McEvoy and McConnachie, 2013; Sharp, 2013). My interlocutors' share similar concerns. If peace and transitional justice processes are dominated by political elites without recognising the local agency of grassroots actors, entrenched power relations remain unchallenged. These power dynamics, perpetuated by the continuation of conflict, highlight the need for bottom-up, locally owned approaches as essential for transformative processes. Echoing this agency-oriented perspective, another interlocutor expressed the need for civil society to create a network and put pressure on the state. They argued that involving all segments of society in such efforts is key to driving change, noting: "Otherwise, waiting for peace means choosing an easy way out" (Interview no:2). This insight underscores the urgency of grassroots action as a catalyst for transformative justice, rejecting passivity in favour of collective responsibility.

## 8.3 Transitional Justice as the Groundwork

Transitional justice provides a valuable framework for addressing the legacies of Turkey's past and holds significant potential for resolving the Kurdish conflict (Budak, 2015). This view is widely shared by my interlocutors, who view transitional justice as a foundation for tackling a deep-rooted social problem and fostering sustainable resolutions. Importantly, they emphasised that as a foundation, transitional justice should not be limited to post-conflict transitions but should also serve as a tool for grassroots actors during the conflict. As one interlocutor explained:

> What we call as transitional justice mechanisms offers us a basis to think as to how to handle a major social problem so that we can move towards permanent solutions. That is why it is so important. Based on what I know and the discussions we have had, it should not be limited to the post-conflict transitions.
>
> (Interview no:3)

Reflecting on what could be done given the limited space for civil society in Turkey was a recurring theme in my interviews. Almost all interlocutors express that the current period could lay the groundwork for an official transitional justice process that will start someday. They emphasised the need for a well-prepared civil society capable of contributing meaningfully when the time comes. While they acknowledged the value of taking initiative in the current situation, most believed the impact would remain limited until the state initiates an official process. This perspective aligns with research suggesting that implementing transitional justice mechanisms during conflict might have limited impact, but such efforts are still critical as groundwork for a future peace process (Sarkin, 2016). Although transitional justice is generally seen as ineffective for initiating political transformation or addressing the root causes of the conflict during ongoing conflict, it can still be beneficial before political transformation begins Hansen (2017). Everything that could be done now counts as infrastructure work, enabling civil society actors to actively and meaningfully engage in the future. As one interlocutor noted, accumulating small experiences now is crucial for building a solid foundation for an eventual official process:

> Every stone we put is meaningful, and every small step counts. Official mechanisms that could only be started with the involvement of the state are not employable right now. However, it makes a lot of sense to do something with the organised activist groups, local administrations or local initiatives.
>
> (Interview no:4)

This quote highlights the potential of mobilising resources that could take meaningful action, stressing the need to identify what is feasible under current conditions, another interlocutor pointed out. Acknowledging the challenges of implementing transitional justice mechanisms during conflict, she underlined the responsibility of human rights advocates. While not every transitional justice mechanism is suitable for the current context, some could be both highly beneficial and relatively easier to implement. As a lawyer and researcher working on dealing with the past and impunity, she noted:

> Is there a ground for a truth commission now? No. However, does that prevent us from contributing to reveal the big picture for when such a mechanism is established? What could be the drawbacks of considering this when the conflict is still ongoing? Obviously, I know what my challenges are. Yet, as a human rights advocate, if I took on the responsibility of reminding the state of its responsibilities and adapted this approach as a lawyer, what could stop me from learning how to make the best use of transitional justice? (Interview no:3)

Examining the most common type of work undertaken by civil society in the realm of transitional justice provides insights into what is most feasible. Activities aimed at truth-recovery and memorialisation, such as archival work, documentation, database creating, reporting, and research, stand out as the most prominent. These efforts are powerfully exemplified in the Saturday Mothers' contributions to transitional justice, discussed in Chapter 6, and the Truth and Justice Commission for the Diyarbakır Prison, analysed in Chapter 7. Other notable initiatives include the İHD's periodic human rights violations reports[1] and weekly gatherings for the disappeared in Istanbul, İzmir, and the Kurdish cities by families and activists,[2] the Truth Justice Memory Centre's "Perpetrator Not-Unknown" website for monitoring human rights trials,[3] Human Rights Foundation of Turkey's daily human rights violations reports and weekly Saturday Mothers/People monitoring reports,[4] Demos Research Centre's Transitional Justice workshops and webinars,[5] and the digital Museum of Memory for Historical Justice[6] are all among such efforts. An interlocutor explained the importance of maintaining such efforts as preparation for future justice mechanisms, asserting:

> In the future, these violations will become more visible and play a role in resolution of the Kurdish conflict and access to justice. This is why we do

1 For annual reports of the İHD, see: https://www.ihd.org.tr/td_d_slug_2/

2 For an example of simultaneous gatherings in Istanbul, İzmir, Batman, and Hakkari, see: *Kayıp yakınları 4 kentte gözaltında katledilenler için buluştu* 7 December 2024 https://firatnews.com/guncel/kayip-yakinlari-3-kentte-gozaltinda-katledilenler-icin-bulustu-206081

3 Truth Justice and Memory Centre describes this website as: "A digital archive where you can find the results of the study monitoring the criminal trial processes regarding grave human rights violations in Turkey's recent past." It can be accessed via https://www.failibelli.org/en/

4 For both daily reports and special reports of the TİHV, see: https://tihv.org.tr/belgeleme-calismalari/ihlallerin-belgelenmesi/

5 For more information on DEMOS' workshops and seminars on transitional justice, see: https://demos.org.tr/projeler/gecis-donemi-adaleti-atolyeleri-seminerleri/

6 This digital museum can be visited via https://bellekmuzesi.org/

> archival work, documentation, data collection, and research. It will be our contribution to transitional justice.
>
> (Interview no:2)

Recording and revealing human rights violations through documentation serves as a function of transitional justice by countering ongoing denial and impunity. Especially in ongoing conflict cases, such as Syria, the act of documentation becomes an act of resistance, helping to keep justice demands alive (Aboueldahab, 2018). Notably, Kurdish lawyers in Turkey believe in the critical importance of documenting current human rights violations as a foundation for accountability in a peaceful future, when addressing past injustices may become feasible (Bostan, 2022). Despite their lack of trust in the Turkish legal system's willingness or ability to deliver justice today, they remain committed to pursuing legal avenues. Therefore, systematically recording violations, ensuring that evidence is preserved for potential future justice mechanisms, and creating memory and archives are important motivations in their persistence.

The collected data could be used in future legal proceedings to hold perpetrators accountable and may also support cases in international human rights mechanisms, such as the ECtHR, when it is impossible to pursue justice in domestic mechanisms. For example, during the 2015–2016 curfews in the Kurdish region, authorities obstructed both national and international human rights organisations from accessing the curfew zones, preventing them from documenting widespread abuses against civilians (Human Rights Watch, 2016). One of my interlocutors described how all entrances and exits to these areas were closed, making it impossible for anyone to enter (Interview no:3). As a result, human rights organisations were unable to observe or report the abuses firsthand. This interlocutor shared how human rights organisations adapted to this challenge by focusing on alternative documentation methods:

> We decided that our most concrete function—considering we didn't have the opportunity to conduct in-person fieldwork—was to collect the investigation folders on these violations and analyse them. This approach would provide the most reliable information and be the most feasible . . . We managed to gather approximately 150 investigation folders and established a database. We then compiled the analysis based on that database into an application for an injunction, which was examined by the ECtHR November last year. We offered it as the third-party view from three institutions.
>
> (Interview no:3)

Another interlocutor underlined the importance of archival work and memorialisation efforts as potential areas for involvement even when establishing official mechanisms is impossible:

> For instance, memorialisation is a crucial mechanism offered to me by the transitional justice framework, and there is no obstacle to pursuing it right

now. I do what I can; I collect what I can under today's circumstances. I cannot make the government apologise, but I can inform people about what an official apology means. For example, I cannot create a new historical narrative, but I can discuss what it should look like.

(Interview no:3)

## 8.4 Transitional Justice as a Precondition for Peace

My interlocutors view transitional justice as a critical component, almost a prerequisite, for peace. They do not envision a peace process as complete without incorporating justice, accountability, truth, and recognition measures. Kurdish grassroots actors' demand for peace has always been closely tied to demands for justice. In fact, the Kurdish political movement and grassroots organisations often conceptualise their peace aspirations as "honourable and just peace (*onurlu ve adil barış*)."[7] In parallel to the concept of Galtung's (1969) positive peace, this concept refers to going beyond ending the armed conflict (negative peace) and physical violence to ensuring social justice and equality (Gurses, 2020). While there is not a fixed definition of the concept, it is associated with achieving a peace process that respects the dignity, rights, and identity of the Kurdish people, addressing past grievances, and ensuring structural changes to prevent future injustices.

Justice and recognition are critical components of sustaining honourable and just peace as the only way to make peace possible is "through confrontation with the past, the transformation of the present and sustainability guaranteed for the future" (Bostan, 2022). Much in line with the perspective that grassroots actors can lead transitional processes, building a just and honourable peace is also understood as a bottom-up process. In Newroz celebrations in March 2021, the HDP co-chair Mithat Sancar framed honourable peace in a comparable way to my interlocutors' description of transition as a bottom-up process:

> We will bring peace to this country together with the peoples of this country. We are not expecting this from those in power but from the democracy forces. We see peace as an honourable and just process, not as something granted by those in power. We know it can only be built from the ground up, together with the peoples. Come, let us find the way to build honourable and just peace together. Let us create a strong march. Let us bring peace and freedom to this country.

(Sendika, 2021)

7 For examples of such statements, see (Evrensel, 2024; HDP, 2018; İHD, 2009; T24, 2024; Yılmaz, 2025).

To build trust in peace and ensure its sustainability with a transformative impact, it is essential to take visible, concrete justice measures that clearly demonstrate a genuine commitment to peace. It is crucial to show that peace being pursued is a just and honourable peace that aims at Kurds' long-standing grievances and truly acknowledges the accountability and justice demand. A Diyarbakır-based lawyer elaborated how peace and transitional justice processes should be interconnected to ensure honourable peace:

> Honestly, I don't think it will work as 'first peacebuilding and then transitional justice' in Kurdistan. This is what people mean by honourable peace, and I think they have deeply internalised it. First there need to be some steps—some confrontation with the past, or perhaps truth commissions as you mentioned. Things like that should happen so that there can be a peacebuilding that people can believe in and trust. That is why, if there is a desire for sustainable peace in Kurdistan, I believe certain things related to transitional justice should take place before a peace table is set up.
>
> (Interview no:17)

In a similar vein, an Istanbul-based Kurdish practitioner emphasised the necessity of implementing justice and peace initiatives simultaneously, asserting that both are essential and cannot exist independently of each other. He referred to the collapsed peace process as an example of the failure to address peace and justice demands together:

> In my view, we can't prioritise one over the other. They work in an interlinked manner. I mean, if there is only peace, then there won't be justice. Or peace won't come if there is only justice. When there is a will to achieve both justice and peace, they will develop together . . . Justice and peace must go hand in hand, they are not independent or separate from each other. If you say, yes, 'we have stopped the conflict, but we won't be able to deliver justice,' it won't create a healthy foundation for peace. In fact, this is exactly what happened in the past. Because they couldn't manage that process properly, because they couldn't deliver peace and justice, or balance it, the peace process ultimately failed . . . The justice dimension was sidelined.
>
> (Interview no:2)

## 8.5 Challenges to Transitional Justice Imaginaries

As my analysis has demonstrated so far, grassroots actors in Turkey have long been working towards the goals of transitional justice, indicating a deep understanding of victims' demands for justice, truth, and accountability. Yet, several challenges restrain their transitional justice imaginaries.

These challenges can be divided into two categories: the first involves limited knowledge of and connections to the established field and practise of transitional justice, while the second concerns the restrictive impacts of ongoing conflict and authoritarianism.

The first challenge lies in the limited knowledge about the state of the field of transitional justice. While various actors have expressed demands for specific transitional justice mechanisms, there has been relatively little implementation in practice. During interviews, those not directly engaged in transitional justice often expressed familiarity with the term but seemed to have limited knowledge of its specific aspects. Those with more experience in the field tended to focus on certain mechanisms relevant to their work, such as truth commissions or trials, but often with limited knowledge of how different approaches and mechanisms may interact.

This lack of a holistic perspective is a significant gap. It is important for transitional justice mechanisms to work simultaneously and holistically because no single mechanism can fully address the complex legacies of mass human rights violations on its own. Instead, different mechanisms serve distinct but complementary functions, and their coordination enhances both effectiveness and legitimacy. Therefore, a well-functioning transitional justice process requires multiple mechanisms operating simultaneously to address complex needs of transitioning societies (Arthur, 2009; Teitel, 2000). In the civil society sphere in Turkey, there has been insufficient work on how these mechanisms function both independently and in coordination with each other. As a result, the current civic space articulates transitional justice objectives in broad, abstract terms but gives insufficient consideration to the specific tools and mechanisms that are most effective and suited to the Turkish-Kurdish context. In other words, discussions remain broad without detailed plans for implementation.

Moreover, most people involved in activities related to transitional justice do not explicitly frame or label their work within the transitional justice framework. This was particularly evident during a series of workshops I co-convened in 2020 with civil society representatives from various organisations.[8] The workshops focused on critical approaches to transitional justice and facilitated discussions on its potential implementation in Turkey. The emphasis was on the role of grassroots actors, highlighting both their past achievements and their continued contributions. For many participants, the workshops served as a reminder of their impact, while for others, they provided an opportunity to examine their work through the lens of transitional justice—often for the first time, beyond legal and official justice frameworks.

8 The online Transitional Justice Workshop Series were organised by the DEMOS Research Association in 2020.

For instance, some participants had been involved in initiatives such as the Truth and Justice Commission for the Diyarbakır Prison. One attendee expressed surprise and delight at realising that their efforts had been part of transitional justice activities. Interestingly, many of these actors had already been employing key concepts from the transitional justice vocabulary, such as dealing with the past, justice, memorialisation, and truth-seeking, even without consciously framing their work within this field. There is, therefore, scope for expanding the transitional justice knowledge and understanding to continue using it more innovatively.

The second challenge relates to the complex picture of the entrenched intersection of armed conflict and authoritarianism. The oppressive and authoritarian regime has limited the ability to act freely in a politically sensitive field. Peace is one of the riskiest topics to be vocal about, and seeking justice and accountability for conflict-related abuses is equally challenging. As is the case in many other contexts, state surveillance and repression often target peace activists, who are also involved and usually the main actors or pioneers of any transitional justice attempts. In particular, the work of those who have been most vocal about the goals of transitional justice has been significantly affected by the repressive policies and crackdown on human rights.

Under an authoritarian regime and amid an ongoing armed conflict, civil society is often compelled to prioritise immediate, urgent, and more pressing issues. The direct impact of conflict on people's lives means that most efforts are directed towards addressing the violence and its immediate consequences rather than tackling issues that may seem secondary, such as transitional justice. In Turkey, civil society organisations that once played a leading role in advocating for transitional justice and confronting past injustices have had to adapt or expand their focus to other areas of human rights. One significant shift has been towards the protection of human rights defenders (Interview no:10).

This shift is driven by two key factors. Firstly, the criminalisation and imprisonment of human rights defenders— including individuals interviewed for this research— have become increasingly pressing and widespread issues. Secondly, donor organisations that previously funded civil society initiatives related to peacebuilding and addressing historical injustices have significantly reduced their budgets for these areas, effectively excluding peace in Turkey as a priority theme. As a result, civil society organisations have had to redirect their efforts to more immediate human rights concerns, often at the expense of long-term justice and reconciliation efforts.

This shift underscores the profound impact of the authoritarian regime, which has disrupted civil society's perception and imagination, constraining their capacity to envision and engage beyond the confines of the current political environment. Although almost all participants agree on the relevance and meaningfulness of transitional justice during the conflict, there is little room for thinking creatively about how to apply transitional justice in the Turkish-Kurdish context. They usually refer to it as a preparation process, finding it unlikely to occur beyond a limited scope before the state initiates an official process.

There is also a personal dimension to limitations on how to think more creatively about transitional justice. Over the last couple of years, many people have faced personal security concerns; some have been detained or imprisoned or dismissed from their jobs. Living under an authoritarian regime's surveillance and the constant fear of losing one's job or freedom makes it difficult to focus on longer-term issues. My interlocutor, a prominent human rights advocate, told me about the activities planned by her association. They wanted to establish an independent institute to work on human rights and collective trauma. They started contacting with potential partners from abroad, but then they had to put it on hold due to the increasing challenges they faced in recent years. She has been involved in human rights work for decades and faced increasing political pressure judicial harassment. She highlighted the psychological impact of dealing with the oppressive regime:

> The last 2–3 years went by in such a chaotic way, we lost our ability to dream. This is the biggest damage done by these men. Myself, for example, due to anxiety, I lost the ability to work and think deeply about something. It will be very difficult to bring it back.
>
> (Interview no:8)

Therefore, there is a noticeable gap between past and current civil society engagement in transitional justice. In the early 2000s, although the conflict was ongoing, discourse around dealing with the past discourse was more prominent and widely embraced, accompanied by a greater number of related activities. For example, in 2007, the Diyarbakir Bar Association organised a conference titled "Dealing with the Past for Truth, Justice, and Peace" (Evrensel, 2007). In his opening remarks, Sezgin Tanrikulu, then chair of the Bar, highlighted the 5233 Compensation Law and several ECtHR cases as potential starting points for dealing with the past. There was also an elevated level of interest in international experiences during this period. Prominent international figures such as Alex Boraine, former Deputy Chair of the South African Truth and Reconciliation Commission, attended the conference, alongside guest speakers from Chile, South Africa, and Ireland.

During that period, there was more focused thinking on dealing with the past, with actors demonstrating a greater ability to draw connections between concrete examples and the broader discourse of dealing with the past. Interestingly however, much of this appears to have been forgotten. My interviews on transitional justice practices in Turkey do not fully reveal the reflections of this wealth of experience. In recent years, topics related to peace and transitional justice have received significantly less attention compared to previous periods. Many individuals who were once actively engaged in these areas of human rights work now recall those days as part of a distant past (Bor et. al., 2021).

Under these conditions it is challenging, and at times impossible, to think ahead and work towards something that may only produce outcomes in a distant, unpredictable future. When the state uses a criminalising and punitive approach to the disrupting voices, civil society actors are limited in what they can do. Even though my interlocutors consistently address the importance of a bottom-up approach to transitional justice and the need for taking the initiative without waiting for a top-down driven process, the reality is that they do not have much space to act under the oppressive rule, and there is not much change expected in the foreseeable future.

## 8.6 Overcoming Barriers: Democratisation and Ending the Impunity

In the light of the existing challenges, I asked my interlocutors what needs to change to be able to apply transitional justice. Most answers relate to democratisation, removal of the impunity culture and institutional reforms, particularly within the judiciary.

First and foremost, a political will needs to be in place to change the political conditions enabling impunity for human rights violations. A prominent human rights defender, faced with several charges, explained how the current political climate reinforces impunity for those promoting violence while criminalising those advocating for peace. She noted:

> Yes, mechanisms such as truth commissions could happen, but much further down the road. First, there need to be legal changes, and a political will for a solution . . . These racist and chauvinist policies have to change, and a more moderate [political] climate needs to emerge. For once, people should be able to speak out without being imprisoned for their thoughts . . . Unless there is a law change, I will be imprisoned myself whenever the judgement becomes definite. I am not as free as them . . . I have never defended violence in my life, and yet, I have been sentenced to this many years in prison.
>
> (Interview no:7)

Another interlocutor, a lawyer and relative of a disappeared person, referred to a fundamental political transformation towards a more democratic country as the only way for justice demands to be fulfilled.

> The only possible way to meet this demand for justice is through political transformation. Will the Kurdish issue be solved by the end of this political transformation? I don't know. But one thing is certain: there needs to be a serious democratic transformation to meet this demand for justice. It

> is a different matter to what extent it will help solve the Kurdish issue. But of course, they are interlinked. The serious democratic transformation, I mean, the change of Turkey's DNA, the foundation of the state, will help.
> (Interview no:24)

As someone who followed the high-ranked military officers' trials and witnessed the structural problems of impunity both personally and professionally, he argued that first of all, impunity as a state policy must be abandoned:

> This is clearly a state policy, a political tendency. This political tendency needs to change fundamentally so that there will be a [meaningful] outcome of these trials. There are thousands of murders and perhaps millions of rights violations. They reached such a high number that it is perhaps not possible to give a judicial response.
> (Interview no:4)

A similar notion of impunity and the protection of perpetrators was raised by another legal expert, particularly in the context of enforced disappearances. He emphasised the critical need for political will to ensure effective judicial processes and deliver justice:

> First, there is need for a political willingness. I mean, a strong political will is required to uncover these incidents. Second, it must be capable of conducting effective investigations. It is not enough just to have public support; this needs to be shared widely with the public. In these processes, what needs to be done is to share information to a certain extent and to keep public support alive. The perpetrators of these incidents are largely state agents.
> (Interview no:16)

This perspective may seem to contradict the idea that transition is a bottom-up process initiated by civil society actors. Yet, recognising political change as a necessary condition for achieving transitional justice goals does not imply postponing these goals to the distant future. On the contrary, all my interlocutors are actively pursuing justice and truth using various avenues. These include engaging in domestic and international judicial procedures, organising and attending gatherings for the relatives of the disappeared in Istanbul and the Kurdish region, documenting human rights violations, and engaging in memorialisation activities. While making the most of existing resources, their efforts underscore the need for profound structural transformation. This necessity does not diminish the importance of exploring every possible avenue to advance justice and accountability demands. Instead, it highlights how even a signal of political change can amplify ongoing efforts, amplify the silenced voices, and nurture the hope that peace and justice are indeed still achievable and imaginable.

This point is illustrated by the developments following then-opposition leader Kılıçdaroğlu's speech in November 2021, where he announced his intention to embark on a journey of reconciliation (*helalleşme*).[9] In this speech, he outlined an extensive list of past atrocities and human rights abuses that he pledged to address if elected (Bianet, 2021). Notably, Kılıçdaroğlu also acknowledged his party's role in some of these injustices and stressed the importance of restoring social relations to build a peaceful future. The speech occurred amidst ongoing public debates about the future of the current government, the formation of new alliances, and the possibility of early elections. At the time, Kılıçdaroğlu was seen as the leading candidate of the opposition for the upcoming presidential elections.[10] Consequently, his speech raised hopes for a new political era that would prioritise reckoning with the past.

This statement generated significant excitement among those advocating for justice and truth. His turn toward addressing past injustices was welcomed by many scholars, researchers, activists, victims, and politicians.[11] While some criticised the language he used,[12] the speech created a platform for widespread debate, sparking discussions in newspaper columns, blog posts, podcasts, and civil society meetings. Civil society responded with notable enthusiasm: 37 civil society organisations issued a joint statement titled "We Are Here for Truth, Equality and Justice" calling for concrete follow-up actions to his reconciliation call.[13] In their statement, they emphasised that "victims and civil society should be at the centre of such efforts." This swift response exemplifies how civil society is ready to take the lead when even a glimpse of hope for formal political action emerges, as noted by my interlocutors, rather than waiting for political leaders to take ownership. While Kılıçdaroğlu's call did not led to tangible actions, the possibility of political

9 *Helalleşmek* roughly means mutual forgiveness between two people, or making amends, and it originates from "helal" (halal), which is used to describe what is permissible in Islam. His choice of term attracted criticism as it was perceived to mean making peace at the expense of justice.

10 This did not prove right, as Erdogan won the presidential elections for the second time.

11 For examples of the written pieces written and podcast episodes recorded in that period, see *Ekonomik Kriz ve Helallesme Uzerine* by Selahattin Demirtas (https://www.indyturk.com/node/441431/haber/demirta%C5%9F-ekonomik-kriz-ve-helalle%C5%9Fme-%C3%BCzerine) (Accessed: 26 February 2025); *Helalleşmeyi Uzlaşma ve Geçiş Dönemi Adaleti Bağlamında Nasıl Tartışabiliriz?* by Güneş Daşlı (https://demos.org.tr/helallesmeyi-uzlasma-ve-gecis-donemi-adaleti-baglaminda-nasil-tartisabiliriz/); and *Ceza yargılaması toplumsal bir yüzleşme alanı değildir.* Guest: Onur Bakıner, Anlasabilirz Podcast by İdil Elveris (https://soundcloud.com/anlasabiliriz-wecanfaway/ceza-yargilamasi-toplumsal-bir-yuzlesme-alani-degildir-konuk-onur-bakiner).

12 For example, on 20 November 2021, Hayriye Eren from the Saturday Mothers movement said that they have always asked for the murderers to be prosecuted and confronted by her family, but she cannot be expected to offer *helalleşme*, as it is different from confronting (https://firatnews.com/guncel/cumartesi-anneleri-yuzlesmek-ve-helallesmek-ayni-sey-degil-163646).

13 The statement was released on April 11, 2022. See the English version: https://en.demos.org.tr/we-are-here-for-truth-equality-and-justice/

change gave momentum to discussions about addressing past injustices. Civil society's engagement with Kılıçdaroğlu's statement highlights the pivotal role of political change in mobilizing demands for justice—even when that change is only a distant possibility.

Political change is seen as requiring institutional reform to open pathways for justice, accountability, and non-recurrence. Institutional reform is a central focus of transitional justice, particularly under the pillar of guarantees of non-recurrence (United Nations, 2010). This includes reforming state institutions to ensure their independence, impartiality, and effectiveness. In the interviews, the need for institutional reform is most prominently highlighted in relation to the judiciary. A key theme that emerges is institutional mistrust in the judiciary, which is closely tied to a culture of impunity. The following quote from a sibling of a disappeared person conveys the frustration of judiciary's indifference and the prevailing impunity. She explained why overcoming impunity must the very first step for meaningfully dealing with the past:

> I think, if you ask me, the files should be opened. Our files are expiring due to the statute of limitations. My brother's case also expired. Unfortunately, many of our disappeared people's cases are expiring. Because the perpetrators are not being prosecuted, they are not being called, not even taken statements of. For example, let's say we are suing someone in our case . . . At the very least, his statement should be taken. But this person's statement is not even taken. At least his statement should be taken. Every file has the name of a perpetrator, I mean the name of the person responsible for this crime. Every file. It is there in the Karakoç file, in the Savaş Buldan file, in the Ferhat Tepe case. I mean, the names are there in all of them. But these names are never summoned, and their statements are never taken. That's why it is very important to start here. These cases should not be closed; they should be reopened, trials should take place, and impunity should be eradicated. Because there is a massive impunity. These people, since they are never prosecuted, are certainly not facing the corresponding legal penalties. This is why . . . I think we should start from here.
>
> (Interview no:23)

Additionally, the judiciary is used as a way of criminalising those advocating justice, especially in recent years under the authoritarian regime. Since the curfew period of 2015–2016 (explained in Chapter 2), people have become fearful of demanding justice in ways they had not before. Families who apply to the ECtHR or file complaints with local courts now face the risk of further violence. As one lawyer noted, this risk is significant:

> For instance, if a father files a complaint about his son being killed by the special forces or the armed forces and calls for an investigation, the possible consequences are as follows: his house may be raided, and he

> may put his family at risk of being taken into custody or investigated for arbitrary reasons. However, there are many families that continue the struggle, no matter the cost. These are the families that are strong-willed and determined. They don't give up. But go see it with your own eyes—the state is everywhere in Kurdistan. It always makes its presence felt: 'I am here.' There is no one who has not been taken into custody. People are exhausted.
>
> (Interview no:9)

Even though families are determined, the authoritarian regime has practically closed the paths for seeking justice through the increased securitisation of the Kurdish region in the aftermath of 2015. Another interlocutor addresses a similar fear of seeking justice, deepened by mistrust in the state:

> For example, that family who identified their son is afraid to file a complaint. I said we should, but they have other children, and they are scared. The state uses the definition of terror in its own favour and as it wants. If you go to the prosecutor with these images, they can immediately arrest you for spreading propaganda for a terrorist organization.
>
> (Interview no:7)

To create the confidence that criminal justice could be pursued, institutional reform will have to primarily aim for an independent judiciary. The following quote shows that an institutional reform in the judiciary will also be seen as proof that there is genuine political change:

> The independence of the judiciary has been completely abolished. It has never been independent, but there were at least some factions within the judiciary with whom you could still communicate. But even those factions do not exist anymore. There is one single perspective dominating. The judges themselves are afraid of being dismissed from their offices. There is no justice where judges are in fear. It is not possible.
>
> (Interview no:7)

When the rule of law is significantly absent and criminal justice system does not function properly, it is hard to imagine that transitional justice mechanisms can be established or that transitional justice goals can be pursued. A comprehensive transitional justice process seems unlikely under the existing conditions, which undermine basic rights and freedoms. A lawyer pointed at this unlikeliness:

> We need a fully independent judiciary. Currently, to say the least, the local courts do not even recognise the Constitutional Court's ruling . . . When Turkey is in this situation, those things we've mentioned—such as

> truth, compensation, justice, reparative measures—I mean, even the vertical punitive process has been abolished. It is a state that has lost its own function to be a state of law, and the punitive law function, let alone the reparative, horizontal justice system. This is the first matter. How are you going to sustain the restorative function?
>
> (Interview no:22)

## 8.7 Phased Approaches to Transitional Justice and Transformation in Turkey

The way my interlocutors describe the terms *transition* and *transformation* draws a three-phased picture of a potential transitional justice process in Turkey. First of all, there is the preparatory phase in which civil society could engage in groundwork for an official transitional justice process. The current context—an ongoing conflict and authoritarian regime—presents a challenging but viable atmosphere to invest in such groundwork. Since the state is unlikely to engage in transitional justice processes, this phase is characterised by grassroots-level, bottom-up efforts. The groundwork includes empowering civil society to effectively contribute to a future official transitional justice process that may potentially take place within a peace process.

A complexity of this first phase is understanding how to carry out this groundwork, what should be prioritised, and how grassroots actors can be empowered to effectively participate in transitional justice efforts. The first phase is challenging also because it demands a strong commitment by civil society actors to continue working towards an official process that may not materialise anytime soon. Nevertheless, my interlocutors believe that a peace process will start sooner or later, and therefore value this preparatory process. Furthermore, as has been shown in the cases of the Saturday Mothers and the Truth and Justice Commission for Diyarbakır Prison, gains can also be made during this phase.

Second, this phase is followed by the transition itself, carried out through transitional justice practices. For a meaningful, far-reaching transitional justice, this phase should include bottom up and top-down efforts working together. Bottom-up approaches, prioritising the grassroots efforts, are essential for addressing the root causes of the conflict, and eventually transforming structural injustices. Top-down efforts, on the other hand, are necessary for institutional support of transitional justice mechanisms and to build trust in new institutions. In the case of the Kurdish conflict, official state recognition of its responsibility is seen as the fundamental first step in opening the door for transitional justice processes and ultimately non-recurrence.

Finally, the phase of transition, or the transitional justice process, will lead to the third phase: sustained, comprehensive, long-term transformation. In an inquiry into the paradigm of "transition", Arthur accentuates an important shift in what transition came to mean around the same period that transitional justice emerged as a field (Arthur, 2009). Until 1970s, transition was understood more with its Marxist connotations, referring to structural change in society and economy. In the 1970s and 1980s, however, it started to mean political reform instead of social transformation, occurring mainly at the legal and institutional levels. Daly notes a tendency in the transitional justice literature to use the terms transition and transformation as identical, but they should be distinguished (Daly, 2002). Transformation refers to more of a radical change while "transition suggests movement from one thing to another". Daly also observes that transition often takes place at the top and fails to reach the grassroots level. Similarly, Quinn argues that transition and transformation should not be equated (Quinn, 2014). They are distinct phases of a broader whole. Transition, as an event, and transitional justice, as a set of practices, are supposed to lead to a more sustained, comprehensive transformation. My interlocutors made a similar distinction between transition and transformation. By long-term transition, they refer to a more comprehensive transformation as a radical social, cultural, and structural change, and they believe that transitional justice can be used as tool to achieve this. In the next and concluding chapter, I will address how a future transitional justice process in Turkey can benefit from a transformative approach.

## 8.8 Moving Forward

In Turkey, grassroots organisations, victim and survivor groups, lawyers, and activists recognise the continued importance and relevance of transitional justice even within the constraints of an ongoing conflict and authoritarian regime. While they consider transitional justice a crucial aspect of their work as human rights advocates, the collapse of the peace process in 2015 and the tightening political climate have significantly diminished its prominence. In periods when the state demonstrated even superficial and pragmatic willingness to engage with the past, civil society efforts were notably more robust and capable of fostering public discussions on accountability and reconciliation. The expansion of political space not only allowed for more open dialogue but also created a sense of hope, making it possible to imagine alternative ways of addressing historical injustices. In contrast, the current political environment—marked by state resistance and diminishing prospects for peace—has rendered transitional justice frameworks increasingly sidelined.

However, the progress made during previous periods of openness has not disappeared—it remains beneath the surface. If the political climate were to shift again, allowing for meaningful discussions without the threat of criminalisation, and if substantive changes occurred in the state's approach to the Kurdish issue, the ideas, initiatives, and momentum from earlier efforts could resurface, revitalising civic space. In such a scenario, engagement with transitional justice would likely take a different yet still meaningful form, evolving in response to the changed political and social landscape, both nationally and globally.

Chapter 7 reminded us that although there seems to be silence in terms of transitional justice presently in Turkey, there is extensive knowledge and experience that can serve as a foundation for future efforts. This chapter draws attention to a clear disconnect between civil society's current commitment to transitional justice and the vigour of their previous efforts, which were more robust. In a political climate more conducive to addressing past atrocities, it was relatively easier to bring past atrocities and crimes to the forefront of civil society's work and facilitate a public discussion around them.

Nevertheless, civil society actors remain committed to pursuing justice and accountability for state violence and conflict-related human rights violations, albeit with less explicit reference to transitional justice frameworks and its specific mechanisms, such as truth commissions. This moment of seeming inertia, however, may present an opportunity to bridge the gap between what is considered necessary and achievable and what is currently being done. By situating their existing wealth of experience within international transitional justice scholarship and practice, grassroots actors can increase their strategic capacity and effectiveness and generate innovative approaches to navigate the challenges imposed by authoritarianism and conflict.

The current period could serve as a foundational phase for a bottom-up transitional justice process. Drawing on lessons learned from past initiatives and global experiences, civil society actors can focus on developing the necessary infrastructure, refining expertise, and fostering a common agenda to guide future official mechanisms. Strengthening connections with the international transitional justice field can help generate detailed, actionable proposals that are both meaningful and achievable in practical terms. Learning from comparative experiences can provide insights into effective strategies, such as truth commissions, reparations programs, and legal reforms that could be adapted to the Turkish-Kurdish context.

Nonetheless, engagement with transitional justice should not be limited to international experiences alone. While global insights are valuable, it is equally important for human rights and peace organisations to take a localised, context-specific approach. If transitional justice is to be an effective and necessary framework, these organisations must collaborate on a detailed analysis of the current situation, prioritising the needs and perspectives of conflict-affected communities. This requires direct engagement with those impacted by the conflict to understand their expectations regarding truth, justice, and accountability.

A crucial step in this process is defining what can be done without state involvement and outlining a roadmap for an eventual official process. To build a bottom-up transitional justice process, as my interlocutors aspire to do, grassroots actors must be better equipped and deliberately build upon what has already been achieved. One effective way to do this is through a case-by-case examination of conflict-related human rights violations, allowing stakeholders to envision and design a transitional justice process that is both practical and feasible if implemented today.

Such preparatory efforts would position grassroots actors as competent leaders of transitional justice initiatives, ensuring they are ready to take a central role when political conditions allow for a more comprehensive reckoning with the past. These efforts should be carried out collaboratively, involving grassroots organisations, victim-survivor groups, legal practitioners, and human rights activists. Their diverse perspectives will help ensure that the process is inclusive, that different demands are considered, and that a wide range of justice mechanisms and reconciliation strategies are explored. By fostering broad participation, transitional justice efforts can be more deeply rooted in local realities and better aligned with the specific needs of those most affected.

The next chapter synthesises the key findings and arguments presented in this book and reflects on the research's broader implications for transitional justice.

## Reference List


Aboueldahab, N., 2018. *Writing Atrocities: Syrian Civil Society and Transitional Justice*. Doha, Qatar: Brookings Doha Center. Available at: https://www.brookings.edu/wp-content/uploads/2018/04/transitional-justice-english_web.pdf

Arthur, P., 2009. How "Transitions" reshaped human rights: A conceptual history of transitional justice. *Human Rights Quarterly*, 31(2), pp. 321–367.

Bianet, 2021. *Kılıçdaroğlu 'helalleşme yolculuğuna' çıkıyor*. Available at: https://bianet.org/bianet/siyaset/253289-kilicdaroglu-helallesme-yolculuguna-cikiyor (Accessed: 13 February 2022).

Bor, G., Daşlı, G. and Alıcı, N., 2021. *From Converging Roads to Narrowing Grounds: The Struggle for Peace by LGBTI+ and Women's Organizations in Turkey*. Available at: https://demos.org.tr/new-research-report-from-converging-roads-to-narrowing-grounds-thestruggle-for-peace-by-lgbti-and-womens-organizations-in-turkey-published/ (Accessed: 14 January 2022).

Bostan, C., 2022. *Games of Justice: Ethnographic Inquiries on Space, Subjectivity and Law in Northern Kurdistan*. Doctoral thesis. Lund University, Sociology of Law Department. Available at: https://portal.research.lu.se/en/publications/games-of-justice-ethnographic-inquiries-on-space-subjectivity-and (Accessed: 26 February 2025).

Budak, Y., 2015. Dealing with the past: Transitional justice, ongoing conflict and the Kurdish issue in Turkey. *International Journal of Transitional Justice*, pp. 219–238. https://doi.org/10.1093/ijtj/ijv002

Daly, E., 2002. Transformative justice: Charting a path to reconciliation. *International Legal Perspectives*, 12.

Evrensel, 2007. *Geçmişimizle yüzleşmeliyiz*. Available at: https://www.evrensel.net/haber/248945/gecmisimizle-yuzlesmeliyiz (Accessed: 27 February 2025).

Evrensel, 2024. *Demirtaş ve Mızraklı'dan mektup: Onurlu, adil barışa inanan herkes barış sürecinin aktif katılımcısı olmalı*. Available at: https://www.evrensel.net/haber/513338/demirtas-ve-mizraklidan-mektup-onurlu-adil-barisa-inanan-herkes-baris-surecinin-aktif-katilimcisi-olmali (Accessed: 26 February 2025).

Galtung, J., 1969. Violence, peace, and peace research. *Journal of Peace Research*, 6(3), p. 185.

Gurses, M., 2020. The evolving Kurdish question in Turkey. *Middle East Critique*, 29, pp. 307–318. https://doi.org/10.1080/19436149.2020.1770448

Halkların Demokratik Partisi (HDP), 2018. *İHD'yi Kutluyoruz*. Available at: https://www.hdp.org.tr/tr/ihdyi-kutluyoruz/12249/ (Accessed: 26 February 2025).

Hansen, T., 2011. Transitional justice: Toward a differentiated theory. *Oregon Review of International Law*, 13, pp. 1–46. https://doi.org/10.2307/840816
Hansen, T., 2017. The time and space of transitional justice. In C. Lawther, L. Moffett, and D. Jacobs (Eds.), *Research Handbook on Transitional Justice*. UK: Edward Elgar Publishing, pp. 34–51.
Human Rights Watch, 2016. *Turkey: State Blocks Probes of Southeast Killings*. Available at: https://www.hrw.org/news/2016/07/11/turkey-state-blocks-probes-southeastkillings (Accessed: 7 October 2021).
İnsan Hakları Derneği (İHD), 2009. *Yaşasın Barış, Yaşasın Halkların Kardeşliği!* Available at: https://www.ihd.org.tr/yasasin-baris-yasasin-halklarin-kardesligi/ (Accessed: 26 February 2025).
Interview no:2, Interview by Author, 2019.
Interview no:3, Interview by Author, 2019.
Interview no:4, Interview by Author, 2019.
Interview no:7, Interview by Author, 2019.
Interview no:8, Interview by Author, 2019.
Interview no:9, Interview by Author, 2019.
Interview no:10, Interview by Author, 2019.
Interview no:16, Interview by Author, 2020.
Interview no:17, Interview by Author, 2020.
Interview no:22, Interview by Author, 2020.
Interview no:23, Interview by Author, 2020.
Interview no:24, Interview by Author, 2020.
McEvoy, K. and McConnachie, K., 2013. Victims and transitional justice: Voice, agency and blame. *Social & Legal Studies*, 22(4), 489–513.
Quinn, J.R., 2014. Whither the transition of transitional justice. *Interdisciplinary Journal of Human Rights*. https://doi.org/10.3366/ajicl.2011.0005
Sarkin, J., 2016. Refocusing transitional justice to focus not only on the past, but also to concentrate on ongoing conflicts and enduring human rights crises. *Journal of International Humanitarian Legal Studies*, 7, pp. 294–329. https://doi.org/10.1163/18781527-00702002
Sendika, 2021. *Kürt halkı AKP'ye cevabı Newroz alanlarından verdi: "Newroz ateşi yandığı sürece kimse bize diz çöktüremez; HDP halktır, kapatılamaz"*. Available at: https://sendika.org/2021/03/kurt-halki-akpye-cevabi-newroz-alanlarindan-verdi-newroz-atesi-yandigi-surece-kimse-bize-diz-cokturemez-hdp-halktir-kapatilamaz-611960 (Accessed: 27 February 2025).
Sharp, D.N., 2013. Beyond the post-conflict checklist: Linking peacebuilding and transitional justice through the lens of critique. *Chicago Journal of International Law*, 14, pp. 165.
T24, 2024. *Kürt Meselesinin Çözümü ve Barış Konferansı: Yeni barış sürecine ve çatışma çözümüne her zamankinden daha çok ihtiyacımız var*. Available at: https://t24.com.tr/haber/kurt-meselesinin-cozumu-ve-baris-konferansi-yeni-baris-surecine-ve-catisma-cozumune-her-zamankinden-daha-cok-ihtiyacimiz-var,1156280 (Accessed: 26 February 2025).
Teitel, R.G., 2000. *Transitional Justice*. Oxford: Oxford University Press. Available at: https://global.oup.com/academic/product/transitional-justice-9780195100648?cc=gb&lang=en& (Accessed: 26 February 2025).
United Nations, 2010. *Guidance Note of the Secretary-General: United Nations Approach to Transitional Justice*.
Yılmaz, E., 2025. Kürt meselesinin en kestirme çözümü: Onurlu ve adil bir barış. *Gazete Duvar*. Available at: https://www.gazeteduvar.com.tr/kurt-meselesinin-en-kestirme-cozumu-onurlu-ve-adil-bir-baris-haber-1748542 (Accessed: 26 February 2025).

# Chapter 9

# Conclusion

## 9.1 Introduction

This study provides one of the first empirical contributions situating Turkey's Kurdish conflict within the transitional justice literature. Turkey serves as a unique case study for transitional justice scholars and practitioners globally, offering invaluable lessons from civil society actors who persist in seeking justice under challenging circumstances.

The book advances our understanding of how transitional justice can be employed in ongoing conflicts, while critically assessing the potentials and limitations of grassroots mobilisation for justice. It examines how victims and their advocates conceptualise their experiences, navigate barriers, and articulate demands for accountability. Furthermore, it offers insights into the impact of authoritarian regimes on civil society-led transitional justice processes.

Human rights activists have long mobilised to counter denial and break the silence surrounding state violence. They have sought to make harm visible and recognised, creating spaces for truth, justice, and accountability. Their efforts have taken various forms, from documenting human rights violations to establishing unofficial truth commissions. The pursuit of truth has consistently been accompanied by demands for justice and accountability, challenging the entrenched impunity surrounding conflict-related crimes perpetrated by state forces. Victims, survivors, practitioners, activists, human rights advocates, and grassroots organisations have embraced the language of transitional justice to demand accountability and recognition.

However, these initiatives have not been systematically analysed through a transitional justice lens. This book positions these efforts as critical to demonstrating the relevance and adaptability of transitional justice in diverse contexts, including ongoing conflicts. Analysing grassroots-led efforts provides invaluable insights into innovative approaches to achieving accountability and recognition. Additionally, it underscores the importance of placing activists, victim-survivor groups, and grassroots organisations at the forefront of transitional justice efforts, including in the design and implementation of transitional justice mechanisms.

DOI: 10.4324/9781003432579-9

The current socio-political circumstances in Turkey allow little room for grassroots actors to engage actively with transitional justice frameworks. Yet, as this book reveals, grassroots justice activists possess a wealth of experience and significant potential to advance transitional justice goals, even under conditions of severe political repression. To address the research questions, I grouped my findings into four key areas.

First, I investigated the development of the Saturday Mothers movement, which is the most systematically organised and longest-lasting organised victim group in Turkey. Second, I explored the construction and complexities of victimhood in Turkey's Kurdish conflict. By moving from the specific example of Saturday Mothers to a broader discussion of victimhood, I drew a detailed picture of the social and political factors that shaped the victimhood debates in Turkey. Third, I switched back to the Saturday Mothers movement, this time to analyse their mobilisation through the pillars of transitional justice. I identified how, through decades-long efforts, they contributed to truth, justice, guarantees of non-recurrence, and memorialisation efforts. Finally, I examined Turkey's transitional justice trajectory by looking into the past efforts and current imaginaries.

This chapter synthesises these findings in a final analytical discussion to answer the overarching research questions. For this purpose, the chapter is structured into three main parts. In the first part, I revisit and briefly outline the key findings and discuss their implications. In the second part, I discuss a transformative justice lens to the transitional justice work in Turkey, specifically answering the overarching question: What future directions does transitional justice work should follow in Turkey? In the third part of the chapter, I provide recommendations for future research and conclude the book with final reflections.

## 9.2 Key Findings and Implications

### *Building an Organised Victims Movement: The Saturday Mothers/People*

Chapter 4 focused on the Saturday Mothers movement to understand how organised victims of state violence can create a sustainable social movement. Saturday Mothers/People began their silent sit-ins in May 1995 as a group of families of the disappeared and human rights activists who asked for the whereabouts of the disappeared. Saturday sit-ins were started by relatives of the disappeared and human rights defenders, who aimed at initiating a constant protest action that will draw attention to the issue of the enforced disappearances and ask for truth and justice. In the beginning, they had two key goals: finding the disappeared and bringing their perpetrators to justice.

Due to heavy police violence, the Saturday Mothers movement had to pause its gatherings in 1999. When gatherings resumed in 2009 after a

10-year break, their demands became more concrete. By that time, there had been court cases opened against some of the perpetrators of the crimes against Kurds in the 1990s. Those cases played a significant role in bringing the Saturday Mothers movement together with more concrete objectives. Justice seemed like a more achievable goal than before, and the movement directed its efforts to achieving an outcome from the trials.

Motherhood identity, partly due to the global image of mothers searching for their children, played a significant role in gathering visibility, legitimacy, and credibility for the movement. Independence from political groups and format of the gatherings (silent and non-violent sit-ins without any slogans or political banners) have been effective tools to further maintain the groups' capacity in conveying their message nationally and internationally. The Saturday Mothers movement carefully adopted these tools and strategies to keep the focus of the movement clearly on disappearances and avoid being instrumentalised or criminalised. Thanks to the mothers' persistent mobilisation, political determination, and the adopted tools, the movement has gained increased support from a wide range of audiences, and their goals and demands have been more visible.

The powerful image of mothers looking for answers to clarify what happened to their children has been preserved throughout the years. As my interlocutors expressed, the focus on mothers is to ensure the focus will always remain on the cases of the disappeared, enhancing this humanitarian aspect of their struggle. They want outsiders to make sense of their protests and empathise and relate with their cause, thus finding it legitimate and supporting it regardless of their political background. Although the families are leading a highly politicised struggle and their relatives were disappeared because of having a particular political stance, foregrounding motherhood enables the movement's demands to be perceived as fair by general public (Interview no:23, 2020).

Staying independent and keeping the focus on the disappearances has not prevented the Saturday Mothers movement from raising broader demands about state violence and the armed conflict. On the contrary, the very nature of their work has required that they publicly, expressly, and vocally draw attention to state violence, the ongoing Kurdish conflict, and the current regime's responsibility for past abuses. They have vocally addressed other human rights issues, making political and historical connections between different facets of state violence and situating their loss and grief within a political framework.

### *The Construction and Complexities of Victimhood*

Chapter 3 established that each context's social, political, legal particularities determine the victim category in each context (Álvarez Berastegi and Hearty, 2019; Saeed, 2016) while Chapter 5 outlined the components of complex, multi-layered victimhood in Turkey's Kurdish conflict. The intersection of ethnicity and gender thickens the conflict-related victimisations aiding them to continue over generations. In that chapter, I explored the implications of the victimhood category for the victims and grassroots actors. Different understandings of, and approaches to, the word *victim* shows that it is a limiting word that does not reflect the complexities of the victimhood. Often, it is associated with passivity, therefore undermining victims' political agency. It is considered to assign an inferior and passive position to those victimised and overlook their political struggle. However, it is still widely used, and no alternative term exists. Although there is not a legislative or institutional framework that regulates the category of victimhood in relation to the conflict, the general legal terminology requires the use of the word victim. Its dominance in the legal terminology is one reason, while the need to address the perpetrator is another.

Most of my interviewees' understanding implies that revealing victims' vulnerabilities automatically means stripping them of their agency. However, I argue that vulnerability and agency are not mutually exclusive; and difficult emotions such as pain, mourning, anger, and despair can coexist with more positively connotated features such as agency, empowerment, and resistance. Instead of thinking in binaries, I advocate for a more complex, multidimensional understanding of victimhood that leaves as much space for vulnerabilities as empowerment. As noted earlier in Chapter 3, vulnerable victims are capable of challenging the conditions that victimised them. They can at the same time be empowered victims, especially through engaging in collective action, as in the case of the Saturday Mothers movement and other organised groups, and making sense of the conditions that led to their victim status. Highlighting only one aspect of victimhood reproduces the aforementioned binary understandings. At the same time, over-emphasising victims' resistance capacity risks leaving less politicised or organised victims out of the discussions.

While analysing the Saturday Mothers movement, I drew attention to a different type of risk. The perceived ideal or innocent victim status of mothers may narrow down the space for different expressions of victimhood, for example of those whose innocence or moral superiority is more easily contested. For example, the families of political prisoners and guerrilla fighters (such as the organisations explored in Chapter 2) who pursue justice and accountability may be perceived as the opposite of the ideal victims undeserving of empathy and justice. Their mobilisation may be more easily and severely illegitimised and criminalised, not only by state authorities but also by the public.

These are critical issues because the identities, images, and perceptions created during the conflict will not dissolve when the conflict has finally ended. Instead, the hierarchies between different victim groups are usually carried over to a peacebuilding process and transitional justice mechanisms.

These identities, images, and perceptions will be crucial in determining which groups are included (or excluded) in those mechanisms, whose voice will be heard and listened to, and whose demands will be taken seriously. Such hierarchies can also define the legitimate, acceptable, ideal actors of a justice struggle. In the context of an official transitional justice process, debates are likely to arise around whose claims and demands need to be heard, made visible, and who are entitled to rights and support.

One-dimensional, homogenous understandings of victimhood fail to capture the reality of complex victims. They help idealise certain victim images, while narrowing down the space for those such as the grieving mother in the case of relatives of the disappeared, and the strong political actors in conflict-affected individuals in general. Moving away from this binary understanding towards a more complex view of victimhood as encompassing different positionalities may enable the transitional justice scholarship to be more aligned with the realities in which the victims suffer, survive, mobilise, empower, and pursue collective goals at the same time.

Brett and Druliolle (2018, p. 2) define victimhood as "victims, their individual and collective identities, and their role in and impact upon post-conflict societies" while politics of victimhood concerns "how victimhood is defined, negotiated and contested, both socially and politically". They argue that the concept of victimhood involves what it means to be a victim in a particular society. A variety of practices, criteria, and actors play a role in shaping the construction of victimhood, and "ideas of victimhood may vary across time and space" (Brett and Druliolle, 2018, p. 2). While analysing the implications of victimhood in Turkey, it is important to note that if a state-led transitional justice process begins, victimhood will develop new meanings. Through the establishment of new mechanisms or new legislation, conflict-related victimhood is likely to be defined as a legal category. If one needs to register as a victim to participate in a truth commission hearing, for example, or to be entitled to reparations in different forms such as psycho-social support and monetary compensation, the implications for victimhood can be expected to change. A new institutional framework could bring some benefits to identifying as a victim, and the social and political discourse around that institutional framework could add new dimensions to how victimhood is perceived.

As I elaborated in Chapter 5, the hesitation to use the term *victim* either to refer to one's own identity or someone else usually relates to the pacifying connotations of the word. A future institutional framework should reflect the complexity of the victimhood outlined in this book to include in a nuanced way the diverse types and dimensions of victimhood. As Huyse (2003) argues, the perception of those victimised matters, and it is worth questioning whether they conform to the victim status or refuse to be labelled as such. If victim-centred transitional justice means that the goals of transitional justice reflect the demands of those most affected by the conflict, it should also take into account the agency of victims in centring their participation. This is critical because it impacts the extent to which victims are acknowledged as active citizens with the capacity to articulate their claims, as well as the legal, social, and political recognition of what they have suffered (de Waardt, 2016).

Transitional justice mechanisms should be designed based on how the beneficiaries of those mechanisms see themselves and prefer to be seen, but they also should go beyond that and be based on a contextual understanding. An official definition of *victim* should address the multi-layered and intergenerational aspects of victimhood. Also, as explained in Chapter 3, victims need to be part of each phase of transitional justice processes, from design to implementation. The active involvement of those affected by the conflict as effective actors is key to ensuring that a transitional justice process acknowledges the victims' agency, and the mechanisms are designed based on their actual needs, demands, and interests. As Brett (2018, p. 295) states: "By taking victims' demands into account, we may develop a peace process in which transitional justice mechanisms ultimately respond to a victim-centred approach".

Often, the victims of a conflict have been marginalised structurally for a long time based on the intersection of ethnicity, gender, and social class (Robins, 2017). In Chapter 4, I demonstrated that in the Kurdish conflict, the multi-layered victimhood means that the Kurdish people have been affected in an intersectional way. Identity is at the centre of the conflict, and it has affected the whole Kurdish populations at various levels. Gendered social relations mean women and LGBTI+ are affected differently within the context of ethnicity-based discrimination. The most widespread forms of victimisations, such as enforced disappearances and displacements, are also gendered violations, which add to women's burdens beyond the immediate impact of the violation. In most cases, these acts are followed by the loss of access to socio-economic resources and a deepening poverty that passes on to new generations. This multi-layered and intergenerational victimhood enforces the existing power hierarchies. For the conflict to truly end and transform, these power relations have to be acknowledged and challenged (Parlevliet, 2010). The recognition of victims' agency plays a crucial role in challenging those power relations. Victims' active involvement in the entire transitional justice process will ensure that a transitional justice mechanism is context-based. It will also challenge prescriptive, elite-driven approaches to transitional justice. Those approaches mostly have a tokenistic approach to victims and rely on elite groups to design and run transitional justice mechanisms on behalf of the victims. Those types of transitional justice mechanisms may be limited in the benefits they can provide for the victims and end up reproducing the existing power hierarchies.

## Saturday Mothers' Contributions to Transitional Justice

Chapter 6 highlighted the key role played by the Saturday Mothers movement in advancing the goals of transitional justice. I argued that their efforts could be assessed through four key pillars of transitional justice: truth, justice, memorialisation processes, and guarantees of non-recurrence. When analysed from this perspective, it is seen that the organised victims can play a leading role even in a setting where there is limited official willingness towards furthering transitional justice. This chapter builds on the background provided in Chapter 5 and Chapter 6 on victimhood and mobilisation around demands for justice and truth. It provides concrete examples of how organised victims, through exercising political agency, become key actors who bring visibility to the transitional justice discourse and gain concrete outcomes.

Due to the nature of enforced disappearances, truth has been the first and most highlighted demand of the Saturday Mothers since their inception. Concurrently, several other grassroots actors have expressed demands for a truth commission. By strongly emphasising the need for a truth commission to reveal the truth behind enforced disappearances, they have contributed to a shared demand for a truth commission from civil society. Not only did they raise demands for truth, but through the unique sit-in format and statement making, they also provided a platform for truth to be shared and circulated publicly. As expressed in one of the interviews (Interview no:23), if it were not for the Saturday Mothers movement, the issue of enforced disappearances would probably be known by a limited audience only, and the practice of disappearance would continue.

Justice, especially after the hopes fade away to find the disappeared alive, has been an equally important demand. Saturday Mothers filed complaints to local authorities numerous times, but their requests were left unanswered. The trials of the perpetrators of most human rights violations in the 1990s in the Kurdish region created new hopes and led to a stronger focus on the justice demands; it was in fact the reason that brought them together after a 10-year break. Seeing the perpetrators of their loved ones' disappearance put on trial for the first time was remarkable. Even after it became clear that these were instrumentalised trials and there was not a real intention to hold the perpetrator to account, the families continued to follow the trials closely.

Memorialisation has been another significant contribution of Saturday Mothers to the transitional justice scene in Turkey. Through the key elements of the sit-ins such as gathering publicly in an organised and regular manner, holding the photos of the disappeared, and sharing their stories and making statements, they added the memory of enforced disappearances to Turkey's sites of memory. Another major element of the sit-in format is the use of Galatasaray Square. Located in one of the busiest streets of Istanbul, the square has become associated with the Saturday gatherings. Through weekly commemorations of the disappeared, they have made Galatasaray Square a site of memory (Nora, 1989), contributing to the visibility of human rights more broadly, not only in their specific cases.

By transforming their suffering into a collective struggle, Saturday Mothers created the longest-lasting and most visible social movement in Turkey. Having a sustainable, persistent social movement enabled them to create a deterrence effect for further disappearances. Thanks to their efforts for, and contributions to, the truth, justice, and memorialisation pillars of transitional justice, they played a preventive role. The book has therefore shown that organised victims can play a tremendous role in mobilising transitional justice in Turkey without a state willingness to start an official transitional justice process. This has implications not only for the Kurdish question but for transitional justice theory and practice in a range of contexts.

### *Transitional Justice Trajectories*

Chapters 6 and 7 illustrated that despite the absence of a transition, bottom-up transitional justice initiatives can take important steps and achieve justice and truth to some extent. However, the research also shows that when the non-transitional context is shaped by an authoritarian regime, bottom-up efforts tend to become criminalised, silenced, and invisible. Chapter 8 makes it evident that although the grassroots actors value working toward transitional justice, the intersection of the ongoing conflict with an authoritarian rule poses serious challenges to taking concrete steps toward transformation. The authoritarian regime has significantly shrunk their capacity, creating a limited civic space to engage with transitional justice.

Chapter 7 and Chapter 8 also showed that there is a gap between the transitional justice practice in Turkey and the use of transitional language. Many individuals and organisations are still actively involved in, and contributing to, key transitional justice objectives such as truth, justice, recognition, and accountability for the conflict-related abuses. However, they rarely label or situate their work within the transitional justice framework. One of the book's main findings is that the transitional justice discourse dropped off the agenda of the grassroots actors as the political regime moved in a more oppressive direction and the prospects for peace became less likely.

The book also shows that transitional justice in Turkey has been fragmented without a systematic plan or an overarching agenda and long-term commitment. Grassroots actors, more loudly at times, have used transitional justice discourse to advocate for truth, justice, non-recurrence, and memorialisation, and to create a change at the official level. In contrast, the government authorities instrumentalised transitional justice discourse to prove that they were willing to break away from the past and make a change, yet in practice have not. The official measures such as the parliamentary commissions and the trials were seen as pragmatic manoeuvres without a long-term or genuine commitment to fundamental political change. The state failed to recognise the broader political setting, which enabled the conflict to happen and ignored the political responsibility behind human rights abuses. The perpetrators of most crimes committed during the 1990s have not been held accountable and the root causes of the conflict remain unaddressed. Sarkin (2016) notes transitional justice efforts in ongoing conflicts tend to remain narrow rather than adopt a holistic transitional justice process. These attempts are often carried out in an uncoordinated manner, and they lack an overarching agenda to achieve wider transitional justice objectives. His claim certainly characterises Turkey, where the past transitional justice initiatives are isolated without an overarching framework.

Since a fundamental political transformation or regime change has not taken place, but there have been some transitional justice initiatives, I have followed Hansen's (2011, p. 23) category "transitional justice in deeply conflicted societies" in non-transitions (see Chapter 3) to situate Turkey within the field of transitional justice. In such cases where there is no fundamental political transition and society remains conflicted, the expectations about what transitional justice could achieve should be realistic (Hansen, 2011). My interlocutors were certainly realistic in their aspirations and understood the limits of the current context, as has been shown. But likewise, they highlight, as did my case study of the Saturday Mothers, that despite the absence of an official transitional justice agenda, or a peace agreement that sets out a transitional justice strategy, it was still possible to use several transitional justice mechanisms and achieve some goals to a limited extent.

Hansen (2011) also argues that transitional justice without a fundamental political change has not been central enough to shape the field. Indeed, transitional justice literature has not focused adequately on the opportunities that transitional justice might offer in the absence of an apparent political will to address the past or a fundamental transformation. Transitional justice literature does not fully capture the settings where there have been different phases and levels of transition, and where the conflict and widespread human rights abuses have not ended. This is an under-researched area. One of my interlocutors, who has expertise in the judicial aspect of transitional justice, emphasised the difficulty of having the literature focused only on transition periods, which makes the methodologies and mechanisms available only designed for transitions. She highlighted the need to focus more practically on transitional justice during conflict and develop a new methodological approach to transitional justice during conflicts (Interview no:3). There is, therefore, a need for a differentiated approach to analyse the potential for, and the challenges and opportunities of, implementing transitional justice in ongoing conflicts and authoritarian regimes.

However, linking the practice of dealing with Turkey's Kurdish conflict that this book elucidated with international transitional justice debates and scholarship can provide new tools to face the challenges presented by the state. Activists, practitioners, human rights advocates, lawyers, and victim movements such as the Saturday Mothers/People can build on their already existing experience in mobilising the transitional justice goals to work towards the end of the conflict. Linking that wealth of experience and the lessons learned in previous transitional justice initiatives with the current situation would empower them and make them even more effective actors. To make these connections, transitional justice scholarship should move towards a differentiated approach to include transitional justice in non-transitions. In other words, adopting the transitional justice framework and terminology has much to offer the Kurdish struggle to have the past officially recognised locally and globally, but the work of grassroots actors in Turkey during an ongoing conflict has a lot to offer the transitional justice field more broadly.

One of the reasons why my interlocutors believe that they should prioritise transitional justice in the current conditions in the absence of any official peace efforts is because they think they were not well-prepared to contribute the last peace process. This reflects the concern that if political actors decide to initiate a peace process again, civil society might not be well-equipped to take action. One of my interlocutors (Interview no:2) clarified:

> During the peace process, we have seen how unprepared we were for such [a] thing. We don't have that type of infrastructure. We didn't have a preparation such as "we are going to put forward these demands when there is a peace process". We just found ourselves in a process like that and entered a position of waiting.

In order not to repeat the same mistake and to play an active role when there is another peace process, they believe in the importance of using the existing situation as an opportunity. This opportunity could be used to do some groundwork for official mechanisms and for capacity-building. In a similar vein, the need for benefitting from the ongoing situation and not letting a top-down approach dominate the transitional justice prospects is another theme that emerged in the interviews.

Therefore, this book reveals that although currently transitional justice is absent, new efforts could be built upon rich knowledge and experience. Civil society can use the ongoing process of non-transition to build relevant infrastructure and ensure a common agenda. That agenda may entail what should be done without state involvement, but it can also deliver a road map to inform an official process. As previously mentioned, a truth commission is a widespread demand to address various atrocities. If a political change happens and that leads to a peace process which involves the establishment of several transitional justice mechanisms, a truth commission is likely to be part of it. In order for such a mechanism to respond to the needs and demands of victims, grassroots actors should develop a clear and comprehensive agenda, if not an outline of how such a body might operate. Thus, they can use the ongoing process to deliver on a comprehensive community-led roadmap toward a truth commission. Otherwise, it is likely that despite their extensive experience, a future transitional justice process will be elite-driven and pushed in directions that is detached from the needs of the conflict-affected communities.

In parallel to the transformative justice-oriented criticisms addressed in Chapter 3, there is always the risk that those with a better access to the international transitional justice vocabulary might dominate any future transitional justice process. This would result in the experts speaking on behalf of victims, primarily because they are the ones who are better connected to the global networks and discourses. For a transitional justice process to be built from bottom-up as my interlocutors wish, grassroots actors need to be better-equipped and build on what has been achieved in a deliberate way. This does not mean they have to adopt the pre-set transitional justice measures and implement them in Turkey. On the contrary, what this book puts forward is there is a wealth of experience available to develop a locally owned and relevant process, and this just needs to be harnessed. As stated in Chapter 1, the knowledge base of transitional justice has always been informed by comparative approaches. Learning from other experiences will enhance the capacity of grassroots actors to develop innovative ideas and combine them with their already-existing experience to ensure the most effective long-term transitional justice approach.

Transitional justice as a field can benefit from incorporating more grassroots voices to move it beyond its prescriptive agenda and the elite-driven approaches (see Chapter 3). There is much to learn from the experience of community-level and agency-oriented efforts and approaches in Turkey that have been outlined in this book. Secondly, transitional justice theory and practice can benefit from the Turkish case by better understanding how processes can work or are limited by ongoing conflicts.

## 9.3 Towards the Adoption of Transformative Justice

The overarching research question of the book was the future directions that transitional justice work could take in Turkey. Some of these directions have been outlined, such as a deliberate exercise in forwarding a truth commission and a host of grassroots-led processes, but this book has also highlighted an appetite for a wider agenda stretching beyond the traditional transitional justice mechanism. The key findings of the research demonstrate that for a future transitional justice process to meet the goals and demands of grassroots actors, it should apply the principles of transformative justice. Lambourne and Rodriguez Carreon (2016) define the aim of transformative justice as finding strategies to foster sustainable peace. For the transitional justice attempts in Turkey to ensure sustainable peace in the long run, there is the need to find "ways in which transitional justice can become more transformative" (Gready and Robins, 2014, p. 355). To develop a transformative justice model that promotes sustainable peacebuilding, Lambourne (2009, p. 30) notes:

> This model requires us to rethink our focus on 'transition' as an interim process that links the past and the future, and to think instead in terms of 'transformation', which implies long-term, sustainable processes

> embedded in society and adoption of psychosocial, political and economic, as well as legal, perspectives on justice. In addition to transitional legal justice mechanisms, transformative justice requires transformation of social, economic and political structures and relationships. It involves recognising and addressing the multiple justice needs and expectations of the local population in a way that draws on the various cultural approaches that coexist with the dominant western worldview and practice.

The premises of the transformative justice model suggested by Lambourne chime with my interlocutors' perspective on several levels. First, her suggestion to move from transition towards transformation aligns with my interlocutors' understanding of transition as a bottom-up, long-term, and non-linear process. As investigated at length in Chapter 8, my interlocutors refer to transition more as a radical transformation that goes beyond a top-down change and reaches the grassroots level. Transformative justice prioritises long-term structural change, which is crucial to addressing the root causes of the conflict in the Kurdish cases as my interlocutors pointed out on numerous occasions.

Second, the emphasis on the change in social, political, and economic structures speaks to the root causes of the conflict as explained in Chapter 2, the multi-layered victimisation and intergenerational aspect of victimhood as elaborated in Chapter 6. As the root causes of the Kurdish conflict remain unaddressed, structural inequalities get deeper and burden the new generations. The intergenerational impact of state violence includes psychosocial and material outcomes such as losing socio-economic opportunities, as well as ongoing cultural marginalisation. Transformative justice offers a useful agenda to address structural violence, socioeconomic issues and challenge the intersecting social exclusion and unequal power relations (Gready and Robins, 2014; Evans, 2016). The need to address the longer-term impact of the conflict, intergenerational harm, and ethnicity and gender as the two key aspects of multi-layered victimisation could also be met by transformative justice.

Feminist scholars have long established that there are no sharp boundaries between conflict and post-conflict periods with regard to gendered experiences (Cockburn, 2004; Yadav and Horn, 2021). Boesten and Wilding (2015) emphasise that although direct and indirect forms of violence against women and LGBTI+ are pervasive during times of conflict, such violence is rooted in pre-existing gender ideologies and structural inequalities. They note that the understanding that gendered violence is not only specific to the conflict lies at the heart of the calls for transformative justice to address gendered harms and consider gender-specific needs. In conflict regions, the everyday experience of queer people, who are part of the racialised and oppressed communities, are shaped by their communities as well as wider political environment (Sandal-Wilson, 2024). This is relevant to the Kurdish conflict as well. For example, Fidan and Göçer (2022) show that LGBTI+ people who live in the Kurdish region experience a higher level of discrimination during conflict compared to peacetime and access to justice is hampered. But they also highlight the criminalisation, marginalisation, and rights violations against LGBTI+ identities during conflict often originate from an already existing cis-heteronormative gender regime. Discrimination against LGBTI+ continues in peacetime, which refers to its structural nature.

As elaborated in Chapter 6, women experience long-term economic, social, and cultural rights violations as a result of the Kurdish conflict. Altekin (2022) emphasises that Kurdish women and LGBTI+ people are exposed to gender-based violence, homophobia, transphobia, sexism, poverty, and heteronormativity while at the same time facing ethnic-based discrimination, racism, and criminalisation. Structural violence, social injustice, and rights violations affect women's and LGBTI+'s everyday life, and they are also strongly interconnected to the root causes of the conflict. Therefore, by adopting a transformative approach to transitional justice, the root causes of the Kurdish conflict can be addressed in a way that the gendered power relations are challenged. Especially if it is combined with a wider strategy to combat gender inequality, the conflict's long-term consequences for women and LGBTI+ may also be repaired. To that end, a future transitional and/or transformative justice process in Turkey should tackle the gendered power relations in society as a key task and take into consideration how it has overlapped with conflict-related social, political, economic, and cultural rights violations.

Third, focusing on the multiple justice needs and expectations will benefit those most affected by the conflict. I discussed in Chapter 6 that my interviews reflect the multi-layered complexities of victimhood in the Kurdish conflict. I argued that to fully capture those complexities, the binary understanding of victimhood needs to be moved towards a more nuanced approach where vulnerabilities and the political agency of victims co-exist. This nuanced approach also requires an understanding that victims are not a homogenous group with the same needs and demands. Since victimhood is constructed and shaped by various social, cultural, economic conditions, and each victim has a unique experience of violence, their justice demands will also vary in line with the victim-centred approach to transitional justice. I suggested in Chapter 4, adopting the transformative justice agenda will ensure that the unique and varied justice demands of those most affected by the conflict will inform the transitional justice process. As Evans (2018, p. 41) puts it:

> Necessary conditions for transformative justice can be seen as the inclusion of the affected communities (not just elites) in shaping agenda for policy and practice, a focus on addressing economic conditions, emphasis on long-term societal changes and attention to the historical and structural roots of contemporary injustices.

In addition to these, participation and empowerment are identified as the key values informing transformative justice practice (Hoddy and Gready, 2020). Gready and Robins (2014, p. 340) define transformative justice as follows:

> Transformative justice is defined as transformative change that local agency and resources, the prioritization of process rather than preconceived outcomes and the challenging of unequal and intersecting power relationships and structures of exclusion at both the local and the global level.

Transformative justice's emphasis on the change that is centred on local agency and ambition to challenge the intersecting exclusionary structures and inequalities (2014, p. 340) mirrors the grassroots actors' perspectives and expectations in Turkey. Gready and Robins (2014, p. 340) also emphasise that transformative justice is based on understanding the populations' needs and realities from a bottom-up perspective instead of coming from "top-down institution of external legal framework or institutional templates". My analysis of the Saturday Mothers' mobilisation, the construction of victimhood with regards to the Kurdish conflict, and the grassroots actors' approach to transition and transitional justice point to the very notions of a bottom-up approach that puts the agency of the victims at the centre when pursuing transitional justice. This book illustrates, repeatedly, that the grassroots actors including civil society members, activists, practitioners, and victims feel strongly that transition and transitional justice must come from the bottom-up in Turkey. This bottom-up approach is centred on the participation and agency of grassroots actors and highlights the importance of them actively partaking in transitional justice efforts.

Of course, achieving widespread transformation is extremely challenging in the current and future context, but a transformative justice agenda nonetheless offers the grassroots actors in Turkey a framework to work with and a set of principles to guide their endeavours. This also reflects the aspirations and approaches outlined in the empirical research conducted for this book and thus should be taken seriously as a basis for future transitional justice trajectories in Turkey.

## 9.4 Recommendations for Further Research

This book highlights a key dilemma: how can transitional justice processes be meaningfully implemented amid ongoing conflict and in the absence of state cooperation? Addressing these questions is critical, as ongoing wars make the subject both relevant and timely. Transitional justice must engage more deeply with these challenges to remain responsive to current realities.

To advance the research agenda in ways that address these pressing issues, future research should focus on how civil society actors can employ specific transitional justice mechanisms to pursue truth and justice in cases of ongoing authoritarian rule. Additionally, studying cases that have not traditionally been the focus of transitional justice scholarship can provide fresh perspectives and new opportunities for learning.

More work is needed to examine how grassroots actors in conflict and post-conflict settings can adopt and operationalise transformative justice principles. As this book has shown, there is a significant gap between transitional justice scholarship and cases where transitional justice initiatives occur without an actual political transition. This gap is even more pronounced in the context of transformative justice. Although transformative justice has emerged as a growing theoretical framework, it is not well understood or effectively communicated to the groups that could benefit most from its application. This underscores the need for further research to bridge the gap between transformative justice theory and practice, with a particular emphasis on contexts of ongoing conflict.

Currently, the transformative justice agenda is not clearly defined or translated into specific mechanisms. Instead, it provides an overarching framework of values and principles that could inform transitional justice processes. A critical area of inquiry is how transformative justice could address issues such as structural violence and socio-economic injustices, which are often overlooked by the standard transitional justice toolkit (Evans, 2018). While transformative justice and transitional justice share a common point of departure, they are distinct from one another (Evans, 2018). If transformative justice is indeed separate, it requires its own set of tools and mechanisms.

The lack of concrete proposals for making transitional justice transformative or for developing a distinct transformative justice agenda has been highlighted by numerous scholars. Gready and Robins emphasise the need for "thicker descriptions and assessments of transformative justice in relation to specific groups (e.g., victims and survivors, women, indigenous groups) and geographical settings" (Gready and Robins, 2014, p. 361). Transformative justice lacks a commonly agreed set of components (McGill, 2019) and "relatively little analytical and political attention has yet been paid to concretizing transformative justice processes" (Evans, 2018, p. 39). Gready (2019, p. xiv) further stresses that "transformative justice itself has work to do. There is a need to more consistently go beyond critique to spell out clearly what alternative approaches might look like".

To advance transformative justice, more empirical studies are required. These studies should focus on real-life examples of how transformative justice can be implemented, connecting practical experiences to the broader transformative justice scholarship. Such research could help establish a more concrete set of tools and mechanisms, moving the field beyond theory and critique toward actionable solutions.

## Reference List


Altekin, O., 2022. *Kürt LGBTİ+'lar, yoksulluk ve barışın olanakları*. Available at: https://demos.org.tr/kurt-lgbtilar-yoksulluk-ve-barisin-olanaklari/ (Accessed: 15 July 2022).

Álvarez Berastegi, A. and Hearty, K., 2019. A context-based model for framing political victimhood: Experiences from Northern Ireland and the Basque Country. *International Review of Victimology*, 25, pp. 19–36. https://doi.org/10.1177/0269758018782237

Boesten, J. and Wilding, P., 2015. Transformative gender justice: Setting an agenda. *Women's Studies International Forum*, 51, pp. 75–80.

Brett, R., 2018. The role of the victims' delegations in the Santos-FARC peace talks. In R. Brett and V. Druliolle (Eds.), *The Politics of Victimhood in Post-conflict Societies*. Cham: Palgrave Macmillan, pp. 267–299.

Brett, R. and Druliolle, V., 2018. Introduction. In R. Brett and V. Druliolle (Eds.), *The Politics of Victimhood in Post-conflict Societies*. Cham: Palgrave Macmillan, pp. 1–22.

Cockburn, C., 2004. The continuum of violence: A gender perspective of war and peace, sites of violence: Gender and conflict zones. In W. Giles and J. Hyndman (Eds.), *Sites of Violence*. Berkeley: University of California Press, pp. 24–44.

de Waardt, M., 2016. Naming and shaming victims: The semantics of victimhood. *International Journal of Transitional Justice*, 10, pp. 432–450. https://doi.org/10.1093/ijtj/ijw011

Evans, M., 2016. Structural violence, socioeconomic rights, and transformative justice. *Journal of Human Rights*, 15(1), 1–20.

Evans, M., 2018. Transformative justice: remedying human rights violations beyond transition. In *Transitional Justice*. Abingdon, Oxon; New York: Routledge.

Fidan and Göçer., 2022. *Yakın Geçmişten Olası Geleceğe Barışı Yeşertmek: 2013–2018 Yılları Arasında Diyarbakır'da Yaşayan LGBTİ+'lar.* Available at: https://turkey.fes.de/fileadmin/user_upload/pdf-files/2022/keskesor-bakad-barisiyesertmek.pdf (Accessed: 16 July 2022).

Gready, P., 2019. Foreword. In M. Evans (Ed.), *Transitional and Transformative Justice: Critical and International Perspectives*. Abingdon: Routledge, pp. xiii-xiv.

Gready, P. and Robins, S., 2014. From transitional to transformative justice: A new agenda for practice. *International Journal of Transitional Justice*. https://doi.org/10.1093/ijtj/iju013

Hansen, T.O., 2011. Transitional justice: Toward a differentiated theory. *Oregon Review of International Law*, 13, pp. 1–46. https://doi.org/10.2307/840816

Hoddy, E.T. and Gready, P., 2020. From agency to root causes: Addressing structural barriers to transformative justice in transitional and post-conflict settings. *Contemporary Social Science*, 0, pp. 1–16. https://doi.org/10.1080/21582041.2020.1812706

Huyse, L., 2003. Victims. In D. Bloomfield, T. Barnes, and L. Huyse (Eds.), *Reconciliation after Violent Conflict: A Handbook*. Stockholm: International Institute for Democracy and Electoral Assistance, pp. 54–66.

Interview no:2, Interview by Author, 2019.

Interview no:23, Interview by Author, 2020.

Lambourne, W., 2009. Transitional justice and peacebuilding after mass violence. *The International Journal of Transitional Justice*, 3, pp. 28–48. https://doi.org/10.1093/ijtj/ijn037

Lambourne, W. and Rodriguez Carreon, V., 2016. Engendering transitional justice: A transformative approach to building peace and attaining human rights for women. *Human Rights Review*, 17, 71–93.

McGill, D., 2019. Tackling structural violence through the transformative justice framework. In M. Evans (Ed.), *Transitional and Transformative Justice: Critical and International Perspectives*. Abingdon: Routledge, pp. 11–35.

Nora, P., 1989. Between memory and history: Les Lieux de Memoire. *Representations*, 26, pp. 7–24.

Parlevliet, M., 2010. Rethinking conflict transformation from a human rights perspective. *Berghof Handbook Dialogue Series*, 2010, pp. 15–46.

Robins, S., 2017. Failing victims? The limits of transitional justice in addressing the needs of victims of violations. *Human Rights International Legal Discourse*, 11, pp. 41–58.

Saeed, H., 2016. Victims and victimhood: Individuals of inaction or active agents of change? Reflections on fieldwork in Afghanistan. *International Journal of Transitional Justice*, 10, pp. 168–178. https://doi.org/10.1093/ijtj/ijv032

Sandal-Wilson, H., 2024. On the (im)possibility of the Kurdish queer. *South Atlantic Quarterly*, 123, pp. 873–880. https://doi.org/10.1215/00382876–11381049

Sarkin, J., 2016. Refocusing transitional justice to focus not only on the past, but also to concentrate on ongoing conflicts and enduring human rights crises. *Journal of International Humanitarian Legal Studies*. https://doi.org/10.1163/18781527-00702002

Yadav, P. and Horn, D.M., 2021. Continuums of violence: Feminist peace research and gender-based violence. In T. Väyrynen, S. Parashar, E. Féron, and C.C. Confortini (Eds.), *Routledge Handbook of Feminist Peace Research*. Abingdon: Routledge, pp. 105–114.

| *Interview No.* | *Date* | *Interlocutors' Organisation/Status* |
|---|---|---|
| 1 | 24 July 2019 | DEMOS Research Association (DEMOS Araştırma Derneği) |
| 2 | 30 July 2019 | Migration Monitoring Association (Göç İzleme Derneği) |
| 3 | 30 July 2019 | Truth Justice Memory Centre (Hakikat Adalet Hafıza Merkezi) |
| 4 | 2 August 2019 | Migration Monitoring Association (Göç İzleme Derneği) |
| 5 | 2 August 2019 | Migration Monitoring Association (Göç İzleme Derneği) |
| 6 | 5 August 2019 | Truth Justice Memory Centre (Hakikat Adalet Hafıza Merkezi) |
| 7 | 6 August 2019 | Human Rights Association Istanbul, Saturday Mothers/People (İnsan Hakları Derneği İstanbul, Cumartesi Anneleri/İnsanları) |
| 8 | 7 August 2019 | Turkey Human Rights Foundation Istanbul (Türkiye İnsan Hakları Vakfı İstanbul) |
| 9 | 8 August 2019 | Lawyers Association for Freedom (Özgürlük İçin Hukukçular Derneği) |
| 10 | 9 September 2019 | Truth Justice Memory Centre (Hakikat Adalet Hafıza Merkezi) |
| 11 | 14 September 2019 | Human Rights Association Istanbul, Saturday Mothers/People (İnsan Hakları Derneği İstanbul, Cumartesi Anneleri/İnsanları) |
| 12 | 2 October 2019 | Rights Initiative (Hak İnisiyatifi) |
| 13 | 8 October 2019 | Tigris Social Research Centre (Dicle Sosyal Araştırmalar Merkezi/DİTAM) |
| 14 | 20 July 2020 | Mesopotamia News Agency (Mezopotamya Haber Ajansı) |
| 15 | 27 July 2020 | Human Rights Association Diyarbakır (İnsan Hakları Derneği Diyarbakır) |
| 16 | 30 July 2020 | Diyarbakir Bar Association (Diyarbakır Barosu) |
| 17 | 4 October 2020 | Rosa Women's Association (Rosa Kadın Derneği) |
| 18 | 5 October 2020 | Relative of a disappeared |

(*Continued*)

(Continued)

| *Interview No.* | *Date* | *Interlocutors' Organisation/Status* |
|---|---|---|
| 19 | 7 October 2020 | Human Rights Association Diyarbakır (İnsan Hakları Derneği Diyarbakır) |
| 20 | 7 October 2020 | Turkey Human Rights Foundation Diyarbakır (Türkiye İnsan Hakları Vakfı Diyarbakır) |
| 21 | 13 October 2020 | Saturday Mothers/People (Istanbul) (Cumartesi Anneleri/İnsanları İstanbul) |
| 22 | 15 October 2020 | Diyarbakir Bar Association (Diyarbakır Barosu) |
| 23 | 17 October 2020 | Saturday Mothers/People (Istanbul) (Cumartesi Anneleri/İnsanları İstanbul) |
| 24 | 21 January 2021 | Social Memory Platform (Toplumsal Hafıza Platformu) |

# Index